A HISTORY
OF
CHINA
IN
MAPS

*Communications
and Transportation*

www.royalcollins.com

A HISTORY OF CHINA IN MAPS

Communications and Transportation

Fu Linxiang

Chief Editor: Ge Jianxiong

A History of China in Maps: Communications and Transportation

Fu Linxiang
Chief Editor: Ge Jianxiong
Translated by Zhang Jing

First published in 2023 by Royal Collins Publishing Group Inc.
Groupe Publication Royal Collins Inc.
BKM Royalcollins Publishers Private Limited

Headquarters: 550-555 boul. René-Lévesque O Montréal (Québec) H2Z1B1 Canada
India office: 805 Hemkunt House, 8th Floor, Rajendra Place, New Delhi 110 008

Original Edition © 2011 by Jiangsu People's Publishing House
This English edition is authorized by Jiangsu People's Publishing House.

All rights reserved. Without limiting the rights under copyright reserved above, no part of this publication may be reproduced, stored in or introduced into a retrieval system, or transmitted in any form or by any means (electronic, mechanical, photocopying, recording, or otherwise), without the prior written permission of both the copyright owner and the above publisher of this book.

ISBN: 978-1-4878-0936-2

To find out more about our publications, please visit www.royalcollins.com.

CONTENTS

Foreword ix
Introduction xiii

CHAPTER ONE
Transportation Systems in the Pre-Qin Period—The Nine Provinces, Four "Remotes," and the Cities 1
1. Nine Provinces in the Book of *Yu Gong* and Waterway Networks 2
2. From the Nine Provinces to the Greater Nine Provinces 8
3. The Concept of Four Remotes and the Western Expedition by King Mu of Zhou 12
4. Cities, Carts, and Trade in the Early Years of Chinese Civilization 15

CHAPTER TWO
Expansion of Communications in the Qin and Han Dynasties— Routes, Silk Roads, and Tower Ships 25
1. Road Networks in the Qin Dynasty 26
2. The Four Royal Patrols by Emperor Qin Shi Huang 31
3. The Lingqu Canal—Bridging the Nanling Mountains 34
4. The Southwest "Yi" Route 36
5. The Rise of Postal Systems and Their Perfection 39

6. Zhang Qian and Gan Ying—the Great Explorers   43
7. Tower Ships (Louchuan) and Sea Routes   47

CHAPTER THREE
Cultural Exchange Between Ancient China and India   55
1. Faxian (法显)—Acquired Buddhist Texts from India   55
2. Geographic Outlook of Ancient Indians and Their Influence on China   61

CHAPTER FOUR
Communications between China and the World in the Sui and Tang Dynasties   65
1. Flourishing Waterways and Land Communications   66
2. Overseas Routes from Guangzhou and Communications with the Arabs   71
3. Xuanzang Goes to India for Buddhist Texts   82
4. Jianzhen Brings Buddhism to Japan   86
5. Japanese Monk Ennin (圆仁) Visited the Tang Empire   95

CHAPTER FIVE
Transportation Development in the Song and Yuan Dynasties   99
1. In Alliance with Goryeo   99
2. Western Expedition by Taoist Priest Changchun   112
3. Zhanchi (Post Stations) and Land and Water Transportation in the Yuan   116

CHAPTER SIX
Prosperous Tourism and Communications in the Ming Dynasty   125
1. Postal Routes and Post Stations in the Ming   126
2. Travels by Merchants   132
3. Leisure Travel by Government Officials   138
4. From Travelers to Geographers   142

CHAPTER SEVEN
Cannons, Western Studies, and Delegates—Communications between China and Europe in the Ming and Qing Dynasties   153
1. Matteo Ricci and His Fellow Missionaries in China   153
2. Cannons from the West   156

3. Western Science and Technology in China   165
4. The Rites Controversy and Chinese Missionaries in Europe   170
5. Tulichen and His Delegates in Russia   177

CHAPTER EIGHT
Trains, Railways, and Contemporary Chinese Politics   **185**
1. Wusong Railways and Cultural Clashes between East and West   185
2. Xiyuan Railway and Attitude Shifts toward Locomotion   192
3. The Beijing–Hankou Railway and Yuan Shikai Fished in Huan River   198
4. Mr. Sun Yat-sen's Blueprint of China's Rail Networks   202

A Brief Chronology of Chinese History   207
Index   209
About the Chief Editor   217
About the Author   219

FOREWORD

The book series, *A History of China in Maps*, is comprised of four volumes: *Territories and Administrative Divisions*, *Ancient Capitals and Cities*, *Communications and Transportation*, and *Ethnic Migration*. Each volume tells one specific aspect of Chinese history with illustrated maps.

Many scholars have pointed out that the keys to understanding history are the five "Ws": what, when, where, who, and why. Any historical facts, regardless of who or what, and anything, be it spiritual or material, have to be connected with specific space. In other words, they have to take place either at a certain point, in a line, or on a surface of the earth. That's why the factor "where" is crucial to understanding history. Just as the late Professor Tan Qixiang said, "History is like a drama, and geography is its stage. Without a stage, there would be no drama at all."

Spatial factors have always played a significant role in history. They are not only important research contents but also indispensable elements to understanding history. Limited by time and energy, no one could be omnipresent; even if one could be there in person, one may not be able to master the entire range or features of the space. Therefore, maps are of vital importance. In ancient times, although limited by cartographic technologies and gadgets, scholars already recognized the significance of maps; when conducting historical research, they almost always had maps by their side.

Tu Jing (图经), a primitive form of chorography, combined records with illustrations, mostly in the form of maps. Some other historical classics were also attached to these maps, which later formed the historical atlas genre. As early as the third century, based on books such as *Zuo Zhuan* (左传), Jia Dan compiled an atlas of places for allied gatherings during the Spring and Autumn Period (770–256 BC) (春秋盟会图). Aside from this, Jia Dan also made the *Hai Nei Hua Yi Tu* (海内华夷图, *Map of Hua and National Minorities inside Seas*).

Based on this prototype, *Yu Ji Tu* (禹迹图, *Map of Yu's Sites*) was carved onto stone tablets in AD 1137. Such tablets have often been found in provincial schools, meaning they might have been used as teaching tools. In AD 1905, Yang Shoujing published *Shui Jing Zhu Tu* (水经注图, *Maps for Records of Rivers*). These ancient maps were printed in red and black ink with explanatory notes. It is a masterpiece of the historical atlas.

With the development of satellite remote sensing technology, information technology and the Internet, accurate images are now made possible by GPS and Google Maps. People tend to think that traditional maps have lost their charm and therefore should be replaced. However, this is not true. No matter how accurate they may be, Google Maps cannot replace traditional maps, nor their comprehensive, abstract, and specific geographic elements.

Modern maps are not sufficient to understand history. What we need are historical maps related to that era. As time goes by, the environment changes too. Features of physical and human geography in ancient times may differ from what we have today. Even if only minor changes have occurred in physical geography, features of human geography may have experienced profound change. Some elements may have disappeared completely, while some new elements have emerged. Historical maps have to be made according to the exact historical facts and corresponding geographic status.

In August 2010, a deadly mudslide took place in Zhouqu County, Gansu, China. While broadcasting the news, TV stations also presented maps on screen to inform the audience where exactly the catastrophe happened. The audience came to understand how far Zhouqu was from Lanzhou, the provincial capital of Gansu Province. Without a map, the audience would be unaware. The same goes for understanding history, which should be illustrated with maps. Otherwise, readers without such a background may find it hard to develop a spatial concept of historical events, even if they receive explanatory notes. This is because some geographic names no longer exist, while some topography has been altered considerably.

For example, in Cen Shen's poem, "A Song of Farewell to Field-Clerk Wu Going Home in White Snow," written in the Tang Dynasty, Cen saw Wu off in Luntai, and watched him disappear among the Tianshan Mountains. However, the modern Luntai is hundreds of miles away from the Tianshan Mountains. It only make sense when readers have learned that Luntai in the Tang was in fact located very close to Urumqi in Xinjiang Autonomous Region, and to the north of the Tianshan Mountains.

Another example is the city name of Nanjing. After the fall of the Northern Song Dynasty, Zhao Gou proclaimed himself as Emperor of the Southern Song in Nanjing. Later, under the increasing threat of Jin's armies from the North, he fled to Yangzhou and then crossed the Yangtze River. It might not be evident if the readers mix up Zhao Gou's Nanjing with the modern Nanjing, located to the south of Yangzhou. It would not make sense for Zhao to flee in the wrong direction! Nanjing in the Northern Song Dynasty was Shangqiu in today's Henan Province. From there, it went south and reached Yangzhou along the Bian Canal. Such a route is logical. A historical map would greatly benefit the readers in clarifying such cases.

Historical maps may also help bring about new research. For example, Professor Tan Qixiang once collected all the data he could of archaeological findings and cultural relics in the bordering areas of Hebei and Shandong provinces. Having marked them on maps, he discovered a region in the shape of a sea-shell, empty of any relics before the fourth century. And this region happened to be the lower reaches of the Yellow River. Based on further research on regional topography, Professor Tan was able to confirm the river had changed its course many times in that era, making it impossible for human inhabitation. This has never been recorded in any historical literature; only maps have provided a reliable means for research.

The four authors of *A History of China in Maps* have made breakthroughs in their work. Maps are not used for illustrations only, but as an essential part of the books—leading readers through comprehensive and accurate descriptions of history.

We have chosen four topics closely related to maps: Ancient Capitals and Cities, Territories and Administrative Divisions, Communications and

Transportation, and Ethnic Migration. Each book is full of ancient place names and other geographic elements. Without historical maps, one cannot fully understand history, no matter how many words have been written. If readers like our concept, it is possible that we will continue to write more books in future, illustrated with maps.

Here I would like to give credit to Jiangsu People's Publishing House. I am very grateful to have been chosen as the chief editor for this book series. I would like to specify what I have contributed: together with the writers and editors, I have determined the topics, style and requirements on the usage of maps. I have given feedback to the authors on their content and structure. And finally, I have written this foreword. Thank you!

GE JIANXIONG

INTRODUCTION

China has a long history of ancient civilization. Over ten thousand years ago, Chinese ancestors were already accomplished fishers, hunters, herders, and primitive farmers. They were trailblazers—where they walked became paths and roads.

In ancient times, people usually lived by rivers and lakes. They invented canoes for fishing and crossing streams. Canoes are known as the earliest water transportation vehicles in human history. Discoveries show that over 7,000 years ago, Chinese ancestors in Hemudu (present-day Zhejiang Province) had already been using wooden oars for canoes. *The Book of Changes,* an ancient Chinese text written more than 2,000 years ago, recorded that Chinese ancestor Fuxi cut a tree trunk and made it into a hull of a boat, then he planed the wood and turned it into oars. This was an important step for human expansion of territory, from land to water.

Inscriptions written on tortoise shells and bronze utensils made in the Shang Dynasty (1600–1046 BC) were clear indicators that carts and carriages had already been invented. Many hieroglyphs indicated that carts made in ancient China already had carriages to transport people, and that oxen and horses had been trained to pull the carts. Out of necessity, roads were paved to match the speed of carts.

In the Xia, Shang, and Zhou dynasties, a primitive transportation network covering land and water came into being. Different transportation vehicles also appeared for different natural conditions. *The Records of the Grand Historian* said that people traveled by cart on land, by ship on water, by sledge on mud, and by *ju* (樏, spike shoes) on hills. Post stations, as government administrations for communications and transportation, had appeared no later than Western Zhou (1046–771 BC). With economic development and the expansion of cities, city roads also appeared and grew.

After Emperor Qin Shi Huang had united China, he ordered large roadways to be built, with capital Xianyang at the center. He also ordered that wheel spans should be of the same width, so that carts could travel without hindrance on different roads in the country. Consequently, a unified national transportation system came into being. Furthermore, the Qin government dug the Lingqu Canal in South China, connecting the Xiang and Pearl Rivers.

In the Western and Eastern Han dynasties, Chinese delegates made it across the Silk Road to the Western Regions. Sea routes to Japan and Southeast Asia were also discovered, and tower ships were invented as an indispensable navy force.

In the era of Wei, Jin, and the Southern and Northern Dynasties, China was divided among war-lords, with continuous fighting disrupting the national transportation system. However, governments in South China were relatively stable. Thus, networks were developed here to some extent. Communications and trade continued to increase. Maritime exchanges with countries in Northeast Asia and Southeast Asia have also increased.

In the Sui and Tang dynasties, China became unified again. As a result, transportation networks greatly improved. Seven major routes, with capital cities Chang'an and Luoyang at the center, not only connected the Tang Empire to the outside world, but also minority tribes on the borders. The Sui government dug the Grand Canal with Luoyang at the center, connecting northern and southern China. Meanwhile, it also served as an important channel for moving food and other goods. In addition, maritime trade became very busy, as exchange between China and Arabian states continued to grow.

During the Five Dynasties and Ten Kingdoms period, wars among the Song Empire and northern kingdoms such as Liao, Western Xia, and Jin spanned over 300 years. It greatly hindered development of transportation networks in China.

Only during periods of truce, could there be serious communications between delegates of different parties.

The Yuan Dynasty only lasted for 97 years, and yet it had the vastest territory in Chinese history. Genghis Khan's expedition to the West, in a way, boosted communications among China, Western Asian, and Eastern European countries. Transportation networks in the Yuan gradually developed in accordance with the unification process in China. The Yuan government trailed new routes not only to Yunnan and Guizhou Plateau in southwest China but also to the Nurgan District in Heilongjiang in northeast China. Thus, communications between Central China and minority groups on the borders were strengthened. Great importance had also been attached to waterway transportation. The Yuan straightened up the Beijing–Hangzhou Canal, which greatly shortened transportation distances. Furthermore, after new sea routes had been discovered, the Yuan Empire expanded its trade with over 100 countries.

In the Ming and Qing dynasties, China eventually became a unified country with different ethnic minorities. With economic development, road mileage increased greatly, further strengthening communications among Central China and minority groups on the borders, such as those in Inner Mongolia and Xinjiang. The Ming Empire had two capitals in Nanjing and Beijing.

Intense water and land transportation networks were built with those two capitals at the center. Sea routes were disrupted because of pirates. At the height of China's marine endeavor, Admiral Zheng He and his fleets set onto the oceans seven times in 28 years. The furthest point Zheng and his fleet reached was Kenya in Africa.

The Qing Dynasty was the last in Chinese history. It also had vast territories. The transportation networks of the Qing laid the foundation for modern China. At the end of the dynasty, the Chinese had already learned about steam powered ships and trains. This marked a new era of transportation history for China. In AD 1902, automobiles appeared in the country. In AD 1906, a driving road from Zhennanguan in Guangxi to Longjinjian, measuring a total length of 50 kilometers, was constructed. Jingzhang Railway, completed in AD 1909, was the first to be built purely from Chinese money. It was designed and supervised by renowned engineer Zhan Tianyou. In AD 1909, aviator and designer Feng Ru built China's first plane. It flew between Beijing and Tianjin in the 1920s.

Development of transportation networks has paved the way for material and cultural communications not only within the country, but also internationally. Taking China as an example, the rise of the lobbying style of scholars during the Warring States era is described in *Zhuangzi · Quqie*: "The footprints of the vassals connect to the borders of the lords, and the tracks of the carriages intertwine for thousands of miles." The prosperity of a large number of merchants and officials traveling during the Ming Dynasty was inseparable from the advanced transportation conditions of the time. On the other hand, the Silk Road, from Central China to the Western Regions, made it possible for the Buddhism of India to be spread in China. Newly discovered sea routes also helped priests and Western civilizations to play their roles in China.

In this book, the author shows the readers some of the most significant and also more obscure events in China's communications and transportation history. This is illustrated with ancient and modern maps; hereby the credits go to the illustrators. Thank you!

CHAPTER ONE

TRANSPORTATION SYSTEMS IN THE PRE-QIN PERIOD
—*The Nine Provinces, Four "Remotes," and the Cities*

The pre-Qin era formed the basis for China's transportation systems. Chinese ancestors paved the way in fruit picking, fishing, and hunting. They not only made the first canoes, oars and carts, but also trained oxen and horses for transportation. As humans expanded their territories, national road systems and waterways came into being in the Xia, Shang, and Zhou dynasties. The book of *Yu Gong* recorded the first water networks in China, enhancing civilization and increasing communication with other peoples.

In the process, such concepts as the "Nine Provinces" and the "Four Remotes" started to appear. King Mu of Zhou's expedition to the West might be the earliest communication between the East and the West in history. The transportation networks not only provided convenience for circulation of products and commodities, but also made cultural exchange possible. Confucius toured different countries, and scholars often served in different kingdoms. Human civilizations advanced greatly because of this.

1. Nine Provinces in the Book of *Yu Gong* and Waterway Networks

The *Book of Documents* was the most ancient history book kept in China. According to legends, it was compiled by Confucius. The book of *Yu Gong* was one chapter in the *Book of Documents*. It was believed that Yu the Great wrote the book himself after he successfully contained the floods. Therefore, it may have been written in the age of the Xia Dynasty. Hence, the *Book of Documents* was regarded as the ancestor of all Chinese history books. According to modern standards, scholars of today categorize it from the Warring States Period.

However, the book of *Yu Gong* recorded water networks in ancient China before the Warring States Period. The networks were cultivated by Chinese ancestors. According to written history, the Chinese lived in groups in ancient times. It is like the road between the hills that is described in the *Mengzi · Jinxin*: "The path on the mountain is so narrow that it becomes a road when people walk on it regularly, but if nobody walks it for a while, it becomes blocked with reeds."

The ancestors noticed that during floods, fallen trees could float in the river. This inspired them to make canoes, the earliest water transportation tools made by humans. In 1977, archaeologists unearthed several wooden oars in Hemudu, Yuyao County in Zhejiang. It was estimated these oars were made 7,000 years ago, as products of the Matriarchal Clan society.

In 2004, among the relics of Tianluo Mountain in Yuyao County, archaeologists discovered two well-preserved and well carved wooden oars. One was 110 centimeters long and its handle was neatly decorated with wooden patterns. The other was 150 centimeters long and retained traces of polish from stone tools. Those were the most well-kept wooden oars among their kind in the Hemudu relics. These oars demonstrated that Chinese ancestors had active water transportation or water networks some 7,000 years ago. *The Book of Changes · Xi (Part Two)*: "To cut the wood for boats, and sharpen the wood for oars, so that the people on both sides of the river may travel to and from each other, and sail to distant places, and make traveling easier."[1] The emergence of the canoe has become the earliest water transport of mankind.

---

1. Li Dingzuo, *Collected Interpretations of the Book of Changes*, vol. 15 (Shanghai: Shanghai Ancient Books Publishing House, 1989).

By the time of Yu the Great, there had been a number of different transportation tools for various natural conditions. According to historical records, sleds were boat-shaped structures made by wooden planks. They were shorter than boats and could travel easily on muddy shores. According to the records, Dayu "walks on the ground in a carriage, on the water in a boat, in the mud in a wooden sled, and on the mountain roads in *ju*. They were always with him, the level and the ink for measuring the level, the circle, and the square for drawing the pattern. He carried them with him at all times when he was engaged in mapping the Nine Provinces, opening the nine roads, building the nine lakes and barriers, and measuring the nine mountains."[2]

Mountains and rivers depicted in the book of "Yu Gong"

Ju was a tool for mountain hiking. It was installed under the shoes. When people went uphill, the *ju* could be adjusted so the front was shorter than the rear.

---

2. "Basic Annals of Xia," in *Records of the Grand Historian*, vol. 1 (Beijing: Zhonghua Book Company, 1959).

Likewise, when people went downhill, the front could be adjusted to be higher than the rear. In this way, people would rarely fall because the shoes provided a flat surface for the climber.

The book of *Yu Gong* covered a wide range of subjects, including the earth, plants, minerals, crop fields, taxes, farm products, handworks, and transportation routes. The Nine Provinces were regarded in the book as a political region. In this region, lords had to pay tribute to the Emperor. There were mountains and rivers, as well as plains in the Nine Provinces. Transportation networks in the region was centered on Jizhou, with water routes playing a dominant role.

Jizhou was the political center of the Nine Provinces. According to the book of *Yu Gong*, tribes of Daoyi (present day part of Liaoning) would pay tributes to the Emperor via the Bohai Sea, Jieshi Mountains, and eventually the Yellow River. However, Hu Wei, a Qing Dynasty scholar held a different view. He wrote that Daoyi referred to Japan and the Korean Peninsula. Youjieshi is generally believed to be located around Changli County, Hebei Province. Therefore, this route refers to the Tribes of Liaodong Peninsula who traveled westward to pay tribute from the Bohai Sea to the ancient Yellow River estuary. The ancient Yellow River now flows into the sea from Tianjin to Huanghua, with many estuaries along the way.

Yanzhou was a province located between the ancient Ji and Yellow Rivers. Compared to modern geography, it would be situated on the borders of Hebei, Henan, and Shandong provinces. Many rivers flowed through this province. In ancient times, the Ji, Yangtze, Yellow, and Huai were referred to as the four major rivers of China. Royal families would hold ceremonies on their banks, and on the five most famous mountains, including Mount Tai and Mount Hua. The flow direction of the Ji River is as large as that of Dingtao, Juye, and Shouzhang in today's Shandong Province. "Luo River" is a tributary of the ancient Yellow River, which flows into the sea in Bin County and Lijin, Shandong Province. Yanzhou was famous for its silk cloth and lacquerware, which were usually transported in bamboo baskets along the Ji River to the capital.

Qingzhou was a province located between Bohai Sea and Mount Tai. Compared to modern geography, it would occupy the East Liaoning and Shandong peninsulas. Many rivers flowed through this province, including the Wei, Zi, and Wen (nowadays the Dawen River). Qingzhou was famous for cereal products in the Mount Tai area as well as silk, pine trees, and precious stones.

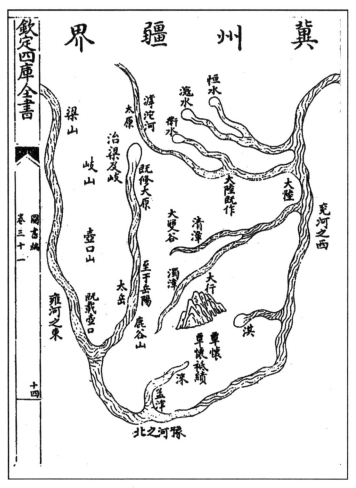

Jizhou and its borders

6 | Chapter One

At the time, Xuzhou was "situated such that it floats on the Huai and Si Rivers and extends to the Yellow River." The Huai River was also one of the four major rivers that flowed into the sea, namely the present-day Huai River and the waste Yellow River in Jiangsu Province. The water source of ancient Si originated from the Bei Mountain of today's Sishui County, Shandong Province, passed through Qufu and Jining and enters the Huai River in the southeast through Pei County and Pi County in Jiangsu Province. The Chinese character "河" is also written as "菏" in the book of *Shuowen Jiezi* and the *Commentary on the Water Classic*, and the ancient He River was also connected with the Si River. Therefore, at that time, Xuzhou's tribute road was from the Huai River to the Si River, then to the Si River, then to the He River, then to the Luo River, and finally to the Yellow River. Tributaries of Xuzhou included five-colored soil, pheasant feathers, phoenix trees in the south of Yi Mountain, floating chimes on the edge of the Si River, true pearl shells of ethnic minorities along the Huai River, dried fish for sacrifice, etc.

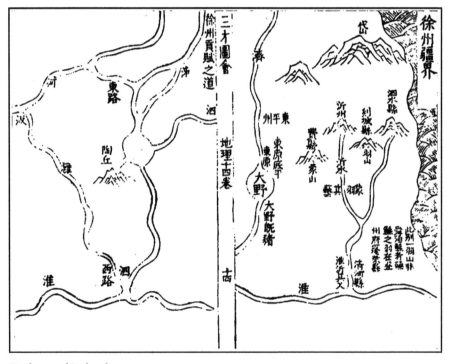

Xuzhou and its borders

Yangzhou was a province located between the south of the Huai River and the East Sea. Today, it would occupy Jiangsu, south Anhui, and east Jiangxi. There were two lakes in the area, namely Pengli (nowadays Boyang Lake) and Zhenzhe (nowadays Tai Lake). Yangzhou was famous for copper, elephant teeth, jade stone, leather, and oranges.

Jingzhou was a province supported by a waterway network consisting of four great rivers in the middle reaches of the Yangtze, i.e., the Yangtze River itself, the Tuo, Qian, and Han Rivers, plus the Luo River—a tributary of the Yellow River which was otherwise disconnected with all other rivers in the region. Luo refers to the present-day Luo River in Henan Province and is a tributary of the Yellow River. The waterway in the middle reaches of the Yangtze River is not connected with the Yellow River Basin and must pass through land transportation in the middle, so it "passes through Luo" and then flows into the Yellow River from Luo River. Like Yangzhou, Jingzhou was known as a major producer of features, yak tails, leather, copper, toon, juniper, cypress, hard rock for arrowheads, bamboo shafts, the chosen weed for sacrifice rituals, handmade headwear, and Yangtze River turtles.

The tribute ships from Yuzhou travel on the Luo River to the Yellow River. Yuzhou is in the south of the Yellow River, which flows from Luo River to the Yellow River, with convenient transportation. The items offered as tribute include lacquer, silk, hemp, satin, fine wool, and whetstone.

The tribute boats in Liangzhou "traveled in Qian River, then left the boats and went ashore on land, then entered Mian River, entered Wei River, and finally crossed Wei River to reach the Yellow River." Qian River is today's Bao River. Mian River, now known as Ju River in Shaanxi, originates from Lueyang County and flows into Han River in the southwest of Mian County. Wei River originates from Weiyuan County, Gansu Province, and flows into the Yellow River in the east. Since the Han River and the Wei River are not connected, they must be connected by land transportation. Among Liangzhou's tribute items, the metals include gold, iron, and silver; the stones include carved stones, arrows, and chimes; and the fur includes animal skins such as bear, fox, and civet skins.

Yongzhou is described as "From the Yellow River near the Jishi Mountain, the tribute ships reached the Longmen and Xi River and met up with ships going upstream from the Wei River to the north of the Wei River." Yongzhou is located in the upper reaches of the Yellow River, from the Jishi Mountain in Linxia, Gansu

Province, to the Longmen Mountain in the northeast of Hancheng, Shaanxi Province. The tribute items include jade and so on.

The Nine Provinces described in the book of *Yu Gong* might have been the imagination of the ancient Chinese. Yet it must have been based on reality. Ancient China must have known that rivers were connected with each other, as in a network. Transportation by waterway had already developed in the era of Yin (殷). In the language, many characters with the word root "ship" (舟) appeared. In other words, there were already ships in different forms at this time. Tribute from the Nine Provinces reflects the local specialties of different regions. Tributes of the Nine Provinces paid to the Emperor may have also reflected commerce carried out via the waterways.

2. From the Nine Provinces to the Greater Nine Provinces

The compilers of the book of *Yu Gong* did not use the actual boundaries of states in the pre-Qin period. That is, they did not use the actual political divisions to describe the geographical areas they knew but used a virtual "county" to divide the areas they knew into nine comprehensive units based on natural geography: Jizhou, Yanzhou, Qingzhou, Xuzhou, Yangzhou, Jingzhou, Yuzhou, Liangzhou, and Yongzhou, which are called "Nine Provinces." In addition to the Nine Provinces depicted in *Yu Gong*, the pre-Qin classics *Zhifang*, *Erya*, and *Master Lü's Spring and Autumn Annals* also have their own concepts of "Nine Provinces," and some were even divided into twelve units and called "Twelve Zhou."

Nine Provinces in *Yu Gong* corresponds to today's geographical region. Mr. Gu Jiegang believes that the region of Jizhou is equivalent to the region to the east of the Yellow River (West River) in the west of Shanxi Province and the north of the Yellow River (South River) in Henan Province, which is transferred from the Taihang Mountains to the west of the ancient Yellow River (East River) in the northeast of Hebei Province. This area is the birthplace of the Yellow River civilization, which is listed as the first in Nine Provinces by the book of *Yu Gong*. To the east of the ancient Yellow River (Dong River), to the south, to Ji River (a section of the Yellow River channel from the north of Jinan in Shandong Province to the Bohai Sea), including the northeast of Henan Province, the south of Hebei Province, and the west of Shandong Province, is called Yanzhou. To the southeast

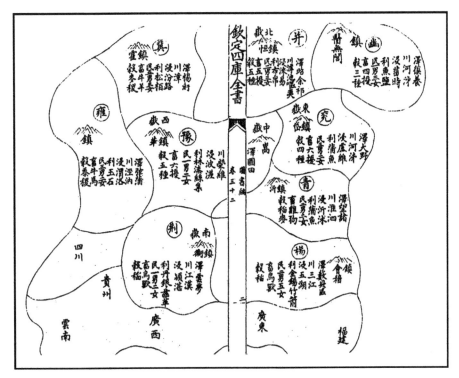

Map of Nine Provinces described in the book of "Yu Gong"

of Yanzhou, today's Shandong Peninsula is Qingzhou. To the south of Qingzhou is Xuzhou, which is located south of Mount Tai and north of Huai River (the old Yellow River on this map), namely, the south of Shandong, the north of Jiangsu and Anhui. From the south of the Huai River to the East China Sea, including most of present-day Jiangsu, Anhui, and Zhejiang provinces and all of Shanghai, as well as the eastern corner of northeastern Jiangxi, Henan, and Hubei provinces, is called Yangzhou. The middle reaches of the Yangtze River to the west of Yangzhou, from the Jing Mountain in the west of Nanzhang, Hubei Province, to the south of Hengshan, Hunan Province, that is, most of today's Hubei and Hunan provinces, and the west of Jiangxi Province, is Jingzhou. From the north of Jing Mountain in Hubei to the Yellow River, including most of today's Henan and the north of Hubei, it is called Yuzhou. To the south of the Qin Mountains, the southern part of today's Shaanxi and Gansu provinces, as well as Sichuan and Chongqing, is called Liangzhou. To the north of the Qin Mountains and to the west of the Yellow River

(West River), most of today's Sichuan and Gansu provinces are called Yongzhou.[3]

According to *Yu Gong*, the Nine Provinces was regarded as a whole region. "Nine Provinces" is described in the book as "the east reaches the sea, the west extends to the desert, and the north and south reach the far reaches of the earth, and the prestige and teaching of Dayu spreads to the Four Seas and Nine Provinces." That is to say, the area of Nine Provinces extends to the East China Sea (today's Bohai Sea) in the east, to quicksand in the west, and far to the north and south. Dayu's prestige and teaching spread all over the world. "Four Seas" is another regional concept of the ancients, who believed that the Nine Provinces mainland was surrounded by the sea in the east, south, west, and north directions. In reality, there are seas in the southern and eastern parts of China. In reality, however, there were only deserts to the north and west. As a whole, "Nine Provinces" in the book of *Yu Gong* reflects the ancient people's recognition of the region of Chinese civilization. "The walking routes of Dayu are divided as Nine Provinces." After the governance of Dayu, the land and water in Nine Provinces was leveled, the soil and tribute were graded, and the national authority was used to formulate the five-suit system. The prestige and enlightenment of the Son of Heaven infiltrated the land of Nine Provinces. The *Book of Documents · Counsels of Dayu* described it as "he was ordered to rule over the four seas and be the ruler of the world." This cultural identity also puts forward requirements for political unification. The State of Qin, located on the Loess Plateau, became the ultimate winner, unifying the "Nine Provinces" by force: "Qin unified the four seas ... divided the world into commanderies and counties."[4]

Within the four seas, other civilizations different from Huaxia also existed. The former was often referred to as "Yi" (夷). For example, tribes to the northeast of Jizhou were called Daoyi (literally meaning Yi on the islands). "Yuyi" in Qingzhou, "Huaiyi" in Xuzhou, "Daoyi" in Yangzhou, "Heyi" in Liangzhou, etc. This shows that there were many civilizations within the region.

In the 3rd century, Zou Yan (305–240 BC), a citizen of Kingdom Qi, invented another concept called the Greater Nine Provinces.

---

3. Refer to Gu Jiegang's annotations of *Yu Gong* in Hou Ren, ed., *Selected Readings of Ancient Chinese Geographic Classics*, vol. 1 (Beijing: Xueyuan Publishing House, 2005), 1–30.
4. "Treatise on Geography (Part One)," book 6, in *Book of Han*, vol. 28 (Beijing: Zhonghua Book Company, 1962).

What the Confucians' called China was only one in the eighty-first of the whole world. The name of China is Chixian Shenzhou. There are Nine Provinces within the divine state of Chixian, which are the Nine Provinces divided by Xia Yu, but they cannot be considered provinces (Zhou). There are nine other states outside of China, like Chixian Shenzhou, which are called Nine Provinces. It is only a state when it is surrounded by a small sea, where the people and even the animals cannot interact with each other. There are nine such states, and there are seas surrounding them, and that is the edge of heaven and earth.[5]

According to his system, the world was divided into a hierarchy of three layers. The Nine Provinces depicted by the book of *Yu Gong* was referred to as Chixian/China. The countries surrounding China were called the "Mid Nine Provinces." They were surrounded by the seas called the Bi Seas (裨海). Outside the Bi Seas, there were 9 other countries, at the same rank as the "Mid Nine Provinces." These were referred to the "The Greater Nine Provinces"—or the world. The world was surrounded by oceans, called the Grand Ying Ocean (大瀛海). The Nine Provinces depicted in *Yu Gong* were relatively small in size. Each only accounted for 1/729 parts of the world.

Sima Qian's evaluation of Zou Yan's theory seems to be not high: "His method, which is really just an 'analogy', extrapolating from the small to the infinite, from the present to the ancient"; it is believed that Zou Yan's thought is based on deduction and comes to a conclusion: "First of all, China's famous mountains and rivers are listed, and the animals and birds that pass through the valley, and the animals and birds that are cultivated by water and soil, and the things that are rare, so it is pushed forward and predict things we cannot see in other parts in the world."[6] However, the reasons for Zou Yan's "the Great Nine Provinces" theory, in addition to the elements of derivation, also reflected people's further understanding of geography at that time. The first is the book *of Yu Gong* Nine Provinces, which is the region where the Chinese civilization is located. In reality, there are seas only in the east and south, and the west and north are land. With the increase of contacts with nomadic peoples in the Western Regions and

---

5. *Records of the Grand Historian*, vol. 74 in book 7, 2344.
6. *Records of the Grand Historian*, vol. 74 in book 7, 2344.

Mongolian grasslands, it is inevitable to contact some other regional civilizations. The ancients may have this idea: there are many civilized regions on the continent where people live, and Nine Provinces may only be one of them, so there is the concept of "Central Nine Provinces." Second, ancient Chinese already knew of the seas and oceans. The Kingdom of Qi (modern east Shandong), where Zou Yan resided, was a peninsula by the sea. After Qin's unification with China, the legend of Xu Fu and Sanshen Mountain confirmed the possibility of maritime exchanges between the Qi people and Japan and the Korean peninsula from one side. The third is the amplification of the concept of the world. *Zhuangzi · Autumn Water* thinks that China is just like only a drop in the bucket and has realized that China is only a part of the world.[7] The Great Nine Provinces might very well stem from communications between ancient Chinese and the outside world.

3. The Concept of Four Remotes and the Western Expedition by King Mu of Zhou

Those regions far away from the Nine Provinces were often referred to as the "Remotes" or hinterlands. According to legend, *Erya*, written by the Duke of Zhou, said in the chapter of "Shidi": "Guzhu, Beihu, Western Queen, and Rixia are the Four Remotes." Guo Pu, a native of the Jin Dynasty, said: "The Guzhu is in the north, Beihu is in the south, the Western Queen is in the west, and the Rixia is in the east, all of which are the Four Remotes of the country."[8] Kong Yingda thought: *"Er Ya* called the Four Remotes the lands far away from the four seas, and it is also said that the country is in the Four Remotes."[9] The emergence of the concept of "Four Remotes" indicates that after the initial formation of the Chinese Civilization Zone (Nine Provinces), cultural exchanges between China

---

7. Hu Axiang, *Magnificent Is This Name: A Study of the Appellations of "China" from Ancient to Modern Times* (Wuhan: Hubei Education Publishing House, 2000), 317.
8. Guo Pu (Jin Dynasty) with annotations and Xing Bing (Song Dynasty) with commentary, *Erya with Annotations and Commentary*, vol. 7, in *Four-Part Comprehensive Collection* version (Shanghai: Zhonghua Book Company, 1936), 75 (upper).
9. Kong Yingda (Tang Dynasty) with commentary, *Erya with Annotations and Commentary*, vol. 1, in *Four-Part Comprehensive Collection* version (Shanghai: Zhonghua Book Company, 1936), 297 (upper).

and foreign countries have begun. The "wasteland countries" shows that the civilization of these regions is quite different from the Chinese civilization.

Guzhu was probably a princedom in the north. Its old town was located in present-day Lulong County, Hebei.

Beihu literally meant "northern windows." It was located in the south, probably at the northern tip of Vietnam. Because of the heat in the region, residents built their windows facing north for cooler temperature.

Rixia means the country located where the sun rises. *Huainanzi · Patterns of Heaven*: "The sun rises in the valley of the rising sun, appears in the west, and wafts over the Fusang, which is called the morning dawn." Probably, it referred to Japan.

There were different theories about the origins of the Western Queen (西王母). According to the research of some scholars, the Western Queen is a Skyth tribe (the nomadic tribes distributed in the west end of the Hexi Corridor and the north and south of the Tian Mountains are called the Skyth in China, while the nomadic tribes scattered in Eastern Europe, Siberia, and Central Asia are called the Scythians in Greece). The word "West" implies both the meaning and the first sound of the Scythia nation. The Kunlun region, where the Western Queen are located, has always been said to be different. Some people say it is on the side of Qinghai Lake on the Qinghai–Tibet Plateau, some say it is on the side of Heaven Lake in Xinjiang, some say it is on the Pamir Plateau, and some people have studied it in Central Asia, Persia, and even as far as Europe. This may reflect the migration process of the Scythians from east to west, from the original southern foot of the Qilian Mountains to the west.

The story of the western expedition by King Mu of Zhou reflected the communications between the Yellow River civilizations and tribes in the Western Regions. The expedition took place in the 3rd century. *The Annals of King Mu, Bamboo Annals,* and *The Records of the Grand Historian* also recorded the story.

Discovery of *The Annals of King Mu* had its own legend. In AD 279, a grave robber called Buzhun unearthed 10 carts of documents written on bamboo slips from the tomb of King Wei in the Warring States Period. The thief couldn't recognize the words and used the bamboo slips for fire. When the local authorities heard about it, they saved the rest of the bamboo slips from being burnt. During the reign of Taikang (AD 280–289), Emperor Wu of the Jin Dynasty ordered the Secretary General to be responsible for sorting out the bamboo slips that had been destroyed, rearranging them in the original order, and transcribing each book again with the official script that was in use at that time, and get 75 ancient books. The *Tale of King Mu, Son of Heaven* has five chapters. The bamboo slips were two feet and four inches long (about 55 cm today) in the Jin Dynasty, each with 40 characters, and were woven together with plain silk ropes. At the same time, there is the *Bamboo Annals*; the latest historical event recorded in the book is "the 20th year of King Jin (299 BC)," "King Jin" refers to the king of Wei Xiang, and this ancient tomb should be the tomb of the king of Wei Xiang.

After King Mu defeated the nomadic tribes in the northwest, the routes between the Kingdom of Zhou and Western Regions were restored. So, King Mu led a group of officials and seven elites in the eight-headed chariot driven by Zao Fu, with Bo Yao as the guide and the best driver at that time, Zao Fu, who drove the carriage. The line was mighty. Starting from Haojing, he crossed the Yellow River to the north and passed through the Qunyu Mountains, places in the territory of the Dog Rong, such as the Xixia clan, Heshou, and Qunyu Mountain. Heading west along the river bend, passing through the Xixia clan in today's Qaidam Basin, he continued westward to Zhuyushi, then traversed the Chongshan, Zhuzhe, and Kunlun hills, arriving at Qunyu Mountain. The mountain was full of jade stones without any soil, so there were "few plants and no birds or beasts." King Mu of Zhou enjoyed his journey and traveled for four days, collecting many jade artifacts. At every stop, King Mu gifted the tribal chiefs with silk, copperware, shell currency, cinnabar, and cassia ginger. In return, the chiefs presented him with a large number of horses, cattle, and sheep. After leaving Qunyu Mountain, King Mu continued westward, traveling another 3,000 *li* before reaching the kingdom where the Queen Mother of the West resided. Based on this journey, the Queen Mother's kingdom should be located west of the Tianshan Mountains in present-day Central Asia. Deeply captivated by Central Asian culture and warmly entertained by the Queen Mother of the West, King Mu was so joyful that he forgot to return home. After bidding farewell at a banquet by the side of the Jade Pool, King Mu took the route through the Black Waters, traveling north for two thousand *li*, passing through the vast plains, and then returning via the Tianshan North Road.

The Records of the Grand Historian, however, recorded a different story. The King of Xuyan in North China took advantage of King Mu's absence and staged a mutiny. After hearing the news, King Mu sped home and defeated the King of Xuyan.[10] According to this record, one could deduct that there were sound communication systems in this era, because information of the mutiny could reach him in such a short period of time.[11]

The western expedition of King Mu also underlined the communications between Yellow River civilizations and tribes in the Western Regions. The Mountain of Jade mentioned in the documents could be Mount Kunlun. Pre-USSR researchers also discovered silk made in the 5th century BC in Altay Prefecture of Xinjiang, China.

One piece of silk was woven with dragon and phoenix patterns, which were typical Chinese symbols used for decoration.[12] In 1977 in Xinjiang, archeologists discovered some cloth and lacquerware made around the Warring States Period. The patterns of rhombus could only be found in inland China at the time. Those discoveries were very similar to the descriptions of the presents given by King Mu to different tribe chieftains on his expedition.

4. CITIES, CARTS, AND TRADE IN THE EARLY YEARS OF CHINESE CIVILIZATION

Chinese cities in their primitive form came into being in the Western Zhou Dynasty. The city structures included: palaces of kings, princedoms, and residencies of masters and nobles. Urban planning came into being around the same time as the cities, and layouts of roads and streets played an important role in ancient urban planning.

Kao Gong Ji (*Records of Examination of Craftsman*) is the earliest handicraft technology document found in China *Kao Gong Ji* at present. It was written in the late Spring and Autumn Period and the early Warring States Period and is an official book of the State of Qi. In the Western Han Dynasty, due to the lack of the "Winter Official Chapter" of the book of *Zhou Guan*, Liu De, the King Xian of Hejian, added it with the title of *Kao Gong Ji*, and Liu Xin changed the *Zhou Guan* to *Zhou Li* when proofreading the book, so later generations also called the *Kao*

---

10. "Hereditary Houses of Zhao," in *Records of the Grand Historian*, vol. 43, book 6, 1779.
11. See Wang Zijin, *Post Offices and Post* (Changchun: Changchun Press, 2008), 28.
12. Lu Jinke, "On the Relationship between China and Altay Tribes in Ancient Times," *Journals of Archeology*, no. 2 (1957).

Gong Ji as *Zhou Li · Kao Gong Ji*. The "craftsmen" here are equivalent to today's architects. They need to operate according to this specification when building the royal city. "Guo" refers to the city, and "Guozhong" refers to the areas within the city.

According to its instructions, each side of the city walls measured 9 *li* (one *li* = 500 meters); there were three gates on each of the walls. Therefore, the total length of the city walls measured 36 *li* and there were altogether 12 gates. Three lanes went through each gate. The middle lane was for vehicles, and the two other lanes were for pedestrians, with men walking on the left and women on the right.

The streets stretching from east to west were called "Wei" (Latitude); the avenues running from north to south were called "Jing" (Longitude). There were nine streets and nine avenues in total running through the city. "The paths of longitude and latitude can all accommodate nine tracks. A track refers to the width of a wheel rut, which is six feet six inches for the carriage. If seven inches are added to the side, it totals eight feet. This is called the nine-track width, which accumulates to seventy-two feet, equating to about eleven steps."[13] Each street or avenue measured a length of 16 meters. The King's Palace was located in the center. Temples for worshiping ancestors were on its left, while temples for ordinary people were on its right. The space in front of the palace was for ministers, who discussed governmental affairs.

The term "环涂" refers to the roads encircling a city. These roads are seven tracks wide, approximately equivalent to 13 meters in modern measurements. The roads connecting the royal city with the cities of the nobles, and the territories of senior officials, are called "野涂" (wild roads). They are five tracks wide, roughly equivalent to about ten meters today. By the Warring States period, different levels of roads, such as "巨涂" (major roads) and "小涂" (minor roads), connected the various states.

According to legends, the first cart/carriage in China was invented by Xizhong in the Xia Dynasty. In the Shang, there were many kinds of vehicles. On one hand, the word root "Che" (车, carriage) appeared on many inscriptions like bones and tortoise shells, as well as other historical recordings. On the other hand, vehicles

---

13. Zheng Xuan (Han Dynasty) with annotations and Jia Gongyan (Tang Dynasty) with commentary, *Zhou Li with Annotations and Commentary*, vol. 41, in *Siku Beiyao* edition, 411 (below).

Transportation Systems in the Pre-Qin Period | 17

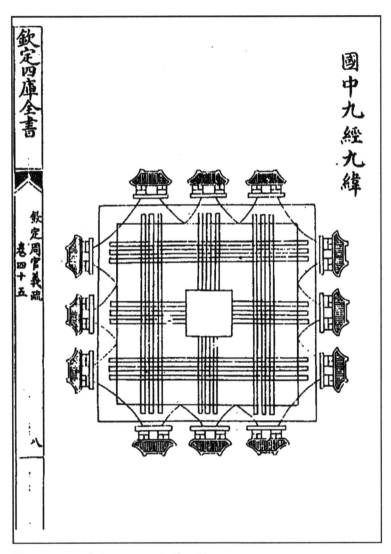

Nine streets and nine avenues in the cities

of the Shang were discovered in Anyang, Henan. There were war chariots and carriages driven by cattle or horses. Carriages driven by cattle were for cargo. Their structures were simple with very large containers. Carriages driven by horses were for people. At the time, only nobles were permitted to ride. They were very sturdy, usually decorated with beautiful design and exquisite craftsmanship.

The *Records of Examination of Craftsman* also recorded how to make carriages in detail. First, it drafted ten requirements on the makings and examinations of wheels, the most important part of a carriage:

a. Are the wheels round enough? If not, then the wheels will slow down the speed of carriages.
b. Are the surface of wheels flat?
c. Are the wheel spokes straight?
d. Are the parts of wheels of equal weight?

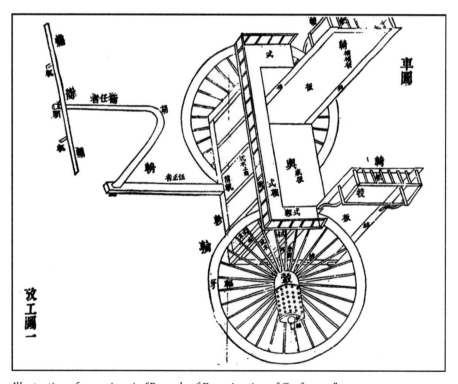

Illustration of a carriage in "Records of Examination of Craftsman"

e. Put the wheels into the water and see if they float at the same level.
f. Are the two wheels from the same carriage of the same size and weight?
g. Are the carriages of appropriate length and size?
h. The wheels should be of appropriate size. If they are too large, then it will be difficult to mount. If they are too small, it will be tiring for the horses.
i. The wood for axles must be of the highest quality. They should be hard and durable.
j. The wood for wheels must also be hard and durable.

Carriage making required different techniques. Therefore, different craftsmen were needed, for example, the so-called "wheel men." This showed a nuanced division of labor. From the recordings of the *Records of Examination of Craftsman*, one could also tell that carriage making techniques in the Zhou Dynasty had already reached a very high level and requirements were very strict.

In the Warring States Period, communication among different states and foreign countries were greatly improved. The transportation of goods and communications among people was very active. The land of Wei: "the surrounding terrain was flat, like the center of a chariot axle, allowing unrestricted access to the vassal states in all directions and without the isolation of famous mountains and rivers. From Xinzheng to Daliang was more than 200 *li*, and with chariots speeding and soldiers running, it did not take much effort to get there."[14] Famous roads at that time included: Chenggao Road—from Chenggao to Hangu Pass, Xia Road—from Nanyang in Chu State to central China, the Stone Ox Road—from Hanzhong in Qin State to the Shu regions.

With the development of land and water routes, as well as the improvement of transportation tools, logistics and goods transportation significantly increased. During the Spring and Autumn Period, different area specialties were recorded in books. For example, some would say the Er fish in the East Sea tasted best. "The apple of Kunlun, the blossom of the longevity tree," "the dill of Yanghua, the parsley of Yunmeng, and the chrysanthemum of Juqu," "the leaves of the red and mysterious trees," "south of Yumao, on the cliff of the southernmost point, there's a vegetable called Jia Tree, its color is like jade." For delicious staple foods, they had "the grain of Xuan Mountain, the millet of Buzhou, the barley of Yangshan,

---

14. "Ranked Biographies of Zhangyi," in *Records of the Grand Historian*, vol. 70, book 7, 2285.

the foxtail millet of the South Sea." For seasoning, they chose "the ginger of Yangpu, the cinnamon of Zhaoyao, the mushrooms of Yueluo, and the fish sauce of Zhanwei," "the salt of Daxia, the dew of Zaijie, its color is like jade." In a time when there was no environmental pollution, people had high standards for drinking water: "The best waters are the dew of Sanwei and the wells of Kunlun." The preferred fruits are "the fruit of Shatang" and "to the north of Changshan, above Touyuan, there are a hundred fruits consumed by the emperors. East of Jishan, where Qingdao (east of Kunlun Mountain) is, there's sweet locust. The oranges of Jiangpu, the pomelos of Yunmeng, the stone ears above the Han River, are brought from there." For the horses one ride, choose the swift "horse of the Azure Dragon and the steed left by the wind."[15]

Commercial transportation led to specialties from different areas being sold in different states.

> In the North Sea, there were horses that were good at running and dogs that were good at barking, and the states in ancient China could domesticate them. In the South Sea, there were feathers, ivory, rhinoceros hides, Zeng Qing (natural copper sulfate), and cinnabar, and the states in ancient China could conduct business. In the Eastern Sea, there were purple coarse linen, fish, and salt, which the states in ancient China could eat and make clothes with. The West Sea had leather and colorful yak tails, which the states in ancient China could use. So those who fished on the lake would have enough timber, and those who cut wood on the mountains would have enough fresh fish; farmers would have enough utensils without cutting or burning kilns and smelting, and craftsmen and merchants would have enough food without cultivating the land. The tiger and the leopard are to be considered fierce, but the ruler is able to skin them and use them. Therefore, there is nothing that the heavens cover, and the earth carries that does not make the most of their virtues and use them to the fullest to adorn the virtuous above and to feed the common people and make them happy.[16]

---

15. (Qin Dynasty) Lü Buwei, "Benwei," in *Master Lü's Spring and Autumn Annals*, vol. 14, in *Siku Quanshu* edition, vol. 848 (Taipei: Commercial Press, 1983), 374.
16. (Qing Dynasty) Wang Xianqian, "Xunzi Jijie," in *Zhuzi Jicheng*, vol. 2 (Beijing: Zhonghua Book Company, 1957), 103.

Consequently, divisions of labor were consolidated. Merchants often liked to cluster and share information; the development of commerce and clusters of merchants made the transportation hubs more cosmopolitan. "They told the merchants to gather and live together, to observe the needs of the seasons, to investigate the availability of local goods, and to find out the prices of goods in the market, and then to carry the goods on their backs and in their arms, to carry them on their shoulders, to lift them on their shoulders, to pull them by heavy ox carts and light wagons, and to carry them from place to place, to exchange what they had for what they did not have, to buy at low prices and sell at high prices. They did these things from morning till night and taught their sons and daughters, talking to each other about ways of making money, showing each other their profits, and telling each other the prices of goods."[17] With the development of commerce and the gathering of merchants, most of the cities located in the transportation hub during the Spring and Autumn and Warring States periods became famous commercial capitals. According to historical records such as the *Records of the Grand Historian* and the *Book of Han*, important commercial capitals include Xianyang in the State of Qin (today's northeast of Xianyang in Shaanxi), Daliang in the State of Wei (today's Kaifeng in Henan), Handan in the State of Zhao, Linzi in the State of Qi (today's Linzi in Zibo, Shandong), Ji in the State of Yan (today's Xuanwu District in Beijing), Luoyi in the State of Zhou (today's Luoyang in Henan), Xingyang in the State of Han (today's north of Xingyang in Henan), Yingdu in the State of Chu (today's north of Jiangling in Hubei) Shouchun (now Shou County, Anhui Province), Wu of the State of Yue (now Suzhou, Jiangsu Province). According to the records of King Qi's Token of the E Place, the King of Chu Huai, unearthed in Shou County, Anhui Province, 50 vehicles or 150 ships can be dispatched for transportation at a time. The prosperity of Yingdu in the State of Chu was described by Huan Tan, a native of the Eastern Han Dynasty, as "in the capital of Hubei in the State of Chu, in the city of E, vehicles are banging against vehicles, and people are crowding each other so that the new clothes people wear in the morning are torn by the evening."[18] Linzi of the Qi State is known as the first capital of the East: "On the

---

17. *Discourses of the States*, vol. 6 (Shanghai: Shanghai Ancient Books Publishing House, 1998), 227.
18. Huan Tan, "Xin Lun," in *Peiwen Yunfu*, vol. 16, under the entry "Zhao Yi Xian," Wanyou Wenku edition, vol. 1 (Shanghai: Commercial Press), 700 (middle).

roads of Linzi, wheels crash against wheels, people's shoulders rub against each other, connecting people's clothes to form curtains, raising their sleeves to form large curtains, sweat can be woven into the rain, families are rich and wealthy, and their ambitions are high." The residents of this rich city have abundant leisure and entertainment activities: "they were always performing and drumming, playing the zither, fighting cock and dogs, and playing chess to have fun."[19]

Apart from the increase of goods transportation, scholar travel among different states also became very popular. "Neighboring countries look at each other, the sound of chickens and dogs hear each other, and the people do not communicate with each other until they die of old age" has changed to "the footprints are connected with the borders of the vassal states, and the car tracks are connected thousands of miles away." One famous example was Confucius in the late Spring

Portrait of Confucius

---

19. *Strategies of the Warring States*, vol. 8, see Fan Xiangyong, *Compilation of Annotations of Strategies of the Warring States* (Shanghai: Shanghai Ancient Books Publishing House, 2006), 539.

and Autumn Period. His first visit to foreign states was made in 518 BC. With the support of Duke Zhao of Lu, Confucius and his students went to Luoyi of Zhou (present-day Luoyang, and China's political and cultural center of the time.) There, Confucius not only read valued books but also talked to many other scholars, including Laozi, the founder of Taoism, and Zhou's official Changhong. Next year, Confucius visited the State of Qi.

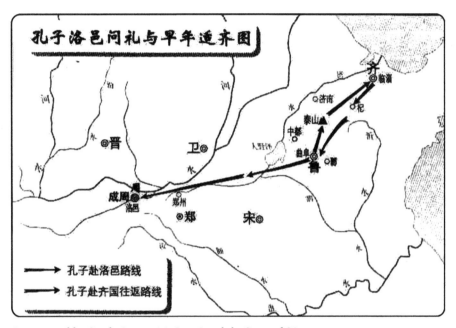

Routes used by Confucius to visit Luoyi and the State of Qi[20]

From 497 BC to 484 BC, Confucius and his students traveled to many states. They were the States of Wei, Chen, Song, Zheng, and Chu. During their visits, which lasted over 10 years, Confucius made speeches wherever he went and published his thoughts. One of his most famous sayings was: "How happy we are, to meet friends from afar!" For a friend to travel from afar, road infrastructure was a minimum requirement.

After Confucius, some other scholars also traveled frequently among different states. For example, Mencius, who was followed by hundreds of people. Su Qin

---

20. Luo Chenglie, *Atlas of Confucius' History* (Beijing: Sinomap Press, 2009), 64.

was famous because he successfully persuaded the rulers of six states to make an alliance against the State of Qin. The six states were: Yan, Zhao, Han, Wei, Qi, and Chu. On the contrary, Zhang Yi, consul-in-chief of Qin, successfully disbanded the alliance. People at that time said that "When he becomes angry, the feudal lords fear; when he calms down, the world is at peace and without incident." The travels of these scholars greatly enhanced communication and political and cultural exchange among different areas of China and brought about social progresses.

CHAPTER TWO

EXPANSION OF COMMUNICATIONS IN THE QIN AND HAN DYNASTIES
—Routes, Silk Roads, and Tower Ships

In the Qin and Han dynasties, land route networks and waterways expanded greatly. Waterways connecting the Yellow, Yangtze, and Pearl Rivers were constructed and communication networks were developed among major economic zones.

After Emperor Qin Shi Huang unified China, he adopted a series of policies and measures to solidify the country, including setting up a "Commandery-County" system. The Qin government not only standardized road width and Chinese characters but also currency. In terms of land communications, roads were built to form a network with Xianyang at the center. In terms of water communications, canals were built to connect central China and the Lingnan districts in the south. In his lifetime, Emperor Qin made five patrols across the country. By doing so, he not only proclaimed his authority but also enhanced cultural exchange among different regions. His patrols also marked the formation of national communication networks.

Territories in the Western and Eastern Han dynasties were greater than that of the Qin. Their land networks were far denser than previously, especially in remote mountainous areas where new trails were blazed. Some famous trails including Yelang Road, Lingguan Route, Baoxie Road, and Ziwu Road connecting Ba-Shu and Guanzhong, Huizhong Road to the western fortress of Xiaoguan, Feihu Road located in the northern part of Hebei and Shanxi to prevent the southern invasion of the Xiongnu, and Qiaodao Road in southern Hunan to Lingnan, etc., which connected central China to southwestern regions, were forged. Meanwhile, tower ships were a landmark in the development of water way communications. Several silk roads were developed, which eased communications between China and foreign countries; international trade played an important role at the time.

1. Road Networks in the Qin Dynasty

In 222 BC, General Wang Ben of Qin defeated the states of Yan and Zhao. A year later, Wang Ben bypassed the Qi defense of its western border, forcing the King of Qi to surrender. By then, the State of Qin had wiped out all of its components and unified China.

Many factors contributed to Qin's victory, with the advanced communications system being one of them. King Hui of Qin wanted to attack Shu in the south, but he was frustrated that there was no way to do it, so he came up with a plan: "Make five stone cattle, put the tail down with gold, and say that it can turn shit into gold. The king of Shu Fuli led the five soldiers to make the road. Qin envoys Zhang Yi and Sima Cuo sought a way to destroy Shu; thus, it was called Shiniu Road."[1] This first road across the Qin Mountains and connecting Sichuan and Shaanxi was opened with the joint efforts of the Qin and Shu people. The road construction in Qin was also very developed. When archaeologists excavated 14 tombs of the Qin and Han dynasties in Fangmatan, Tianshui, Gansu Province in 1986, they found seven maps painted on pine boards in Tomb No. 1. These maps were drawn around 300 BC. There is a traffic line beside the main river in the No. 4 drawing, which is equivalent to the Fangmatan–Huangjiaping section of today's Shuidongli Highway, reflecting the general situation of the traffic from Tianshui to the south of Qin Mountains during the Warring States Period, and is of great significance in the history of transportation.[2]

The Qin people were also gifted in building bridges and carriages. They built the first floating bridge over the Yellow River, and the first two-wheel carriage

---

1. (Northern Wei) Li Daoyuan, *Commentary on the Water Classic*, annotated by Chen Qiaoyi (Beijing: Zhonghua Book Company, 2007), 645.
2. See Zhang Xiugui, *Research on China's Historical Geography and Ancient Maps* (Beijing: Social Sciences Academic Press, 2006), 551.

in China's history. The Qin boasted plenty of carriages. It was recorded that even when the Marquis of Xiang was removed of his title in 271 BC, over 1,000 carriages followed him on the way to his fiefdom. The Qin were also proficient in water transport and had many types of fast boat for men and cargo.

> In the west of Qin, there was Ba and Shu, and the ships were used to carry grain. They were anchored at Wenshan and traveled in parallel, going down the river for more than 3,000 *li* to the Chu capital. A boat carrying 50 men and food for three months was floated in the water. The journey was long but effortless, and in less than ten days, they could reach the Han Pass and confront the Chu army.[3]

Han Pass, also known as Jiang Pass and Qutang Pass, is one of the passes of the State of Chu in the Spring and Autumn Period on the Chijia Mountain on the north bank of the East Yangtze River in Fengjie, Sichuan Province. This record may be exaggerated, but it also reflects that there were many types of ships in the State of Qin at that time, including those specially loaded with goods and those specially transported with people, and the speed of navigation was relatively fast.

The newly incorporated Yandi, Qidi, and Jingdi are far away from the Guanzhong area, which is inconvenient to control after Qin Shi Huang unified China. Therefore, the country is divided into 36 commanderies politically. In terms of the system, "one law is used, one measure was used, and one written language is applied."[4] One of the measures of "using the same unit of measure" is to "clear the river and clear away the obstacles," open up the passes between the six countries, repair the roads, and establish a new national transportation system. In Emperor Qin Shi Huang's era, a new national communications network was built with the capital—Xianyang—in the center. These were the eight major roads:

a. Sanchuan the East Sea Route: This was the major route from west to east, stretching from the Guanzhong area to the seas (the Huanghai and the East Sea). It also had the largest amount of cargo transportation in the Qin era.

---

3. "Ranked Biographies of Zhangyi," in *Records of the Grand Historian*, vol. 7, 2290.
4. "Annals of the Qin Shi Huang," in *Records of the Grand Historian*, vol. 1, 239.

b. Nanyang Nan Commandery Route: Setting out from Xianyang to Nanyang and then to Nan Commandery. This was an important route connecting central China to the middle reaches of the Yangtze River.
c. Handan Guangyang Route: It connected the Guanzhong area with the North China Plain.
d. Longxi Beidi Route: It connected the Guanzhong area with the northwest regions, i.e., the eastern part of the Silk Road.
e. Hanzhong Bashu Route: It went through the Qinling Mountains to Shu and the Ba Commanderies in southwest China.
f. Zhi (Straight) Route: It set out from Xianyang to the Jiuyuan fortress in the north and was completed in 212 BC. This was an important route for transporting supplies to the Jiuyuan garrison. The purpose of building the Zhi Route is to prevent the nomadic Xiongnu from going south and transporting materials to the military town of Jiuyuan City through this road. In the event of war, the follow-up cavalry troops of the Qin Dynasty can arrive at the Jiuyuan front from the capital of Xianyang in three days and three nights through the Zhi Route. Therefore, this is a military highway. Sima Qian once visited the whole course of the straight road: "I went to the northern border and returned by the Zhi Route, and along the way, I saw the Great Wall and forts that Meng Tian had built for Qin, digging mountains and filling valleys to connect to the Zhi Route, which would have been an abuse of the people's manpower and resources."[5]
g. Beibian Route: the Qin administration built a new Great Wall based on the walls of previous warring states. Along the new Great Wall, the Qin built a side path running from west to east, for better inspection.
h. Binghai Route (Seaside Route): It started from Liaodong Peninsula in the north to the southern tip of Hangzhou Bay in Southeast China. This route went along the eastern coast.[6]

In 220 BC, Emperor Qin ordered the building of "driveways," effectively large, fast roads. The main purpose of the driveways was for the Emperor to inspect

---

5. "Ranked Biographies of Meng Tian," in *Records of the Grand Historian*, vol. 88, book 8, 2570.
6. Wang Zijin, *Communications in Qin and Han Dynasties* (Beijing: Press of Chinese Communist Party School, 1994), 28–32.

his territory. According to Jia Shan, a native of the Western Han Dynasty, "The Bohai Sea has everything from the ancient borders of Yan (north of Hebei and west of Liaoning) in the east to the ancient Wu and Chu (Anhui and Hubei) in the south (you can feel it all once you get there). The width of the road reaches 50 meters, and a pine tree is planted every three *zhang* (a unit in Chinese lineal measurement slightly longer than ten feet). This is the driveway, which radiates from Xianyang to all counties in the country. The driveway was so magnificent that later dynasties would not alter it."[7] The construction of driveway has become an important part of traffic construction in the Qin and Han dynasties.

Portrait of Qin Shi Huang

The Qin administration had strict standards for building driveways. The first criterion for the construction of the road is "the road is fifty steps wide, and there should be a tree every three *zhang*." According to Kong Yingda, "Driveway, namely middle road, is the royal road where the emperors would gallop, so it is called driveway, which means a place where the emperors can walk (and run)

---

7. "Ranked Biographies of Meng Tian," in *Records of the Grand Historian*, vol. 88, 2570.

their carriage and horses."[8] The middle of the driveway is the royal road, and there are side roads on both sides. The way between the royal road and the bypass road is similar to the way that urban roads are separated by street trees today. Trees are also used as a sign of isolation, and a pine tree is planted every three *zhang*. Roads must be 50 steps (69 meters) wide, and every 7 meters a tree should be planted. The royal road intended for only the Emperor was located in the middle of the driveway. There were two sideways next to the royal road, separated by trees every 7 meters.

In Xianyang, Shaanxi, an ancient avenue was discovered. It was 50 meters in width and looked very similar to the ancient driveway system. Driveways were discovered in Chunhua, Xunyi, Huangling, Fu County, Ganquan and other places in Shaanxi. The widths of the road is 50 to 60 meters. Another view is that "three *zhang* and a tree" means that the middle royal road is three *zhang* wide, and the width of "fifty steps wide" includes the middle royal road and the side roads on both sides, and the royal road and the side roads are separated by pine trees. The provisions of the Han Dynasty are the same as the latter point of view: "Let the envoys have the right to run on the sides of the road, and not to run in the middle of the road that is three *zhang* wide."[9] The second is "build thick outside, hide with the golden spine," which is the technical rule of pavement construction. It requires that the subgrade construction should be solid and form wide and gentle slopes on both sides. When building the road surface, the road must be compacted with a metal cone to make it high and above the surface to divide the water. The high level of construction standards made the driveway a highway used by the Qin Dynasty.

One anecdote stated that Prince Liu He of Han once traveled from his palace to Dingtao on the driveway. He covered a total length of 135 *li* within a day, driven by seven horses. For those times, the speed was impressive. It was said that his servants tried their best to follow the prince on the sideroad, however, their horses were so outpaced that they dropped dead halfway.[10]

These ancient driveways were highways, and horses were the fastest carriers. However, at first there were no measures to block out other traffic. Strict rules

---

8. Zheng Xuan (Han Dynasty) with annotation and Kong Yingda (Tang Dynasty) with commentary, *Annotations and Commentaries on the Book of Rites*, vol. 4, in *Sibu Beiyao* edition, 47 (upper).
9. "Bao Xuan," in *Book of Han*, vol. 72, Yan Shigu's annotation cited Ru Chun, book 10, 3094.
10. *The Book of Han*, vol. 63, book 9, 2764.

were implemented by the Qin, forbidding other carriages to use the royal roads.

The Han administration maintained these regulations. It was said that once Emperor Cheng of Han, then still a crown prince, was summoned by his father Emperor Yuan. The crown prince wouldn't travel across the royal driveway. He had to detour, underlining the regulations. This case shows that the implementation of the system at that time was quite strict. After Emperor Yuan knew it, he issued a special order to allow the prince to cross the driveway. The sidewalks on both sides of the driveway are for senior officials to use. The middle- and lower-level officials or other personnel must obtain permission to use them. Those who violate the regulations will have their horses and carriages confiscated.

2. The Four Royal Patrols by Emperor Qin Shi Huang

Even though the Qin Empire had united China, there were still nobles of the other six states who sought opportunities to rebel against the Qin. This is why the "Commandery-County" system was implemented.

At the time, communication was still primitive. Royal patrols were effective means for Emperors to project authority. In addition, between Qin and the six countries, although the scholar-bureaucrat class has already had various forms of mobility, the ideological and cultural differences, and customs between countries or regions are extremely obvious. Sima Qian has a very vivid description of this difference in the *Records of the Grand Historian · Biography of the Merchant Colonies*. Confucius traveled all over the countries to the west in order to spread his theory. Qin Shi Huang traveled eastward in order to integrate the cultural differences between the East and the west. From the 28th year of the first emperor (219 BC), Qin Shi Huang "patrolled commandery and county to show his strength and conquer the world." He made four official patrols in total.

His first was from the capital, Xianyang, to Jibei Commandery (present-day Tai'an, Shandong), south of Wei River, Hangu Pass (present-day Henan), Sanchuan Commandery (present-day Luoyang), Dong Commandery (Henan), and Xue Commandery (Qufu in Shandong). Emperor Qin Shi Huang chose a different route back to the capital. He went via Jiaodong Commandery (present-day Jimo, Shandong), Langya Commandery (Jiaonan, Shandong), East Sea Commandery (Dancheng), Sishui Commandery (Pei County, Jiangsu), Jiujiang Commandery

(Anhui), Hengshan Commandery (Huangzhou, Hubei), Nanyang Commandery, and Wuguan and eventually reached the capital Xianyang.

Emperor Qin Shi Huang accomplished three major events during his first patrol. One was to pay tribute to Mount Tai. During the Spring and Autumn Period and the Warring States Period, in the minds of the Qilu people, Mount Tai was the highest mountain. The emperors of the world should go to the highest Mount Tai to sacrifice to God, indicating that they were ordered by "heaven." The sacrifice on Mount Tai is called "Feng," and the sacrifice on Mount Liangfu, a small hill under Mount Tai, is called "Chan." Qin Shi Huang did this, on the one hand, to identify with Qilu culture, on the other hand, to publicize his merits. In the inscription, he declared that he "personally visited the distant people, climbed Mount Tai, and visited the eastern part of the country." The ministers accompanying the emperor recalled the past when the emperor unified the country and respectfully glorified his achievements. The state's policy was implemented, production and life were well organized, and everything was in accordance with the state's law. This clear and correct political proposition must be passed on to future generations and cannot be changed for all time. Second, when he was in Langya County, he felt very good. He ordered 30,000 families to be relocated to live under Langya Terrace and exempted them from taxation for 12 years. He also built the Langya Terrace and erected a stone monument with inscriptions praising the merits of the Qin Dynasty and expressing his ambition." In the Langya Terrace stone carving, Qin Shi Huang publicized the breadth of the territory of the Qin Dynasty: "Between heaven and earth and the southeast and northwest is my emperor's land, west to the desert, south to Lingnan, east to the sea, and north past Daxia (said to be the area of Jinzhong), and wherever there are people, they submit to the Qin." Third, he sent thousands of young girls and boys, led by Xu Fu, to the seas in search of immortal beings.

During this tour to the east, there were also several things that hit the confidence of Qin Shi Huang. First, in Pengcheng County, Sishui Prefecture (Xuzhou, Jiangsu Province), Emperor Qin Shi Huang "fasted and prayed, and tried to salvage the tripod (*ding*) of the Zhou from the Si River. He had thousands of people dive into the water to look for it but did not find it." The tripod of the Zhou symbolizes the Nine Provinces (the world) and the power of the Son of Heaven. Although Qin Shi Huang won the world, he failed to win the Tripod of the Zhou, and his image was hurt. Two, it was in Changsha County, in Mount

Xiang (Mount Jun, also called Mount Dongting), when the Emperor wanted to cross the Dongting Lake, when they arrived at the Xiangshan Hall (香山祠), they encountered strong wind and again failed to pass. He asked Boshi, "What is the God of Xiang?" Boshi replied, "When Qin Shi Huang learned that Xiang Jun was the daughter of Yao and wife of Shun, he was furious and had all the trees on the mountain cut down, leaving the hills bare and ochre red." This gale also seems to challenge the authority of Qin Shi Huang.

The following year, Emperor Qin made another trip to the east. He followed the same route out, and then chose a different path when he returned. He went northwest via the Zhang River valley, and then via Shangdang Commandery to the capital.

In 215 BC, the Emperor made a third trip. This time, he went to inspect the northeastern part of his empire. He went via Hangu Pass, commanderies of Sanchuan, Henei, Handan, Julu (present-day southwest of Pingxiang, Hebei), Hengshan (north of Shijiangzhuang, Hebei), Guangyang (southwest of Beijing), Youbeiping (present-day Ji County, Tianjin), and finally Jieshi. When he returned, he went via commanderies of Yuyang (present-day southwest of Miyun, Beijing), Shanggu (Huailai, Hebei), Dai (present-day Yu County, Hebei), Yanmen (Youyunan, Shanxi), Yunzhong (northeast of Tuoketuo County, Inner Mongolia), Shang (southeast of Yulin, Shaanxi), and finally Xianyang. The place where Qin Shi Huang passed this time was the middle and lower reaches of the Yellow River, originally belonging to Wei, Han, Zhao, Qi, and other countries, so there were many city walls and embankments that were harmful to traffic and "a beggar-thy-neighbor approach" for defense. Qin Shi Huang ordered "destroy the city walls, break the embankments," which was conducive to improving traffic conditions. He passed by on the return journey to the northern border area of the Qin Dynasty. The purpose of his was to investigate the border defense.

In October 210 BC, Emperor Qin Shi Huang made his fourth patrol, also his final trip. His youngest son Huhai and Counsellor-In-Chief Li Si accompanied him. This time, the Emperor went to inspect the southeast area of his empire. He set out from Xianyang, and went via the Dan and Han Rivers. In November, he reached Yunmengze (present-day Dongting Lake). After paying tribute to ancient Chinese leaders Yao and Shun in the Jiuyi Mountains, he went along the Yangtze to Kuaiji Commandery. In Kuaiji, he paid his tribute to Yu the Great. Then he went via Wu County (Suzhou), Jiangcheng (Jurong, Jiangsu), Yangzhou, Langya,

Chengshan, and Linzi. When he reached Pingyuanjin (southern Shandong Plains), Emperor Qin Shi Huang fell ill. He died in Shaqiu Pingtai (present-day Guangzong, Hebei). Li Si ordered the corpse of the Emperor to be placed in a carriage with ice and transported back to Xianyang.

3. The Lingqu Canal—Bridging the Nanling Mountains

The Nanling Mountains were also referred to as the Five Ling Mountains: Saishang Ling, Qitian Ling, Dupang Ling, Mangzhu Ling, and Yuecheng Ling. Lingnan districts were located to the south of the Nanling Mountains. After Qin Shi Huang unified the six countries, in order to show the power of Qin, while sending Meng Tian to lead the troops to defend the northern border, he sent Tu Sui to lead the water army to attack Baiyue in Lingnan area: "Recruit 500,000 soldiers and arrange them into five armies. One army guards the mountains of Tancheng; one army guards the fortress of Jiuyi; one army guards the area of Panyu; one army guards the border of Nanye; one army guards the dam of Yugan. These five armies should put on their armor for three years straight."[11] It can be seen that this war was fought very hard. One reason was the difficult road conditions, which made it impossible to transport many supplies.

There was a stretch of terrain that sloped gently between Dupang Ling and Yuecheng Ling called the Xiang–Gui Corridor. Here, the Xiang and Li Rivers almost met, with only 40 kilometers between them. Emperor Qin sent Jian Lu to dig a canal connecting the two rivers. The canal was called Lingqu because it was located in the Lingling Commandery (present-day Xing'an County, Guangxi). The Qin people built dams and opened canals on the Haiyang River, one of the sources of the Xiang River. The main projects included Huazui, Daxiaotianping, Nanqu, Beiqu, etc. Huazui is a diversion dam. The Haiyang River, a tributary of the Xiang River, looks like a plowshare and is built of stone. The point at the corner is opposite the flow direction of the river. It divides the Haiyang River into two parts; one flows into the Nanqu and the other flows into the Beiqu. The Daxiaotianping are stone barrages built at the end of Huazui, which are shaped like a "herringbone" embankment and slightly lower than the river embankment.

---

11. He Ning, "In the World of Man," in *Collected Interpretations of the Huainanzi*, vol. 18, 1289.

The section close to the east bank of the river is called Datianping, which is connected to the mouth of Beiqu. The section close to the west bank of the river is called Xiaotianping, which is connected to the mouth of Nanqu. The function of Tianping is to raise the water level of the Xiangjiang River and block the river for water storage. In dry seasons, it could lift the water level of the Xiang River up to 4 meters, which would then flow into the Li; thus smooth water transportation was guaranteed. In case there were floods, the canal could direct the water into rivers and seas.

In the flood season, the flood peak overflows the top of Tianping Dam and flows into the old channel of Haiyang River, reducing the water potential so that the water in the channel can flow up without overflowing, dry without running out, and always maintain the safe flow. The southern part is about 34 kilometers long and is the main channel of Lingqu. Of the 4.5 kilometers, manual cutting was used, making it the most dangerous section. The rest uses the original channel. The Beiqu is more than 3 kilometers long and is a supporting project of the Lingqu. Its function is to enable ships in the Xiang River (or Li River) to smoothly transfer to the Li River (or the Xiang River). The flow of the southern and northern parts is three to seven, so there is a saying, "Seven in Xiang River and three in Li River."

After the Han Dynasty, the canal was dredged and rebuilt, and new projects were added. During the reign of Baoli (AD 825–826) of Tang Dynasty, when Li Bo presided over the construction of the canal, he created 18 sluice gates (steep gates), which were mostly built in shallow and narrow channels where the water was turbulent. After being blocked by the steep gate, the water level is raised, the flow is gentle, and it is convenient for navigation. Its function is like the ship lock of later generations. The regional inspector Yu Mengwei rebuilt it into a stone dam that could transport boats of thousand *hu* of carrying capacity. Lingqu Canal "set thirty-six sluice gates. When one ship sails through one gate, it will release one gate in return. In this case, the water could be reserved. The water can climb up to the mountain and pour down from high places." Therefore, the Song people are praised for their "unparalleled achievement in managing the water of Lingqu Canal."[12] Shipping on the canal didn't stop until 1937 when the Xiang–Gui railway

---

12. (Song Dynasty) Huang Xia, "Huangshi Richao," vol. 67, in *Siku Quanshu* edition, book 708, 629 (below).

was built. However, it continued to serve local people in terms of irrigation and daily water usage.

4. The Southwest "Yi" Route

The Southwest "Yi" referred to the minority groups living in southwest China. To be exact, they lived in the western and southern parts of Ba-Shu (present-day Sichuan). In the Qin era, the government had limited control over the routes in the Bashu and Dian Lake areas. In the early years of the establishment of the Han Dynasty, Liu Bang had no time to take into account the border defense because of the volatile domestic political situation. The Xiongnu in the north continued to invade the south. Zhao Tuo in Lingnan established himself as the king of Nanyue, and the Wuchi Road in the southwest was also forced to give up. After the Rule of Emperors of Wen and Jing, the national power of the Han Dynasty became stronger and stronger. After Emperor Wu of Han came to the throne, he expanded his territories to southwest China. One of his major movements was to build the Southwest "Yi" Route.

The Route was composed of two parts. One headed toward the West "Yi" and the other headed toward the South "Yi." The former was called the Lingguan Route, while the latter was known as the Yelang Route.

Yelang is an ancient country established by ethnic minorities in southwest China. During the Qin and Han dynasties, it had traffic with Ba-Shu and Nanyue, but the road was extremely dangerous. "The gaps between mountains and rivers in the map are just several inches, while in reality, they are hundreds of miles apart, and the terrain is precipitous. It seems easy to travel while indeed it is hard to go through."[13] In the Han Dynasty, Tang Meng was sent as a delegate by the government to Nanyue. The locals gave him some wolf berry jam. Tang was curious because wolf berries were specialties in Ba-Shu (Sichuan). How could they appear in Lingnan regions? Tang Meng inquired and found out that it was transported through the Zangke River. Zangke River stretches for several *li*, directly under Panyu City, and connects Yelang in the northwest. Tang Meng knew that there was a waterway between Shu and Lingnan. In the sixth year of

---

13. "Biographies of Yangzhou," in *Book of Han*, vol. 64 (Part One), book 9, 2778.

Jianyuan (135 BC), Tang Meng wrote to Emperor Wu of the Han Dynasty that he used Yelang soldiers to fight against Nanyue: "It is heard that Yelang has more than 100,000 well-trained soldiers. We could take the waterway and win by surprise."[14] Emperor Wu of the Han Dynasty appointed Tang Meng as the general in charge of the forces, leading thousands of soldiers and 3,000 logistics personnel to pass into Yelang from Ba-Shu, intimidating Yelang's attachment, and setting up Qianwei County (now southwest of Yibin, Sichuan). In the fifth year of Yuanguang's reign (130 BC), more than 1,000 troops were sent to Sichuan. In 130 BC, the Yelang Route was built via Bo Route (僰道, present-day Yibin, Sichuan) and Nanguang (Junlian) and ended in Pingyi (Bijie). In the next year, postal offices were set up on route.

Lingguan Route was built around 130 BC, having been proposed by Sima Xiangru. "The Western Yi, Qiong, and Zuo, may be established as commanderies." Emperor Wu of the Han Dynasty appointed Sima Xiangru as the general in

Portrait of Emperor Wu of Han

---

14. "Ranked Biographies of Southwest Yi," in *Records of the Grand Historian*, vol. 116, book 9, 2994.

charge of the forces, sent an envoy to Western Yi, built Yuesui County, and built the Lingguan Route. It started from Jianwei in the east, via Yelang Route, Maoniu (south of Hanyuan, Sichuan), Yuexi Commandery, Dali, Baoshan and eventually reached Dianchi Lake in today's Yunnan.

It cost the Han administration much expense and human resource to build the Southwest "Yi" Routes. For example, it took Tang Meng two years for his men to build the Yelang Route. "Tang Meng had already plundered and opened Yelang and took the opportunity to open the road to the south-western barbarians, conscripting soldiers from Ba, Shu, and Guanghan to participate in the construction of the road by tens of thousands. The road was not built for two years, with many soldiers dying and the money spent costing hundreds of millions. The people of Shu and the people of Han said that it was inconvenient."[15] The opening of the Lingguan Route was held with the financial and human resources of the four counties in Ba-Shu, which were very rich then. Due to the restriction of the natural environment, such as terrain and climate, and the reluctance of the southwest ethnic minorities to conform, the development project has been carried out for several years but still not completed, so it has become a project carried out with the strength of the whole country.

> In order to build these two roads, the Western Han Dynasty requisitioned tens of thousands of people to dig them, but because of the shortage of food in the "Southwest Yi" region, the Han Dynasty had to transport food from the Ba-Shu region in order to solve the problem of feeding these tens of thousands of people. For years, the road was impassable, and the barbarians attacked many times, and the officials sent soldiers to kill them. It was learned that the rent of Ba and Shu was not enough to make it. Therefore, the officials recruited rich farmers to till the Southwest Yi and hand in grains to the government. These farmers would get money from town officials. As far as the county of Canghai in the east, the cost of corvee is the same as cultivating the Southwest Yi.[16]

In the meantime, the wars between the Han Empire and Xiongnu tribes in the north continued, costing the former a fortune in terms of military expense.

---

15. "Sima Xiangru," in *Records of the Grand Historian,* vol. 117, book 9, 3046.
16. "Pinghuai," in *Records of the Grand Historian,* vol. 30, book 4, 1421.

Emperor Wu finally gave up his expansions in southwest China, and focused on the northern wars. Nevertheless, the Southwest "Yi" Routes made it easier for numerous tribes in the Yunnan and Guizhou Plateau to communicate with people in Ba-Shu. Han culture, therefore, spread via these routes to southwestern minority groups. However, communications were limited, and Han culture had little influence on those southwestern regions.

5. The Rise of Postal Systems and Their Perfection

Post was a form of communication in ancient China. It was a system controlled by the government which served political and military purposes. It was composed of posts and post offices. These post offices passed on documents and also provided accommodation for officers and delegates. There are already "传" (transmission) and other words in the oracle bone inscriptions. "驲" is a borrowed word. In ancient times, riding by carriage meant "驲" and "传," while riding by horse meant "遽" (a fast car or horse that delivers mail) and "驿" (post). Later post stations were mainly set up by horse, so the word "驿" was often used.

In the Western Zhou, systematic postal services came into being. "In the capital and on the roads in the wilderness, there were huts for every ten *li*, where food and drink were provided; for every thirty *li*, there were lodgings, where there was a road chamber and a committee for the road chamber; for every fifty *li*, there was a market place, where there was a waiting hall and a collection of good for waiting hall."[17] Post offices were set up based on distance and had different scales. In the Warring States Period, post offices also provided accommodation to officers and delegates passing by. Later, the Qin administration reformed the postal system. For example, a chamberlain in central government was put in charge of the national postal service. In local governments, organizations were set up to be responsible for different postal services. For example, "Chuan" (传) was responsible for sending documents by carts/carriages; "You" (邮) was responsible for sending documents by foot; and "Yi" (驿) was for sending the posts by horses. Today, Guantao County in Hebei Province, formerly known as Taoqiu, was

---

17. Zheng Xuan (Han Dynasty) with annotations and Jia Gongyan (Tang Dynasty) with commentary, *Annotations and Commentaries on Rites of Zhou*, vol. 13, in *Sibu Beiyao* edition, 133 (upper).

established here by the State of Zhao during the Warring States Period and later evolved into the name of the county.

After the unification of the six countries, Qin changed the post and transmission system. In the central government, the imperial servant under the prime minister is responsible for the national post service: "It is said that King Mu of Zhou set the position of Taipuzheng and appointed Bojiong as the Taipuzheng, managing the horses. Qin followed this convention."[18] Locally, the commandery, county, and township are responsible for the establishment of "mail" (邮), "pavilion" (亭), "transmission" (传), etc. Vehicle delivery is called "transmission," delivery by walking is called "mail," and horse delivery is called "post." The stopover station set for the post and transmission is called "home," and the stopover station set for the post is called "pavilion."[19] The pavilion is also a part of the grass-roots administrative organization below the county level. "There is one pavilion every ten *li*, one township every ten pavilions," they are responsible for local public security, taking care of travel, transferring service, etc., and also have the function of delivering documents. Liu Bang, the Emperor Gaozu of the Han Dynasty, served as the pavilion chief of Sishui in the Qin Dynasty and escorted the servicemen to work in Lishan for the county, which was also part of the transportation organization. In the Western Han Dynasty, the post and transmission were in charge of officials such as Daxingling (officials in charge of foreign affairs) under the prime minister. In the Eastern Han Dynasty, it was changed to "Facao" (equivalent to current judges), who was subordinate to the captain. At the local level, it is managed by the "post supervisor" of the prefectural and county officials. The specific management of the post house includes the "post house master" and "post house assistant." The management and staff of the post house include the "post order officer," "post assistant," and "post guard." The management of the post house includes the "pavilion chief" and so on.

Both the Qin and Han set concrete standards on the distance between two posts. Normally, there should be a post every 10 *li*. In some special areas, the distance could be lengthened up to 20 or even 30 *li*. There were also specific regulations on the internal set up of posts.

---

18. (Tang Dynasty) Du You, *Tongdian*, annotated by Wang Wenjin et al., vol. 25, book 1 (Beijing: Zhonghua Book Company, 1988), 705.
19. See Wang Zijin, *Thousands of Miles of Mail Transmission: Post Stations and Delivery*, 39.

There were 12 families in each mail office. Twenty-four in the Chang'an post and 18 in the police post. In the event of the death or the departure of the postman, the replacement acts as a postman and also takes possession of his land and house. The registration of the postman would not be canceled. In dangerous areas and in border areas, where it was not possible to set up a postal service, the two priests of the gate pavilion, the pavilion father, and the thief catcher were responsible for the transmission of documents. Those who were afraid of harm and could not put mail in the vicinity would post their things with the help of the gate pavilion and the thief catcher. In Beidi, Shangxi, and Longxi, it was 30 *li* a post; if the land was dangerous and it could not be mailed, one had to go in and out at his convenience. Each post had facilities to provide food and drink, with a well and a mill. For officials traveling on official business who did not have servants, the postal service cooked for them; for those who did have servants, the cooking utensils were lent to them, and water was provided.[20]

It means that one post should be composed of 12 postal families. However, as the work near the capital was vast, a post there could be staffed with 24 postal families. Posts related to military service would usually have 18 postal families. If postal personnel died or left, a successor could inherit the former's land and houses. The number of postal families remained the same, regardless of how many people there were within the family. Responsibilities of postmen were to send documents and urgent papers. They shouldn't have any other work besides postal services. In places where the environment was extremely poor and there was no postal service near the border, the gatekeeper, the thief catcher, and others would take its place. Beidi County, Shangjun County, and Longxi County had one post every 30 *li*.

On borders and in places where the environment was impossible to set up postal offices, detectives could serve as postmen. A post office should be equipped with utensils for cooking food, wells for water, and grinds for food processing. For government officers passing by, post offices should provide water and drinks. If officers came with servants, post offices should provide them with cooking

---

20. Zhangjiashan Han Tomb No. 247 Bamboo Slip Organizing Group, *Zhangjiashan Han Tomb Bamboo Slips (Tomb No. 247)* (Beijing: Cultural Relics Press, 2001), 169.

utensils. If without, then postmen should cook for the officers.

There were also specific regulations regarding the time frame of posting documents. Policies in the Qin Dynasty stated that postal documents must be stamped with the date and exact time of arrival. In the Han Dynasty, policies specified that postmen should travel 200 *li* per 24 hours. If the documents didn't arrive on time, then there would be punishment. The pavilion of the Han Dynasty was also "one pavilion within ten *li*," which was the same distance as the setting of the mail office, while the post office was "one pavilion within thirty *li*."[21] Therefore, in the *Book of Han*, the post and the pavilion were often referred to as "the post pavilion," such as "the post pavilions are mostly damaged," "to repair the post pavilions," "let the people know the intention of the emperor and let officials in charge of the post pavilions raise livestock."

Hotels at the post offices were provided for officers of high rank in the government. Local officers would come to the hotels and pay their respect. There were many records of the Hotel in the historical records of the Han Dynasty and the Three Kingdoms Period. For example, the "Handan Hotel" was recorded in the *Records of the Grand Historian*, and the official name of the specific person in charge was "Li Zi"; in the State of Qin, there was "Guangcheng Hotel," where Lin Xiangru once lived; Liu Bang once talked with Li Shiqi in "Gaoyang Hotel." There is "Chenliu Hotel" in the *Book of Han*, "Handan Chuan She" in the *Book of the Later Han* and the Hotel in Gaoping County in the *Records of the Three Kingdoms*. There were kitchens and stables in the Hotel.

In the border areas of the Han Dynasty, due to the urgency of military affairs and the popularity of horsemanship, the communication form of "post" was initially promoted. Yan Shigu of the Tang Dynasty explained the relationship between "post" and "transmission" when explaining the history of Tian Heng's "riding to Luoyang": "Chuan is like a post today, the ancient people use a carriage to call a transmission vehicle, and then use a single horse to call a ride for transmission."[22] Therefore, it was often called "post" in later generations. In the Eastern Han Dynasty, post-horses were generally set up, "one post-horse within thirty *li*."

---

21. "Treatise on the Western Regions," in *Book of the Later Han*, vol. 88, book 10 (Beijing: Zhonghua Book Company, 1965), 2920.
22. "First Annals of Gaodi (Part Two)" in *Book of Han*, vol. 1, book 1, 58.

6. Zhang Qian and Gan Ying—The Great Explorers

The Xiongnu were a nomadic tribe in northern China. After Emperor Qin Shi Huang had unified the country, he sent General Meng Tian with 300,000 soldiers to fight against the Xiongnu, who were forced to give up Hetao District. However, between the Qin and Han dynasties, the Xiongnu occupied Hetao once more. In 200 BC, Emperor Gaozu of Han led 320,000 soldiers to battle against the Xiongnu, but was defeated in Baideng. In the 14th year of Emperor Wen (166 BC), the Xiongnu cavalry arrived at Yong (now Fengxiang, Shaanxi) and Ganquan (now near Chunhua, Shaanxi) and burned a palace. Seeking appeasement, early Han Emperors adopted a policy of marrying their daughters to Xiongnu tribe chiefs.

The Xiongnu expanded their territories to the Western Regions and conquered some 20 small kingdoms there. In 160 BC, the Kingdom of Dayuezhi (present-day north Afghanistan) was defeated by the Xiongnu. Xiongnu killed the King of Yuezhi and made his skull into a big wine cup. Its people had to move to Amu Darya in Central Asia.

Emperor Wu, however, wished to change the status quo. He planned to make an alliance with the former Dayuezhi people to fight the Xiongnu. Zhang Qian was chosen to lead a 100-person delegation to the Western Regions. They set out in 139 BC from the capital of Chang'an. As soon as Zhang Qian and his party entered the Hexi region, they were captured by the Xiongnu and escorted to the Xiongnu Chanyu Royal Court (Hohhot, Inner Mongolia). Once, when the Xiongnu were unprepared, Zhang Qian and his entourage, such as Gan Fu (Tangyi Fu), finally escaped and headed for the Western Regions again. They took Gushi (Turpan, Xinjiang) to enter the Tarim Basin and then went upstream along the Tarim River, walking for dozens of days, passing through Yanqi, Qiuci, Shule, and other countries, crossing the Congling Mountains, and came to Dayuan (Fergana, Uzbekistan), where they received a friendly reception. Then, after spending a few days in Kangju (Kazakhstan), they finally found Dayuezhi. However, at this time, Dayuezhi lived in the Guishui (Wuhu River, now the Amu Darya River) Basin, with fertile land and a happy life for the people; he had no intention of revenge and did not want to return to their hometown. Zhang Qian waited for Dayuezhi for more than a year and finally returned without success.

When returning, Zhang Qian chose another way to enter the Han territory from the Qiang region. They crossed the Congling Mountains, crossed the

Yeerqiang River, and the Hotan River and advanced along the southern line of the Tarim Basin. Unexpectedly, he was detained by the Xiongnu on the way. More than a year later, Zhang Qian and Gan Fu were able to escape when the Xiongnu Chanyu died, and internal chaos occurred. When returning to Chang'an, only Zhang Qian and Gan Fu were left in the original 100-member mission, which lasted for 13 years.

Zhang Qian reported the situation of the Western Regions in detail to Emperor Wu of the Han Dynasty. Zhang Qian's introduction greatly expanded the geographical vision of the Han people. At this time, the situation between the Western Han Dynasty and the Xiongnu had changed. In the second year of Yuanshuo (127 BC), the Han General Weiqing recovered the Hetao area, and the main threat of the Xiongnu to the Han was transferred from the north to the Hexi area. Emperor Wu of the Han Dynasty, who was determined to "fight against the four barbarians and repel the territory," was determined to lift the threat from the west and defeat the Xiongnu completely. Based on his own knowledge and experience, Zhang Qian put forward the proposal of sending another mission to the Western Regions and uniting with Wusun to jointly fight the Xiongnu.

In 115 BC, Emperor Wu sent Zhang Qian for a second time to the Western Regions. This time, Zhang was equipped with over 300 men, including several assistants and many valuables. When necessary, the assistants would be sent to different neighboring kingdoms. The accompanying personnel were equipped with two horses each and carried thousands of cattle and sheep, as well as tens of millions of gold coins, silk, and other properties. At this time, the Hexi Corridor was under the control of the Han Dynasty. Zhang Qian and his party successfully arrived at the Wusun Kingdom in the area from Ili to Balkash Lake on the northern Tianshan Road. During his stay in Wusun, Zhang Qian sent deputy envoys to visit Khotan, Dayuan, Kangju, Dayuezhi, Daxia, Anxi (now Iran), Shendu (now India), and other countries for diplomatic activities. At this time, Kunmo, the king of Wusun, was not willing to join the Han Dynasty to attack the Xiongnu because of his old age and infirmity and hesitated. Zhang Qian couldn't get a positive reply from Wusun, so he returned to Chang'an with the mission of Wusun that year.

Soon, the deputy envoys sent by Zhang Qian and envoys from the Western countries came to Chang'an. Since then, the relationship between the Han Dynasty and the countries in the Western Regions has been increasing. "The envoys are looking at each other across the street. The number of envoys in one country ranges from several hundred to more than a hundred. Envoys who travel afar would go for eight or nine years; those who travel near would be out for a few years."[23] Not only did they send envoys to the countries in the Tarim Basin, such as Qiuci, but they also sent envoys to countries such as Antiochia (now northwest of the Persian Gulf).

Ten years later (105 BC), the King of Wusun sent the official delegates with thousands of good horses to visit Chang'an and setup alliance with the Han Empire. During the reign of Emperor Xuan of the Han Dynasty, the Western Protectorate-General was set up in Wulei (east of Luntai, Xinjiang). There were more than 50 countries in the Western Regions to the east and south of Wusun (around the Balkash Lake), which were within the sphere of influence of the Han Dynasty: "It contains fifty countries. The officials of different levels, accounting for 376 people, are all granted the seals of the Han Dynasty, while officials of Kangju, Dayuezhi, Anxi, Jibin, Wuyi, etc., are not included in the list because of their long distance. Their tribute to the Han Dynasty would be reported, while not recorded in the official documents."[24] The opening of the Silk Road opened a channel for cultural exchanges between China and the West.

In the Eastern Han Dynasty, the Silk Road was absolutely open. In the 16th year of Yongping of the Emperor Ming of Han (AD 73), the Han troops marched northward to the Xiongnu and then to the Western Regions. In the third year of the Yongyuan era (AD 91), Ban Chao settled in the Western Regions, served as Du Hu, and lived in Qiuci. Ban Chao took a series of military measures: "Reset the Wuji Commandant responsible for 500 soldiers and stationed at Gaochangbi. Also, set the Duke of Wubu to station at Buhoucheng. These two military bases are five hundred *li* apart." Six years later, Ban Chao defeated Yan Qi again." Therefore, more than fifty countries become dependent states. Countries such as Antiochia and Anxi are 40,000 *li* apart, and their tributes are considered again."

Ban Chao was a man who liked to make contributions. In the ninth year of Yongyuan (AD 97), he decided to send Gan Ying as an envoy to Daqin (Rome). According to the *Records of the Later Han Dynasty*, the Han people at that time also called the State of Great Qin Lixuan, which was west of the sea of Antiochia. Antiochia is located in Syria and Iraq today. Before Gan Ying, the envoys sent

---

23. "Ranked Biographies of Dayuan," in *Records of the Grand Historian*, vol. 123, book 10, 3170.
24. "Western Regions (Part Two)," in *Book of Han*, vol. 96, book 12, 3928.

by the Han Dynasty to the Western Regions reached Wuyi as far as possible, and none of them reached Antiochia. Gan Ying went through many hardships, starting from Pi Shan, southwest to Jingxuandu, passing Kophen, and then to Alexandria Prophthasia to leave the country after more than 60 days. Alexandria Prophthasia was a big country, which was called Paichi at that time. Gan Ying and his party traveled southwest for more than 100 days to reach Antiochia. The capital of Antiochia was on the mountain, with a circumference of more than 40 *li*. Gan Ying was in the west of Antiochia and was going to Daqin by boat. At this time, the following scene appeared:

> In the ninth year of Emperor Yongyuan's reign, Banchao, the Du Hu, sent Gan Ying to Daqin and arrived at Antiochia. As they were approaching the sea and wanted to sail across it, the boatman said to Gao Ying, "The sea area is wide, and if we encounter a favorable wind, we can pass by in March. However, if we encounter a headwind, it can take two years to pass. Therefore, every ship that wants to cross the sea must prepare food for three years. Moreover, being on the sea can easily evoke nostalgia for one's homeland, leading to multiple deaths." After listening, Gan Ying stopped moving forward.[25]

Gan had never traveled by sea, so he gave up the plan and returned home. Scholars later deducted that the Anxi people had wanted to monopolize the silk trade (specifically silk supply to the West), thus they prevented direct contact between the Han and the Romans.

Although Gan Ying did not complete his mission, he significantly extended the Silk Road, helping it reach the Persian Gulf. He probably set a record in being the first Chinese to have reached what is today's Syria and Iraq.[26] Second, when he arrived at the capital of Anxi and the hometown of Antiochia, he had a deeper and more detailed understanding of Central Asia, West Asia, and the State of Great Qin than anyone before, thus expanding the knowledge of the Han people in the extraterritorial world: "Afterwards, Gan Ying passed through the Anxi Kingdom and arrived at the Antiochia Kingdom. He looked toward the Qin

---

25. "Western Regions," in *Book of Han*, vol. 88, book 10, 2918.
26. Yang Gongle, "The Routes and Significance of Gan Ying's Attempt to Visit Daqin," *World History*, no. 4 (2001): 117.

country from the west sea, where he was more than 40,000 *li* away from Yumen and Yangguan. recorded all kinds of local products, wrote down the detailed situation, and examined the true conditions."[27] Sima Guang had spoken highly in the *Comprehensive Mirror for Aid Government*: "Ban Chao, the Du Hu (Western Regions Protector), therefore sent Gan Ying to the Qin empire and the Antiochia Kingdom, fully exploring the west sea. This expedition was unprecedented, and all the local specialties and valuable products were recorded and collected."[28]

7. Tower Ships (Louchuan) and Sea Routes

The tower ship was the main ship of the navy in the Qin and Han dynasties, so the navy was also called "tower ship" and "tower ship army." The shape of the tower ship was huge, and it was usually fully equipped. There is a kind of ship called tower ship. There are three stories on the boat, and the standard for combat is set up. Flags were set up, crossbow windows were opened, and spears were stored. Catapults, big stones, and iron juice were prepared, forming a fortress in the ship. If suddenly encountering a storm that human power could not control, it was also a very inconvenient situation. However, it was necessary to establish a large-scale naval force.[29]

The tower ship originated from the State of Yue in the Spring and Autumn Period. Qin soldiers attacked Lingnan Baiyue in five ways and used tower ships. During the reign of Emperor Wu of the Han Dynasty, in order to prepare for the war with the ethnic minorities in the south, the tower ship army was vigorously built, and a training base for the navy was set up in Chang'an. In the third year of Yuanshou (120 BC), "At this time, the Yue Kingdom planned to wage war with the Han Dynasty through ships, so they built a large-scale Kunming Lake surrounded by temples. The ship was more than ten *zhang* high, and the flag on it was very magnificent."[30] Kunming Lake was basically an artificial lake. It was a small lake originally built to prepare for the war with the King of Yunnan. During the "great

---

27. "Western Regions," in *Book of Han*, vol. 88, book 10, 2931.
28. *Comprehensive Mirror in Aid of Governance*, vol. 48, book 4 (Beijing: Zhonghua Book Company, 1956).
29. Du You (Tang Dynasty), *Tongdian*, vol. 4, annotated by Wang Wenjin, et al., 4122.
30. "Treatise on Food and Commodities (Part Two)" in *Book of Han*, vol. 24 (Part Two), book 4, 1170.

repair," Kunming Lake had become a lake with a radius of 40 *li*, where tower ships could be built and sailors trained. There used to be "hundreds of tower ships" in Kunming Lake, which were all the training ships used for naval drill and review.

The function of the tower ship was equivalent to that of the tower car in a land war. At that time, the weapons were mainly bows and arrows. Therefore, compared with civilian ships, the building ships should be tall, usually three or more floors. Soldiers could shoot arrows from a high position, and the power of weapons was easily used. The tower ship was fully equipped, with a towering watchtower or *doulou* (斗楼) and paddlers rowing below. There was a thin retaining wall about three feet high outside each floor to defend from the enemy's arrows and stones. There was an arrow hole in the middle of the retaining wall, from which soldiers shot arrows. The whole tower ship was surrounded by combat cells made of hardwood, and the key parts were covered with leather to prevent attack by the enemy.

Besides tower ships, navies were also equipped with other kinds of boats. For example, some were built for one or two soldiers only. According to the records of Liu Xi of the Han Dynasty in the *Shiming*, the ships that were divided by function were: when attacking, the ships that ran in the front of the whole fleet were "first boarded," which means to board against the enemy; the long and narrow "solemn" boat was used to shuttle between the enemy ships and disrupt the enemy array; the fastest was "*Chima* Boat," which was painted red; the "ship" on the upper and lower floors was protected by boards on all sides to prevent the enemy's arrows. According to the size of the ships, there were "scout ships" with a capacity of more than 2,500 *dou*, and there were cabins on the ship to watch the advance and retreat of the enemy; "with a capacity of more than 1,500 *dou* and shaped like a mink and with a short boat shape, which was not easy to overturn; A "boat" of the capacity of less than 1,000 *dou* could only carry one or two people and was suitable for individual combat.

The tower ship army in the Han Dynasty played a great role in consolidating the unity of the country and communicating the water transportation between the coastal areas and various water systems. In 112 BC, Emperor Wu ordered 100,000 navy soldiers to quell the rebels to the south. "Send Lu Bode, the Fubo General, to Guiyang and the Huang River; send Yang Pu, the Louchuan General, to Yuzhang and the Zhen River; send Yan, the Gechuan General, to Linglin and the Li River; send Jia, the Xialai General, to Cangwu." They all mobilized convicts and ten thousand boats from Jianghuai and areas to the south. The lord of Yuezhi sent gifts and also dispatched convicts from Ba-Shu, recruited troops from Yelang, navigated down the Zangke River, and all met up at Panyu."[31] One could deduct from their routes, that there were waterways to South China from what is modern Sichuan, Hunan, Guangxi, and Jiangxi provinces. There were also sea routes from Zhejiang to Fujian.

In the Han Dynasty, "now the troops were sent thousands of miles away, carrying food and clothing, penetrating deep into the Yuejiang region, crossing the mountains on shoulders, towing boats against the water, traveling hundreds or thousands of miles through deep forests and bamboo thickets, with rocks touching the boats under the water, jungles full of vipers and snakes, and epidemics such as vomiting, diarrhea and cholera constantly prevalent in the hot summer months."[32] Despite many harsh natural conditions, the Han Dynasty's army in the war against southern Guangdong was relatively smooth in general. The following year, it captured southern Guangdong and set up Nanhai, Cangwu, Yulin, Hepu, Jiaozhi, Jiuzhen, Rinan, Zhuya, Daner, and other counties. Nanhai County is in today's Guangdong Province; Cangwu County, Yulin County, and Hepu County include today's Guangxi and western Guangdong Province; Jiaozhi County, Jiuzhen County, and Rinan County were in the north and south and middle of today's Vietnam. But it was quite difficult to fight the battle in Fujian today. At that time, Fujian was the territory of Yu Shan, the king of the Dongyue. In the first year of Yuanfeng (110 BC), under the pressure of the Han army, the Dongyue split killed Yu Shan and surrendered to the Han army. Emperor Wu ordered the people of Yue in Fujian to move between the Yangtze and Huai Rivers. Today, Fujian Province belongs to Kuaiji County in the Western Han Dynasty. Because it was mountainous, the land traffic between the west and Yuzhang County (Jiangxi) and the north of Kuaiji County (southern Jiangsu and Zhejiang) were all mountain trails, deserted, and difficult for outsiders to enter. It was even more difficult for a large number of troops to travel. First, there was no food available locally. Second, it was difficult to find where the target was. Therefore, in the Han Dynasty, only one Ye County was set up in today's Fuzhou City to get in touch with other commanderies and counties by sea.

---

31. "Annals of Emperor Wu," in *Book of Han*, vol. 6, book 1, 186.
32. "Biographies of Yan Zhu," in *Book of Han*, vol. 64, book 9, 2779.

The tower ship bases in the Han Dynasty were mainly located in Yuzhang (Nanchang, Jiangxi), Xunyang (southwest of Huangmei, Hubei), Lujiang (south of Lujiang, Anhui), Zongyang (Anqing, Anhui), and Kuaiji (Suzhou, Jiangsu) in the Yangtze River Basin, as well as Juzhang (west of Cixi, Zhejiang), Bochang (at the mouth of Xiaoqing River in Boxing, Shandong), and other places along the Yangtze River. These bases were also major shipbuilding bases. In the middle and lower reaches of the Yangtze River, in addition to the tower ship building bases, the shipbuilding bases also include Yiling (Yichang, Hubei), Jiangling (Jiangling, Hubei), Wuchang (Yicheng, Hubei), and other places. At the end of the Eastern Han Dynasty, Sun Quan built new large ships in Wuchang and carried out navigation tests at Fankou. The *Wei Wen's Letter to Sun Quan* said, "Choose six ships with the maximum load capacity and carry the load of 500 *dan* from Mianshui to Fankou."[33] During the Western and Eastern Han dynasties, the most important ship base was in Panyu (present-day Guangzhou). It used the most advanced ship building techniques—archaeologists discovered many ship models in tombs dated from the Han, showing how all kinds of boats and ships were built in Panyu. Located by the South Sea, it became a hub for overseas trade and ship building.

One such leader, who enjoyed sea travel was Emperor Wu. He traveled by sea at least seven times. His major trips are listed below. In 110 BC, Emperor Wu set out from Mount Tai and arrived at Jieshi in the north. In 106 BC, he went up to Langya. In 102 BC, he went by sea first and then climbed Mount Tai.

In the Eastern Han Dynasty, it was also known as the "Seaside Route," which was formed along the coast of the present Bohai Sea and the Yellow Sea. The terrain here was flat, and the construction was easy, so land transportation was convenient. It was also an important economic and cultural center in the Qin and Han dynasties. Therefore, Emperor Qin Shi Huang and Emperor Wu of the Han Dynasty toured here many times. Jieshi, where they arrived, was the gateway of the northeast counties. From Jieshi to the east along the sea, Liaoxi Commandery, Liaodong Commandery, and the Korean Peninsula can be reached. In the first year of Yuanshuo (128 BC), 280,000 people, including the king of Dongyi Huinanlu, fell to the Han Dynasty and became Canghai County. "歲" means "Hui" or "Hui Mo." In the Han Dynasty, it was distributed in the

---

33. *Imperial Reader*, vol. 770, book 4 (Beijing: Zhonghua Book Company, 1960), 3414 (below).

north of the Chen-Han and the south of the Goguryeo, Wozu, and other parts, mainly in today's Korea. Since the Han Dynasty had not defeated Korea at that time, the connection between the Han Dynasty and Canghai County was only by sea. In the spring of the third year of Yuanshuo (126 BC), Canghai County, which had been established for more than one year, was abolished. In the second year of Yuanfeng (109 BC), the king of Korea attacked and killed the Liaodong Duwei of the Han Dynasty. Emperor Wu of the Han Dynasty decided to send troops to attack Korea, gathering people who had been sentenced to death all over the country, and sent General Yang Pu and General Xun Zhi of the Lou Chuan to lead a team of criminals to attack Korea. The next summer, the Koreans beheaded their king, Youqujiang, and the Han Dynasty set up Lelang, Lintun, Xuantu, and Zhenfan commanderies with their land. So far, the offshore route connecting the Yanqi region and the Korean peninsula has been formed.

The maritime traffic between the Liaodong Peninsula and the Shandong Peninsula was common in historical records in the late Eastern Han Dynasty. Taishi Ci, a native of Huang County, Donglai County, and Bing Yuan, Guan Ning, a native of Zhuxu County, Beihai County, all "avoided chaos in Liaodong." The exchanges between the Liaodong Peninsula and the lower reaches of the Yangtze River were extremely frequent during the Three Kingdoms. For example, in the first year of Sun Quan's Jiahe reign (AD 232), General Zhou He and Governor Pei Qian led a fleet of hundreds of ships to Liaodong by sea.

To the south of the "Binghai Route" was the sea route along the East China Sea and the South China Sea, which had been fully formed in the Eastern Han Dynasty. The tribute fu of Jiaozhi County, the southernmost part of the territory of the Han Dynasty, could only be transported by sea because it was more difficult and dangerous to go by land. It was transported northward along the coastline through Dongye (Fuzhou) and then to the Yangtze River Basin by inland waterway. Many ships were damaged and drowned because of the heavy wind and waves at sea. After the eighth year of Emperor Zhang Jianchu's reign (AD 83), the land road between Lingling (today's Xianggui Corridor) and Guiyang (today's Qitianling Route) was opened, and the water and land transport and commercial exchanges continued. At the end of the Eastern Han Dynasty, the shipping conditions of this sea route were still relatively poor. Xu Jing, Yuan Pei, and others "sail through Dong'ou, Min, and Yue kingdoms. After sailing for thousands of miles, there was still no sight of the Han country. However, they ran out of food and had nothing to eat. More than half of the crew members died."[34] During the Three Kingdoms Period of Wu, this route became the key maritime route operated by the State of Wu. In AD 230, General Wei Wen and some 10,000 of his men went by sea to the Island of Taiwan.[35] This was the first time that any administration in mainland China had any direct rule over the island.

Located next to the South Sea, Lingnan regions held significant advantages over other parts of China in terms of sea transportation. Ships could sail directly to the Pacific and Indian oceans. Ports in Lingnan served as a hub, where goods and food from Southeast Asia could be passed onto other parts of China. One of the reasons why Emperor Qin ordered the conquering of Lingnan was because he wanted rare items, such as emeralds and rhino horns traded in the region.

There were many ports in Lingnan, the most important being Panyu (present-day Guangzhou). In the Qin Dynasty, Panyu was in the Qin County of Nanhai. At the end of the Qin Dynasty, Zhao Tuo established a separate regime in the Lingnan region, ruling Guilin and Xiangjun, with Panyu as the capital. After Emperor Wu of the Han Dynasty pacified South Vietnam, Panyu remained the prefecture of the South China Sea, and its contacts with the mainland continued to increase. Panyu was among the nine major capitals of the country in the early Han Dynasty, recorded in *Records of the Grand Historian · Biography of the Merchant Colonies*. The rhinoceros horn, elephant tooth, emerald, pearl, and other products in Lingnan were famous in the Central Plains, and the merchants in the Central Plains who went to trade made a lot of profits. However, the Lingnan area did not produce these goods. According to later records, they were imported from overseas.

After Emperor Wu united Lingnan, he sent a delegation to Southeast Asia, bringing with them silk and gold to trade with pearls and other precious stones. As ships at the time were quite small, they could only sail along the coast. They all set out from such ports as Xuwen (present-day south Xuwen, Guangdong) and Hepu. All ships with imported goods would cluster in Panyu. The route of the voyage at that time, according to historical records, was as follows:

---

34. "Biographies of Xu Jing," in *Records of the Three Kingdoms*, vol. 4 (Beijing: Zhonghua Book Company, 1959), 964.
35. "Annals of Sun Tuan," in *The History of Three Kingdoms*, vol. 47, book 5, 1136.

Since Rinan County was a barrier and blocked the road, it took about five months by boat from Xuwen and Hepu to reach Duyuan Kingdom; about four more months by boat, and it would arrive in Yilumei Kingdom; about twenty more days by boat, it would arrive at Chenli Kingdom; it took about ten days on foot to reach the Fugandulu Kingdom. It took about two months by boat from the Fugandulu Kingdom to the Huangzhi Kingdom, which had the same customs as the Zhuya Kingdom. Its state was vast, with many registered permanent residences and many foreign objects, which have been rarely seen since Emperor Wu's time. There was Yichang, belonging to the Huangmen, who, together with the applicants, had entered the sea as a bright pearl, a wandering wall, a strange stone and a foreign body, and a golden cross. The leader of the translator is called Yizhan, who is under the management of the Huangmen. Together with the recruited people, they would go near the sea to buy pearls, rare stones, and novel products so that they could carry gold and various colors of silk. All the countries to which they came were coupled with food, and the barbarian merchant ship sent them. It was also beneficial to trade, plagiarism, and murder. There were also those who pursued interests that would rob and kill people. Some were drowned in the storm, and those who did not die would return after many years. The circumference of a large pearl is about two inches. At the beginning of the reign of Emperor Ping, Wang Mang assisted the government and wanted to show off his prestige, paying tribute to the King of Huangzhi, and ordered his envoy to present a rhinoceros. From Huangzhi to Pizong, it took eight months; the ship could travel for two months to Sunan and Xianglin. To the south of the Huangzhi, there was a long way to go, but there was no country. The Han envoy left Huangzhi Kingdom and headed south, finally arriving at Yichengbu Kingdom, and the translators of the Han soon returned.[36]

The sea route to Southeast Asia was regarded as the "Silk Road on the Sea." It went via the Kingdom of Duyuan (modern day Java), Kingdom of Huangzhi (southeast India), and the Kingdom of Yichengbu (Sri Lanka). Other names on the route were no longer available. There were many disagreements regarding these names within the academic circle.

---

36. "Treatise on Geography," in *Book of Han*, vol. 28, book 6, 1671.

In Eastern Han, some merchants also came to China via the "Silk Road on the Sea." In AD 131, delegates from the Yetiao and Dan kingdoms (modern Java and Sumatra) came to China. In AD 166, the Emperor of Daqin also sent delegates with rhino horns and elephant tusks. It was believed that Daqin was in fact the Roman Empire.

Discoveries in modern Guangzhou also proved the colossal scale of foreign trade between China and other countries. There was one ornament made of glass containing a very low percentage of lead and barium. This was different from the glass made in China but very close to what was made in the West. In the tombs of the Nanyue King, elephant tusks, very similar to those in Africa, were discovered.

In the Three Kingdoms Period, Guangzhou Port became the starting point of the Silk Road on the Sea. Zhu Ying and Kang Tai, from the Kingdom of Wu, traveled by sea extensively and visited more than 100 territories along these routes. In the fifth year of Huangwu (AD 226), Qin Lun, a businessman of the State of Great Qin, came to Jiaozhi Commandery from Haido. Wu Miao, the governor of Jiaozhi, sent him to Jianye (Nanjing, Jiangsu) to meet Sun Quan.

The Silk Road on the Sea meant that the sea business had entered a new phase; China had advanced ship building industry and marine technology. The main product for export was silk, which implied that silk was plentiful in China and its silk production had reached a high level.

CHAPTER THREE

CULTURAL EXCHANGE BETWEEN ANCIENT CHINA AND INDIA

There is a Chinese proverb, which is: "The general trend under heaven is that there is bound to be unification after prolonged division and division after prolonged unification." The period of the two Han dynasties was a period of unified dynasties in Chinese history. In the late Eastern Han Dynasty, although it was already a separate warlord regime, the emperor surnamed Liu still remained high on his throne and maintained formal unity. In AD 220, Cao Pi proclaimed himself Emperor of Wei, and China entered the Three Kingdoms Period. In AD 266, Sima Yan proclaimed himself Emperor of Western Jin, and later defeated the Shu and Wu kingdoms. Thus, China was unified again in AD 281; however, this did not last long. China was divided again into the Southern and Northern Dynasties, the separate regime "blossomed everywhere" and appeared successively. During war, Buddhism, which came to China at the end of Western Han, became a spiritual haven for administrators as well as ordinary people. When Buddhism flourished in China, cultural exchange between China and India reached a new level.

1. Faxian (法显)—Acquired Buddhist Texts from India

There were two major routes for monks to spread Buddhism in China. One was by land via the famous Silk Road, travelling from mid-Asian countries to the Yellow

Print from "Biographies of Faxian"

River in China. One of the most prominent monks from the Western Regions was called Kumārajīva (鸠摩罗什).

The other was by sea via the Indian Ocean. One of the first monks to use this path was Kang Senghui (康僧会). He arrived in Jianye (present-day Nanjing), capital of the Wu Kingdom in AD 247. There, he built temples and made Jianye a famous center of Buddhism in Southern China. The Buddhist center of Northern China was located in Luoyang. During the Southern and Northern Dynasties, several monks came by sea helping to spread Buddhism and translated Buddhist scriptures, which played a great role in the early spread of Buddhism in China.

As time passed, people realized that the Buddhist texts brought by the monks might not really satisfy their needs. First, they didn't know what Buddhist scriptures China needed. Furthermore, some of the scripts were not complete;

some translations seemed to be far from the original versions. Therefore, some Chinese monks decided to travel to India in search of better Buddhist scripts. Zhu Shixing was the first to set out, followed by Zhu Fahu and Kang Falang, among many others. However, when traveling on foot, most were halted by difficult natural conditions. The furthest they reached was the Western Regions, i.e., modern Xinjiang and neighboring Central Asian countries. Only one or two monks reached India. Against this background, the 62-year-old Faxian began a difficult journey to Tianzhu for lessons.

Faxian (c. AD 337–422), whose surname was Gong, was born in Wuyang County, Pingyang Commandery (Xiangyuan, Shanxi Province). When he was three years old, he was ordained as a monk, and when he was 20 years old, he was officially ordained. In the first year of the Hongshi reign of the late Qin Dynasty (AD 399), Faxian saw that the Buddhist scriptures were incomplete. In order to promote the long-term development of Chinese Buddhism, he resolutely went west with his four companions, Huijing, Daozheng, Huiying, and Huiwei. Faxian and his party set out from Chang'an and went west through Dunhuang. It is difficult to describe the harsh natural environment along the way. "There are many evil spirits and hot winds in the Shahe. If one encounters them, he is doomed to death. There were no birds above and no animals below. Up and down, far and wide, there was no living thing in sight, and the signposts were the dead bones that lie here."[1] The Shahe here is the desert zone between Dunhuang and Shanshan. In case of a strong wind, the desert moves with the wind, making it difficult to distinguish the direction. "There was snow in Congling in winter and summer. There were also poisonous dragons. If they lost their will, they would spit poisonous wind, rain and snow, and flying sand and gravel. In this case, there none can survive. Everyone in that land was called Snow Mountain Man."[2] After entering the country of Tianzhu, the road was still dangerous: "The road was hard and steep, the cliffs were dangerous, the mountains were stone only, the walls stand on thousands of feet, and the eyes were dazzled. If you want to enter, you will find no way to walk into it."[3] When crossing the Little Snow Mountain (Sefedeco Mountains), his companion Huijing was frozen to death: "Snow Mountain was

---

1. Zhang Xun, annotated, *Annotated Record of Faxian* (Shanghai: Shanghai Ancient Books Publishing House, 1985), 6.
2. Zhang Xun, annotated, *Annotated Record of Faxian*, 24.
3. Zhang Xun, annotated, *Annotated Record of Faxian*, 26.

Chapter Three

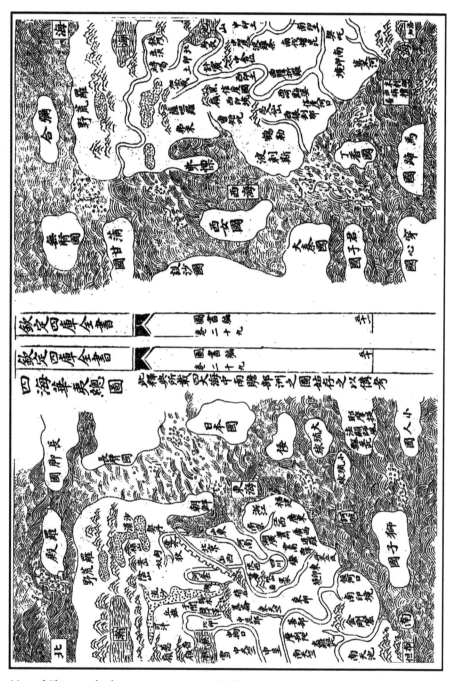

Map of China and other countries surrounded by the seas

covered with snow in winter and summer. When a cold storm arose in the north of the mountain, everyone was silent. Huijing was unable to make progress again. His mouth frothed, and he told Faxian: 'I'll not survive, so you should go without me, or else both of us will die.' So, he died. Faxian touched him and cried sadly: 'That you can do if your wishes cannot be fulfilled and your fate is such!'"[4]

After the tour in Middle Tianzhu (India), Faxian, and Daozheng returned to the center of Buddhism—the Magadha kingdom. Magadha kingdom, that is, Patna in Bihar, India, is the most famous country in the middle reaches of the Ganges River in ancient India and also the important tourist destination of Sakyamuni's "enlightenment and Buddhahood." At that time, there were many Buddhist temples and eminent monks. Faxian had studied Sanskrit and written laws here for three years. After seeking the *Mahasangha-vinaya*, the *Dharma of the Savador*, and many other Buddhist sutras, he remembered that the purpose of this journey to the west was to make the Dharma circulate in China and decided to return to the east with what he had learned. The fellow Daozheng, seeing that there were some good Buddhist conditions here, was already unwilling to return.

Faxian had to go home alone. He decided to go east along the Ganges River and return to China by sea. At the entrance of the Ganges River to the sea, in the Tamalitti Empire (the former capital is in Tamluk, southwest of Calcutta, West Bengal, India), Faxian saw the prosperity of Buddhism here and lived here for two years, writing Buddhist scriptures and painting Buddhist statues. In AD 409, he reached Sri Lanka and stayed for a couple of years, acquiring more Buddhist texts, such as two commandments of *Misha Sai Law* and *Zazang*, as well as the Buddhist scriptures such as *Chang Ahan* and *Za Ahan*.

"Faxian went to the Han area for many years and learned about the foreigners, mountains, rivers, and plants. His partners grew apart, and they either stayed or died. They looked at their own shadows and got very sentimental. Suddenly, he saw the merchant offering a white silk fan in the Jin area beside the jade statue. He felt so sad that his eyes were full of tears."[5] By then, Faxian had already been away from China for over 10 years. One day, he came across a white Chinese silk fan, placed next to the Buddha as a tribute. This little fan reminded him of China. He was so homesick that he burst into tears.

---

4. Zhang Xun, annotated, *Annotated Record of Faxian*, 51.
5. Zhang Xun, annotated, *Annotated Record of Faxian*, 151.

In AD 411, Faxian set out for China from Sri Lanka. Over the years, he'd acquired several Buddhist texts and paintings to bring back. Although the sea route was neither as cold as Congling nor as hot as Shahe, it was still dangerous. Faxian was on a Chinese merchant ship in Simhaladvipa, which could carry more than 200 people. He was towing a small boat behind him in case of damage to the big ship. When they met sea storms, the ship leaked. Fortunately, Chinese ships were already built with advanced technology preventing sea water from flooding the entire ship. At that time, Chinese ships had adopted the waterproof compartment technology, and one leakage would not affect the whole ship. After repairing the island, the merchant ship continued to sail eastward for about 90 days to Yavadvipa. At that time, sea navigation depended on the sun, moon, and stars to identify the direction. In case of rainy days, the ship would be blown away by the wind, which increases the sailing time. Finally, they reached Sumatra.

Five months later, Faxian boarded an Indian ship heading for Guangzhou. The preparatory sailing time was about 50 days. The ship had a "sea master" who was particularly responsible for observing the sun, moon, and stars to determine the course. One night after sailing for more than a month, when they passed by Xisha Island, they were hit by storms. The Indians thought it was the monk who brought them bad luck and wanted to dump Faxian on one of the islands. Faxian argued and finally persuaded them to continue. Due to the continuous overcast days and the sailor's observation error, the ship deviated from its course, and then it could only sail in a northwest direction. It took nearly 20 days longer than the normal voyage to Guangzhou to the south bank of Lao Mountain in Shandong Province. After that, the merchant ship went south to Yangzhou. Faxian passed through Pengcheng (Xuzhou) to Jingkou and arrived at Jiankang (Nanjing), the capital of the Eastern Jin Dynasty, in the ninth year of Yixi (AD 413). In AD 413, Faxian started translating the Buddhist texts he had fetched. In AD 416, Faxian completed his travelogue, which is known today as *A Record of Buddhistic Kingdoms*.

Faxian set out from Chang'an in the first year (AD 399) of the Hongshi reign of the late Qin Dynasty and returned to Jiankang in the ninth year (AD 413) of the Yixi reign of the Eastern Jin Dynasty. The journey lasted for 15 years. The contribution of Faxian to the west is mainly reflected in three aspects: first, he reached places that had never been reached by any Chinese before, and he was unswervingly determined to finally achieve his intended goal. "He was the first one who followed the sea and land, traveled extensively to the west, studied abroad in India, and returned with the classics." The second was *A Record of Buddhistic Kingdoms*. written after he returned home, which records the situation of India, Khotan, Qiuci, and other countries. The historical materials retained in India were mostly mixed with myths, while Khotan and Qiuci had no biographies, so they are very valuable historical materials. Third, the Buddhist scriptures *Fang Deng* and *Nirvana Sutra*, which Faxian brought back through hardships and dangers, "opened one of the branches of Buddhism" and made important contributions to the development of Buddhism in China and the rise of Chinese Buddhism.[6]

2. Geographic Outlook of Ancient Indians and Their Influence on China

Faxian mentioned the term "Middle Kingdom" many times in *A Record of Buddhistic Kingdoms*. According to Sanskrit, "Middle Kingdom" referred to the regions from the Himalayas to the Ganges River. Those outside the regions were referred to as remote. These concepts showed the world outlook of the ancient Indians, whose notions influenced the Chinese greatly by way of Buddhist texts.

The second volume of the *Sakyamuni Chronicle*, "The Commanding Chapter," records the ancient Indians' understanding of the world, believing that the world is composed of Mount Sumilu and four continents. Sumilu Mountain, also called Xumi Mountain, is located in the middle of the sea. It is about 80,000 years away from the sea. The sun and moon revolve around the mountainside of Sumilu Mountain. In the sea outside Sumilu Mountain, there are four continents: the eastern continent is named Vitiha (i.e., Shengshen), the southern continent is the Shanbu, the western continent is named Qutuoni (i.e., Niuhuo), and the northern continent is named Kulu (i.e., Zuolu). One of the four continents is called "Four Haves." They are like the petals of lotus flowers and surround Sumilu Mountain.

Tianzhu, where Sakyamuni lives, is located on Lubu Island. Shanbu Island was located in the sea to the south of Sumi Mountain (Sumilu Mountain), with 240,000 *li* from east to west and 280,000 *li* from north to south. The four solstices

---

6. Tang Yongtong, *History of Buddhism during the Han, Wei, Two Jin, and Northern and Southern Dynasties*, vol. 1 (Beijing: Zhonghua Book Company, 1983), 271.

of Middle Tianzhu (India) were as follows: "The east reaches 58,000 *li* to Zhendan (Zhendan is also the name of Shenzhou). They are as far as the Jindi Kingdom in the south, the Ajuzhe Kingdom in the west, and the Anotatta Lake in the north." In the center of Shanbu Island, "there is a big pool called Anavatapta. It was called Wurenao in the Tang Dynasty, and it referred to Anotatta Lake. In the south of Xiang Mountain and the north of Daxue Mountain, on the top of the mountain, you can find a special place. There are eight hundred miles around the pool and four banks of treasure decorations." Obviously, the ancient Indians had realized that the Pamir Plateau, located in Central Asia, is the roof of the world. "Therefore, a pool is divided into four rivers, each of which flows into a sea according to the terrain. Therefore, water flows into the East China Sea to the east of Congling, into the South China Sea to the south of Daxia, into the West Sea to the west of Xueshan, and into the North Sea to the north of Daqin."[7]

This concept of the world geography of the ancient Indians has also had an important impact on the Chinese people's understanding of where the source of the Yellow River is. Our ancestors had long been active in the Yellow River Basin, but mainly in the middle and lower reaches of the Yellow River. Where the source of the Yellow River is, was unclear for a long time. On the one hand, the source of the Yellow River is located in a cold and swampy area, which is not suitable for human habitation and is not easy to investigate. On the other hand, the source of the Yellow River is located in central and southern Qinghai Province. For a long time in history, it was not under the control of the Central Plains, nor could it be investigated. Therefore, in *Classic of Mountains and Seas*, written from the end of the Spring and Autumn Period to the beginning of the Han Dynasty, it is believed that the Yellow River originated from the Kunlun Mountains. As for where Kunlun Mountain is, there are different opinions. However, the ancient Indians have a perception that there is a big river in "China," which originates from one source and flows in four directions. After the rise of Buddhism, it inherited this concept and incorporated it into the Buddhist scriptures: "There is a mountain called Baoshan in the middle of the snow mountain, and its height is 20 yojana." The snow mountain was 800 *li* tall. On top of the mountain was Anotatta Lake, with a width of 400 *li*. Its water is cold and clean. Seven treasures are built, seven fences, seven nets, seven rows of trees, various colors, and seven

---

7. (Tang Dynasty) Daoxuan, *The History of Buddha's Country*, 8.

treasures are combined to the east of Anotatta Lake was the Ganga River, which flows out of Niukou and into the East China Sea from the Wubai River. There is the Xintou River in the south of Anotatta Lake, which flows out of Shizikou and into the South China Sea from the Wubai River. To the west of Anotatta Lake is the Pocha River, which flows out of Makou and into the West Sea from the Wubai River. In the north of Anotatta Lake, there is the Situo River, which flows out of the mouth of the elephant and into the North Sea from the Wubai River."[8] The Anotatta Lake in the "Long Agama Sutra," which is called the Anavata Pond in the *Records of the Western Regions of the Tang Dynasty*, is the mythical Heavenly Pond. The Ganga River is now the Ganges River, and the East China Sea is now the Bay of Bengal. The Xintou River is now the Indus River, and the South China Sea may refer to the Arabian Sea. The Pocha River is the current Amu Darya River, and the West Sea is roughly the current Aral Sea and the Li River. The Situo River refers to a river in the north of Snow Mountain (western Himalayas). After Buddhism was introduced into the Congling area of Central Asia from Central India, the monks referred to the rivers in Xinjiang as the Situo River.[9]

Many rivers in the western region have disappeared into the desert in the lower reaches. The ancients did not understand this phenomenon and thought that these rivers were buried underground and would flow out of the ground again at some place in the east to form the Yellow River. Zhang Qian accepted this view when he sent an envoy to the Western Regions: "In the west of Khotan, all water flows to the west and flows to the west sea; in the east, water flows to the east and flows to the salt marshes. The salt marshes sneak underground, and its south is the source of the river."[10] The formation of the two sources of the Yellow River said: "The river has two sources: one is from Congling Mountain, and the other is from Khotan. Khotan is located at the foot of the Nan Mountains. Its river flows northward, joins the Congling River, and flows into the Puchang Sea in the east. Puchang Sea, a salt marsh, extended to Yumen and Yangguan for more than 300 *li*, covering a vast area of 300 *li*. The water pavilion house, which does not increase or decrease in winter and summer, is thought to sneak

---

8. "Long Agama Sutra," in *The Newly Corrected Tripitaka*, vol. 1 (Taipei: Buddha Education Foundation Publishing Department, 1990), 116 (below).
9. Zhang Xun, "On the Formation of River Sources," in *Collected Works of Zhang Xun* (Beijing: China Ocean Press, 1986), 181–182.
10. "Records of the Western Regions," in *Records of the Grand Historian*, vol. 123, book 10, 3160.

underground, and the south is out of Jishi, which is said to be the Chinese river."[11]

With the continued spread of Buddhism to the east, the monks of the Western Regions traveled eastward to the Yellow River Basin, and after being exposed to the Han culture, they naturally linked the Kunlun Mountain, the birthplace of the Yellow River, with the Anotatta Mountain, where it is located, and the Yellow River with the Situo River. In the last years of the Eastern Han Dynasty (AD 189–220 years), when Meng Kangxiang, a monk of the Central Indian Kingdom, translated the *Buddhist Sutra the Origin of Things*, he expressed this view in his preface: "The so-called Kunlun Mountain is the center of Yanfulidi. The mountains are all precious stones, and there are 500 caves in Zhouzao. The caves are all gold, and 500 Arhats often live there. The Anotatta Spring is surrounded by mountains outside and flat in the mountains. All the banks of the spring are gold, with four animal heads flowing out of its mouth and circling one turn each, returning to its side and throwing it into the four seas. The water that comes out was thought to be the water of the Yellow River."[12] One hundred years after the *A Record of Buddhistic Kingdoms* was written, Li Daoyuan, in the Northern Wei Dynasty, also adopted the theory of the source of the Yellow River and the relevant records in the *A Record of Buddhistic Kingdoms* many times when he annotated *Water Classic*. This wrong understanding has affected modern times.

---

11. "Records of the Western Regions (Part One)," in *Book of Han*, vol. 96 (upper), book 12, 3871.
12. "Sutra Preface Spoken by the Buddha on Rising Actions," in *The Newly Corrected Tripitaka*, vol. 4, 163 (below).

CHAPTER FOUR

COMMUNICATIONS BETWEEN CHINA AND THE WORLD IN THE SUI AND TANG DYNASTIES

Communications and transportation were hindered during the Southern and Northern Dynasties. After the Sui reunited China, regional communication networks became synchronized. Emperor Yang of the Sui Dynasty started construction on a large scale: the Grand Canal not only connected the northern and southern parts of China but also strengthened ties between central government and regions to the south of the Yangtze.

In the Tang Dynasty, infrastructure was a central government priority. New roads were constructed and old roads were repaired. National communications networks were also built connecting major cities in China. There were seven routes stretching out from the bordering prefectures, connecting the Tang to minority tribes and countries overseas. Cultural exchange with other territories brought different religions into China for the first time, including Buddhism and Islam. Buddhism also adjusted to Chinese culture, while Chinese influence spread to neighbors in Asia forming a Chinese cultural circle. "The order of the Han Dynasty is in the northwest, so the northwest calls China the Han Dynasty; the order of the Tang Dynasty is in the southeast, so the barbarians call China the Tang Dynasty."

1. Flourishing Waterways and Land Communications

Regions to the south of the Yangtze prospered as the Southern Dynasties established their capitals in South China. The regions surrounding the Sui capital of Daxing (present-day Xi'an), however, had been deteriorating in land fertility and could no longer support the growth of the population. Food had to be transported from Jiangnan in southeast China. Thus, it became the top agenda of the Sui to strengthen its reign in these farm-rich areas.

Emperor Yang of Sui decided to move the political center east. He ordered the building of the capital, Luoyang, and the Grand Canal, connecting North and South China. Geographically speaking, Luoyang was more central compared to Daxing. Therefore, transport links were better and costs were lower.

Emperor Yang of the Sui Dynasty was very aware of the general situation of the world. He believed that "the river is far away, and the troops are not in a hurry," and the political center must be moved eastward. So, while building Luoyang, the capital of the East, he also dug the South and North Grand Canal, aiming to "control the three rivers, consolidate the four fortresses, connect the land and water, and facilitate people's paying tribute."[1] Compared with Daxing City (Xi'an), the capital city, Luoyang, has a moderate geographical location, and the transportation of grain can avoid the natural danger of Sanmenxia of the Yellow River. The distance was shortened, and the transportation cost was reduced. The grain in the south of the Yangtze River can be transported conveniently by water. In the first year of Daye (AD 605), the Jiqu Canal was opened. It led the valley water from the west of Luoyang to the east of Yanshi to Luo River and then led the Yellow River from Luo River to the east of Banzhu (east of Sishui Town, Xingyang, Henan), and then led the Yellow River to the east. It passed through Kaifeng, Sui County, Shangqiu, Suzhou, and now the other bank of Xuyi to the Huai River. This section was also known as Tongji Canal and Bian River in history. In the fourth year of Daye's reign (AD 608), the Yongji Canal was opened again, and the Qin River was connected with Qing and Qi Rivers, and then the old Baigou Road and the current South Canal were followed to reach Ji County (Beijing), Zhuojun, a military town in the north. In the sixth year

---

1. Zhu Yu, "Pingzhou Ketan," vol. 2, in *Siku Quanshu*, book 1038, photocopy ed. (Taiwan: Commercial Press, 1983), 295.

of Daye (AD 610), the Jiangnan River from Jingkou (Zhenjiang, Jiangsu) to Yuhang (Hangzhou, Zhejiang) was also dredged. Together with the Guangtong Canal opened by Emperor Wen of the Sui Dynasty in the fourth year of his reign (AD 584), the North and South Grand Canal was formed. The Grand Canal reaches Chang'an in the west, Zhuojun in the north, and Yuhang in the south, with a total length of more than 2,000 kilometers. It connects the five major basins of the Hai River, the Yellow River, the Yangtze River, the Huai River, and the Qiantang River from the north to the south, forming a water transport network with the political center of Chang'an and Luoyang as the axis, controlling the military town in the north, and connecting the Jiangnan Economic Zone in the south. In the Tang and Northern Song dynasties, the Grand Canal was still the lifeline of water transport.

While excavating the South and North Grand Canal, Emperor Yang of the Sui Dynasty also built a large number of driveways for galloping: "The canal (referring to the Grand Canal) is 40 paces wide, and there are royal driveways built beside the canal, with willows. From Chang'an to Jiangdu, there are more than 40 palaces."[2] In the third year of Daye's reign (AD 607), men from more than ten counties north of the Yellow River opened the Taihang Route and built straight driveways to Bingzhou (southwest of Taiyuan); the imperial road from Ji (Beijing) to Yulin (twelve cities in the northeast of Zhunger Banner, Inner Mongolia), which was three thousand *li* long, was also built.

On the basis of the Sui Dynasty, the Tang Dynasty continued to open up new roads, improve road traffic facilities and add post stations. At the height of the Tang Dynasty, there were not only a large number of post stations serving officials but also a large number of commercial facilities serving ordinary passengers on the post road network, with Chang'an in the western capital and Luoyang in the eastern capital as the core. "Every store had donkeys for passengers to ride on, which could travel for tens of *li* in a flash. It was called donkey post. There were shops in Jingxiang and Xiangyang in the south, Taiyuan and Fanyang in the north, and Shuchuan and Liangfu in the west for business travel."[3]

---

2. *Comprehensive Mirror in Aid of Governance*, vol. 180, Daye of Sui Dynasty first year, third month, Wu Shen day, book 12 (Beijing: Zhonghua Book Company, 1956), 5618.
3. (Tang Dynasty) Du You, *Tongdian*, annotated by Wang Wenjin et al., vol. 7, book 1, 152.

Chapter Four

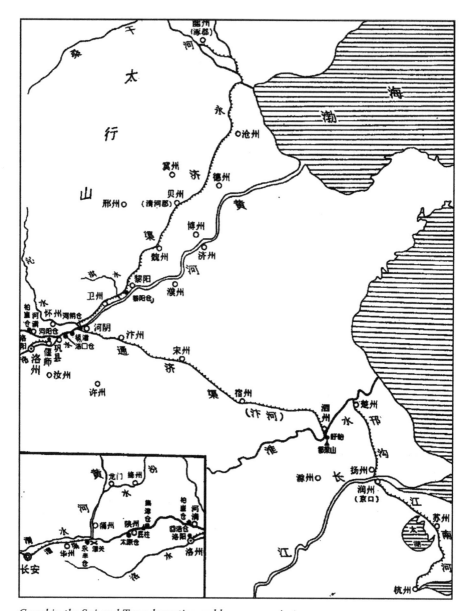

Canal in the Sui and Tang dynasties and large granaries[4]

---

4. Zou Yilin, *Chunlu Theses on History and Geography* (Tianjin: Tianjin Classic Literature Press, 2005), 120.

The busiest post road in the Tang Dynasty was between the eastern and western capitals—Chang'an and Luoyang. Emperor Taizong of the Tang Dynasty visited Luoyang many times, and Emperor Gaozong of the Tang Dynasty, Emperor Wu Zetian, and Xuanzong of the Tang Dynasty often traveled to and from Chang'an and Luoyang. Officials from Hebei, Henan, Jianghuai, Lingnan, and other places had to pass through Luoyang before going to the capital. Therefore, in the second year of Zhenyuan (AD 786), the post road from Chang'an to Bianzhou (Kaifeng) was designated as the "Dalu Post."[5] According to research, there were the following post houses from Chang'an, the capital of the Tang Dynasty, to Luoyang, the capital of the East City, 865 *li* apart: Inside Chang'an, there's the Duting Relay Station. Heading east, one would exit Chang'an through the Tonghua or Chunming gates, then pass through the Changle Relay Station (also known as Lesui Station, located east of Changlepo in Xi'an), Baqiao Relay Station (also called Zishui Station, present-day Baqiao Street), Huichang County (Lintong) Relay Station within the city, Yinpan Relay Station (east of Lintong's Yinpanpo), Xinfeng County (northeast of Lintong's Xinfeng Town) Relay Station within the city, Xishui Relay Station (also known as Xiyuan or Xikou Station, east of Xinfeng's Xi River), Duhua Relay Station (west of Weinan's Liangtian), Weinan County Relay Station within the city, Dongyang Relay Station (east of Weinan), Chishui Relay Station (west of Hua County's Chishui), Zheng County (Hua County) Pude Relay Station, Fushui Relay Station (west of Huayin's Fushui), Changcheng Relay Station (approximately ten *li* west of Huayin), Huayin County Relay Station within the city, Dong Relay Station (east of Huayin at Huayue Temple), Guanxi Relay Station (west of the old Tongguan's Xiguan Town), Tongguan Relay Station (by the Yellow River), Huangxiang County (northwest of Lingbao) Relay Station within the city, Pando Relay Station (west of Lingbao's Huangxiang Town's Pando) to Hucheng County (Huangxiang Town) Relay Station within the city.

East of Hucheng County, there are two relay routes: the northern route continues along the south bank of the Yellow River through Chousang Relay Station (north of Lingbao) to Taolin County Relay Station (northeast of Lingbao's old city). The southern route goes through Hongnong County (Lingbao's Guolue

---

5. "Relay Station," in *Institutional History of Tang*, vol. 61 (Shanghai: Shanghai Classics Publishing House, 1991), 1250.

Town) Bairen Relay Station to Taolin County, where it merges with the northern route. Starting from Taolin County Relay Station, the route heads east, passing Quwo (southwest of Shan County), Taiyuan Warehouse (southwest of Shanxi's Qilipu) to Shan County's Gantang Relay Station (old city of Shan County). The direction then shifts southeast through Qiaoshan to Xieshi City Relay Station, Jiaxiang Relay Station, Yongning County's Luqiao Relay Station (northwest of Luoning), Sanxiang Relay Station (northwest of Yiyang), Fuchang County (west of Fuchang in Yiyang) Relay Station within the city, Liuquan Relay Station (west of Yiyang's Liuquan), Shou'an County (Yiyang) Gantang Station, Sanquan Relay Station (east of Yiyang's Miaocun), Ganshui Relay Station (where Ganshui meets Luo River), and Lindu Relay Station (west side of Luoyang), and finally arriving at the Eastern Capital's Duting Relay Station.[6]

The communication network was centered around Chang'an and other key cities. Major routes to the rest of the country included:

a. from Chang'an eastward to Luoyang, northeastern Youzhou (Beijing), and Yingzhou (Chaoyang in Liaoning Province);
b. from Chang'an westward to Anxi Protectorate (Gaochang, to the east of Tulufan in Xinjiang) and Beiting Protectorate (north Jilinsa'er in Xinjiang);
c. from Chang'an southward to Jingzhou (Jiangling in Hubei), Hongzhou (Nanchang in Jiangxi Province), and Guangzhou.

Major routes from Luoyang to the rest of the country included:

a. from Luoyang westward to Chang'an, Southward to Jingzhou, and northeast to Yangzhou and Fuzhou;
b. from Luoyang eastward to Bianzhou (Kaifeng) and northeast to Dengzhou (Penglai in Shandong Province);
c. from Luoyang northward to Taiyuan and Daizhou (Dai County in Shanxi Province).

---

6. See Wang Wenchu, "A Study on the Relay Routes between the Two Capitals during the Tang Dynasty," in *Studies on Ancient Transportation Geography* (Beijing: Zhonghua Book Company, 1996), 46–81.

Other major hubs included Bianzhou (Kaifeng), Youzhou (Beijing), Taiyuanfu, Liangzhou (present-day Wuwei in Gansu Province), Yizhou (Chengdu), Jingzhou (Jiangling), Guangzhou, and Yangzhou.

There were seven major routes to foreign countries or minority districts:

a. From Yangzhou to Andong, reaching modern Heilongjiang Province;
b. From Dengzhou to Goryeo and Bohai, reaching the Korean Peninsula;
c. From Xiazhou to Datong and Yunzhong, reaching Suiyuan;
d. From Dalad Banner to Huihu, reaching modern Mongolia and the Yenisei River in Russia;
e. From Anxi to the Western Regions (i.e., the famous Silk Road), reaching Persian and Mediterranean countries;
f. From Annan to India;
g. From Guangzhou to overseas countries.[7]

Two other major routes went to Tibet and Yunnan. The Tubo Route, reaching Luoxie in Tibet (present-day Lhasa), was formed in the era of Emperor Taizong, enhancing cultural and economic exchange between Han Chinese and Tibetans.

In the early years of the Tang, administrators named six major tribes in the Erhai Lake District in Yunnan as "Liu Zhao." In AD 738, with support from Tang government, the chief of Nanzhao conquered other tribes in the area. Since then, many routes were constructed to Yunnan from central China.

2. Overseas Routes from Guangzhou and Communications with the Arabs

Guangzhou Port was known as Panyu Port in the Qin and Han dynasties. The area was blessed with favorable natural conditions. "The mountains and the sea are vast and open; the higher is the mulberry soil, the lower is the fertile land, and the birds and animals at the foot of the forest, everything is here. Sea monster fish and turtle, turtle alligator and fresh crocodile, rare and strange foreign

---

7. *The New Book of Tang Dynasty*, vol. 43, in *Geography*, book 4 (Beijing: Zhonghua Book Company, 1975), 1146.

matter, thousands of species and thousands of categories, which were too many to be counted." In the 15th year of Jian'an in the Eastern Han Dynasty (AD 210), Sun Quan sent Bu Zhi, the governor of Poyang, to be the governor of Jiaozhou and occupy Lingnan. When Buzhi came to Panyu, he climbed up and looked far "to see the vastness of the huge sea and the Yinfu of the original place. He said: "The fertile land of Sicheng Island should be the capital."[8] In the 22nd year of Jian'an (AD 217), Bu Zhi moved to Panyu, which was under the jurisdiction of Jiaozhou. Since then, Panyu has become the transportation center of Lingnan. In the fifth year of Wu Huangwu's reign in the Three Kingdoms (AD 226), the population of Lingnan increased. Sun Quan, taking into account the large size of Lingnan, divided Jiaozhou into two and newly established Guangzhou. Soon, they were merged into one place again. In the seventh year of Yong'an (AD 264), Sun Xiu once again divided Jiaozhou into two parts. Guangzhou was to the north of Hepu and governed Panyu of Nanhai County (now the old city of Guangzhou, Guangdong). Afterward, sea routes were developed from Panyu to Southeast Asia, South Asia, and West Asia. In the Southern and Northern Dynasties, Faxian, the famous monk, returned from India via Guangzhou.

Guangzhou Port became the largest of its kind in the country during the Tang era. From AD 630s, the Arabs launched a series of wars under the banner of Islam and established the large kingdom of Dashi across Asia, Africa, and Europe. The Dashi kingdom had a vast territory and attached great importance to maritime traffic. Seagoing ships could sail directly to the coast of China. In the 9th Century, Arabian geographer/explorer, Ibn Khurdadhbih, recorded the four big ports of Tang in his journal. "From Shuanfu to Lūqin, China's first port (Lūqin) is 100 farsakh by land and sea. In Lūqin, there were Chinese stones, Chinese silk, and high-quality Chinese ceramics, and it was the place where rice was produced. From Lūqin to Hanfu (Khānfu), there were four itineraries by sea and 20 itineraries by land. Hanfu (Khānfu) was China's largest port. There were various fruits, vegetables, wheat, barley, rice, and sugarcane in Hanfu (Khānfu). From Hanfu (Khānfu) to Khānju, it was eight days' journey. The specialties of Khānju are the same as those of Khānfu. From Khānju to Qntū, it was 20 days

---

8. (Northern Wei Dynasty) Li Daoyuan, *Water Classic Commentary*, vol. 37, in *Water Classic Commentary with Verification*, 873.

journey. The specialties of Qāntū were the same as those of Khānfu and Khānju. These ports in China were each bordered by a big river in which ships could sail. These were all tidal rivers."⁹

From AD 785 to 805, Counsel-in-Chief Jia Dan compiled a record of all seven major routes from the Tang Empire to other countries.

> If starting from Guangzhou Southeast seabound, it is 200 *li* from Tuen Mun Mountain (Tuen Mun, southwest of Kowloon), and if the sailing wind goes westbound, it will arrive at Jiuzhoushi on the second day (the seven islands on the northeast coast of Hainan). Within two days' sail toward the south, one can get to Xiangshi (now known as Duzhu Mountain, in the southeast of Hainan); three days to the southwest, to Culao Cham Mountain (Champo Island, Vietnam, which was 200 *li* east of the Huan Kingdom by sea (i.e., Linyi, in the south of Vietnam). With another two days' sail to the south, one could arrive at Lingshan (Vietnam Guiren Yanzi Cape). Sailing for one more day, one could get to the Mendu Kingdom (Guiren, Vietnam). On another day, people could arrive in the country of Guda (Nha Trang, Vietnam). With another half day's sailing, people could reach the Pentulang Chau (Van Lang, Vietnam). In another two days, one could arrive at Juntunong Mountain (Kunlun Island in southern Vietnam). On the fifth day, they arrived at Haixia (Malacca Strait of Singapore), which was called "Zhi" by the people of the South and the North, with Luoyue (the southern end of the Malay Peninsula and the area of Singapore) on the north bank and Foshi (the southeast of Sumatra) on the south bank. Traveling for four or five days to the east of Foshi Kingdom, one gets to the country of Haling (now Java), the largest in South China. From the west of the Xia (gorge), in three days, you arrive at the Gege Sengqi Kingdom (probably an island in today's Barlavento Archipelago). It's an isolated island to the northwest of where the Buddha passed away. The locals are largely fierce and hostile, making seafarers dread them. To its north coast is the Geluo Kingdom (west coast of Kedah, Malay Peninsula). West of Geluo is the Gegulu Kingdom (southwest of the Kra Isthmus, Malay Peninsula). From Gege Sengqi,

---

9. Ibn Chordadhbeh (Arab), *Book of Roads and Kingdoms* (Beijing: Zhonghua Book Company, 1991), 71–72.

after four or five days of travel, you arrive at Shengdeng Island (the area around Medan in the northern part of Sumatra). Five days westward brings you to Polu Kingdom (around the northern part of Sumatra near Banda Aceh). After six days, you reach the Pa Kingdom's Galan Island (Nicobar Islands). Four days northward leads to the Shi Zi Kingdom (Sri Lanka). Its northern coast is about a hundred *li* from the southern coastline of Tianzhu (South India). Four days westward, passing through the Meilai Kingdom (around Cochin in southwest India), you're at the southernmost region of South Tianzhu. Heading northwest, after passing over ten small countries, you reach the western border of Brahman (India). Two days northwest from there, you arrive at the Ba Kingdom (in the region of Broach in northern India). After ten days, passing through five small western Tianzhu countries, you reach Ti Kingdom (east of Karachi in Pakistan). There's the Milanta River, also known as the Xintou River (Indus River), which originates from the northern Bokun Kingdom, flowing westward into the sea by the north of the Ti Kingdom. From the Ti Kingdom, a twenty-day journey westward, passing through over twenty small countries, leads to the Tiro Luhe Kingdom (near Abadan by the Persian Gulf), also called the Luohe Yi Kingdom. The locals set up a beacon in the sea, and at night, a torch is placed atop it, guiding seafarers. A day's journey westward takes you to the Wula Kingdom (east of Basra in Iraq) by the Frillah River (Euphrates River) of the Tang Dynasty, flowing south into the sea. Small boats sailing upstream reach Molo (Basra) in two days, a stronghold of the Tang Dynasty. Another overland journey northwest for thousands of miles leads to the capital city of Momen King, Fuda (Baghdad).

From the southern boundary of Brahman, the route from the Meilai Kingdom to the Wula Kingdom follows the eastern coastline. To the west of this coastline lies the Tang Dynasty's territories, with its southernmost region called the Sanlan Kingdom (probably somewhere on the East African coast). From the Sanlan Kingdom, twenty days northward, after passing over ten small countries, you arrive at the She Kingdom (probably in the region of Yemen). Another ten days, passing six or seven small countries brings you to the Saiquhejie Kingdom (northeast coast of Oman), located on the western coastline. Six or seven days westward, passing through six or seven countries, you reach the Meixun Kingdom (Sohar port in Oman). Northwestward for ten days, passing over ten small countries, you come to the Bari Monan Kingdom (possibly on the eastern coast of Saudi Arabia). A day's journey brings you to the Wula Kingdom, where the route merges with the eastern coastline.[10]

This voyage records the Tang Dynasty's route to Arab, starting from Guangzhou, sailing south through the Pearl River Estuary to the port of Tuen Mun, then turning southwest, passing near the northeastern tip of Hainan Island via the Qizhou Ocean, reaching the southeastern seas of present-day Vietnam, then sailing south via the Mekong River Estuary and through the Singapore Strait to reach Sumatra Island. From there, via the Java and Malacca Straits, cross the Indian Ocean to reach Sri Lanka and the southern tip of the Indian Peninsula. Then along the west coast of India to the ports of Opola and Basra in the Persian Gulf. This route connected several major regions, including China, India, Persia, and Arabia, and was the longest maritime route from the Tang Dynasty to foreign countries, approximately 14,000 kilometers.

The trade between Guangzhou and Southeast Asian countries was very active in the Tang Dynasty. It was recorded that there were four major sea routes to these countries:

a. From Guangzhou via Southeast Asian countries to Sri Lanka, Arabian countries, and the Persian Gulf;
b. From Guangzhou via Southeast Asia to Sri Lanka and Iraq;
c. From Iran via Sri Lanka to Southeast Asia and Guangzhou;
d. From Sri Lanka, through Java and Vietnam to Guangzhou;
e. Between Guangzhou and Southeast Asia.

At that time, the countries in Southeast Asia that had regular trade with Guangzhou included: Linyi, Zhenla, Dandan, Panpan, Duohe Luo, Chitu, Piao Country (Myanmar), Sri Vijaya, Duopodeng (present-day Sumatra), Heling (Java), Persia, Dashi (Arab), Brunei, India, Jibin, Simhaladvipa, and the Daqin Empire, among others. In the ninth year of the Tianbao era (AD 750), "there were ships in the river from Brahmins, Persians, and Kunlun, too numerous to count; they carried incense, medicine, and treasures, piled up like mountains. These ships had a draft of six or seven *zhang*. Countries like the Simhaladvipa, Arab, Gutang

---

10. "Geography Section 7 (Part Two)," in *New Book of Tang*, vol. 43, book 4, 1153 (below).

Country, Baiman, and Chiman came and settled, with a wide variety of types."[11] "As for the various countries overseas, such as Danfuluo, Liuqiu, the Maoren, and the states of Yidan, as well as Linyi, Funan, Zhenla, and Kadaram, they are countless and lie on the southeastern edge of the world. Sometimes, they wait for favorable winds and tides to pay tribute. The barbarian and foreign merchants' ships cross the seas to trade."

Guangzhou Port had two outer ports, Tuen Mun and Boluomiao. Tuen Mun is located in Qingshan Bay, New Territories, Hong Kong today. The port faces south, the Kau Keng Shan and Qing Mountains are distributed from east to west, and the Dayu Mountain is its barrier. Boluomiao is located in Nangang Miaotou Village, Huangpu today, also known as Gudou Village and Fuxu town. All ships entering and leaving the port stop here, pay a visit to the sea god, and pray for the blessings of the gods. There are terminals such as Guangta and Lanhu inside the port. Guangta Terminal is in the area of Guangta Street, Guangzhou, near Fan Fang. Guangta was built for navigation. During the Qing Qianlong period, a foreign ship was dug up from the south of Guangta. Lanhu Terminal is located in the area of Liuhua Lake Park today, which was an important terminal for inland navigation in Guangzhou at the time, and the South Sea County Office was built nearby.

With the development of communications from Guangzhou to foreign countries, economic and cultural exchange between Lingnan and central China also flourished. For example, the supply of salt and seafood from Lingnan would not only satisfy demand in the Yangtze and Huai regions, but there was also enough for storage. However, there were only two routes of communication between Guangzhou and the inland. One was through Qitian Mountain to Chenzhou in Hunan, and the other was through Dayu Mountain to Ganzhou in Jiangxi. The Qin Dynasty set up Hengpu Pass on Dayu Mountain, which was one of the roads connecting the inland to Lingnan. However, this road was treacherous and dangerous, with mountainous terrain making transportation of goods reliant solely on manual labor. In November of the sixteenth year of the Kaiyuan reign of the Tang Dynasty (AD 728), the court ordered Zhang Jiuling to open a new road through Dayu Mountain. The new Dayu Mountain Road

---

11. Zhenren Yuankai, *The Record of the Eastern Expedition during the Great Peace of Tang*, annotated by Wang Xiangrong (Beijing: Zhonghua Book Company, 2000), 74.

was not constructed through the Xiaomei Pass as it was in the Qin and Han dynasties, but a new road was built at the narrow passage east of the Xiaomei Pass, shortening the mileage and improving road conditions, allowing several carts to pass at the same time. "Open and vast with five tracks, stretching out in four directions. Through this, the labor of transportation is transformed, and the depths and heights lose their danger. Thus, those kinds like those with pierced ears and chests, and those with extraordinary treasures and rare gifts, find rest and reprieve as if they were in the capital or on an islet."[12] Along the way, there were post stations and inns built. Personnel and goods from the mainland and Lingnan could travel and communicate with each other more conveniently, forming a major transportation route from Chang'an, Luoyang, Bian River, Huai River, the Jiangnan Canal, Hangzhou, Qiantang River, Chang Mountain, Yu Mountain, Xin River, Poyang Lake, Gan River, the Dayuling Pass, Zhen River, Bei River, and Guangzhou. These factors made Guangzhou Port the largest of the four major ports of the Tang Empire.

The volume of foreign trade from Guangzhou Port to other countries in the Tang era exceeded any dynasty before it. During the Tang Dynasty, due to the chaos caused by the rebellion of Feng Chongdao, only four or five foreign merchant ships arrived in Guangzhou each year. In the fourth year of the Dali period (AD 769), Li Mian was appointed as the governor of Guangzhou, and the inspector of Lingnan, and he pacified the rebellion. Li Mian was an honest official, and when foreign ships entered the port, he did not board the ships for inspection. It was reported that in AD 770, there were over 40 foreign ships in Guangzhou Port.[13] "Ships from foreign lands sail in the South Sea, and every year they reach Annan and Guangzhou. Among them, ships from the Simhaladvipa are the largest, with several *zhang* in height, loaded with various precious goods. When the ships arrive, they report to the local government, and the county is bustling with excitement."[14] These foreign ships had pigeons on board; whenever there was an accident, the pigeons would carry messages for help.

---

12. (Tang Dynasty) Zhang Jiuling, "Preface to the Carving of the Dayu Mountain Pass," in *Qujiang Anthology*, vol. 17, *Siku Quanshu* version, book 1066, 186–187.
13. "Annals of Li Mian," in *Old Book of Tang*, vol. 131, book 11 (Beijing: Zhonghua Book Company, 1975), 3635.
14. (Tang Dynasty) Li Zhao, "Supplement to the History of the Tang Dynasty (Part Three)," in *Siku Quanshu* version, book 1035, 449 (upper).

Goods imported to Guangzhou included pearls, shells, ivory, rhinoceros horn, and rosewood, as well as various fragrances and plants: frankincense, camphor, benzoin, sandalwood, spikenard, sappan wood, gall nuts, black pepper, white cardamom, Arihun (阿日浑), Aniruddha, myrrh, purslane, and figs, etc. According to Arabic records, goods exported from Guangzhou included silk, precious swords, flower-patterned satin, musk, agarwood, saddles, mink fur, ceramics, girdles, inner cinnamon, galangal, etc. Pieces of Tang Dynasty porcelain or Tang Sancai fragments have been found in various places such as Cairo in Egypt, East Africa, Xilafu of Persia Gulf, and Samara in Iraq, indicating that the export of porcelain also accounted for a considerable proportion. In the Abbasid Caliphate, there were many artisans from China: "Silk weaving shuttles, gold and silver craftsmen, painters, and Han craftsmen who specialized in drawing were represented by people like Fan Shu and Liu Ci from Jingzhao. As for those who specialized in weaving, there were individuals like Yue and Lü Li from Hedong."[15]

Records from the Sui and Tang eras also showed that slaves were imported from foreign countries to China. In the Sui Dynasty, Chen Leng "recruited people from the southern countries to join the army, including some from Kunlun, who spoke the language quite well and sent someone to comfort them."[16] These Kunlun people were also known as "Kunlun slaves" and were tall and dark-skinned, often doing heavy manual labor. The poem "Kunlun Er" by Zhang Ji depicts them vividly: "Kunlun's home is in the southern state of the sea, the barbarian visitors who come to the Han land, their language is understood by Qin and Ji, the waves have just passed the Yu Lin State. The golden ring wants to fall through the ear, the snail bun is long, and the fist is not wrapped around the head. They love their skin as black as lacquer, half-undressed when they walk with wooden cotton fur."[17] These Kunlun people came from the remote Nai and Gantang countries: "Nai Country, Kunlun people also, located in the south of the forest city, go to the Jiaozhi Sea for three months. Customs are the same as Brahmans. Extremely remote, never communicated with China before. In the second year of the Tang Dynasty's Zhenguan, the tributary mission arrived in October." "Gantang

---

15. (Tang Dynasty) Du You, *Tongdian*, annotated by Wang Wenjin et al., vol. 193, book 5, 5280.
16. "Liuqiu Country Records," in *Book of Sui*, vol. 81, book 6 (Beijing: Zhonghua Book Company, 1973), 1825.
17. (Tang Dynasty) Zhang Ji, *Zhang Siye Collection*, vol. 5, in *Siku Quanshu* version, vol. 1078, 41 (upper).

Country, located in the south of the sea, Kunlun people also. In the 10th year of the Zhenguan era of the Tang Dynasty, envoys from the Zhujupo country arrived for a tribute on the same day."[18] This phenomenon still existed in the Song Dynasty: "Many wealthy people in Guangzhong kept ghost slaves, who were very strong and could carry hundreds of pounds. They spoke with a desire for lust and had a simple nature and were also called wild people. Their skin was black as ink, their lips red and teeth white, their hair was curly and yellow, with male and female, born in the mountains beyond the sea."[19] Some records in the Song also had similar descriptions, and it was suspected the Kunlun people originated from Africa.

The officers in charge of foreign trade in the Tang were often local administrators such as commanders-in-chief or governors. As the scale of foreign trade upgraded, experts were needed. In AD 722, the Maritime Trade Superintendency was set up.[20] Its officers were often trusted eunuchs or military commissioners of Lingnan districts. In the first year of the Guangde reign period of the Tang Dynasty (AD 763), a drama took place where the eunuch commissioner of maritime trade, Lü Taiyi, led an army to expel Zhang Xiu, the governor of Lingnan, and his subordinates looted the city of Guangzhou.[21]

When foreign ships came to Guangzhou for trade, they had to carry out procedures such as "taxing ships," "gathering the market," and "accepting tributes." "Taxing ships" refers to collecting import duties on ships. According to Arabian records, the import tax could be as high as 30 percent. Records in the Tang also showed that high rates were used by local officers to extract money for themselves. This created rifts among local administrators and foreign merchants. This is repeatedly documented in Tang Dynasty literature: "In the South Sea, there are abundant profits from the maritime trade, and treasures converge. The former governor (referring to the governor) made laws to promote prosperity and wealth, and whoever was in charge of the South Sea would never refuse to return.

---

18. (Song Dynasty) Yue Shi, *Records of the World during the Era of Great Peace*, ed. and annotated by Wang Wenchu, etc., vol. 177, book 8 (Beijing: Zhonghua Book Company, 2007), 3385. See also *Institutional History of Tang*, vol. 98–99.
19. Zhu Yu, "Pingzhou Ketan," vol. 2, in *Siku Quanshu* version, book 1038, 290 (below).
20. See Wang Jie, *Management of Foreign Trade Overseas in Ancient China* (Dalian: Dalian Maritime University Press, 1994), 53.
21. "Annal of Daizong," in *Old Book of Tang*, vol. 11, book 2, 274.

Lu Jun (referring to the governor of Lingnan) is benevolent and forgiving, and his governance is honest and clean. He asks the commander of the army to lead the maritime trade and customs and has not engaged in any prior activities."[22] Wei Zhengguan "took over as the governor of Lingnan. Since the beginning of the maritime trade in the South Sea, the governor must take ivories, rhinoceros horns, and bright pearls to sell to the lower classes. Wei Zhengguan, since his arrival, has taken nothing, and officials consult him for his cleanness."[23]

"Due to the governor's income and grandeur, the city is divided into three layers, and the commander holds six banners, one banner, and one army, with no difference in majesty from the son of heaven. The purple and red colors fill the city, and the residents of the city are forced to give way." In AD 758, armed merchants from Iran and Persian countries attacked the city of Guangzhou. They robbed warehouses and set local houses on fire. Local governor Wei Li fled. As a result, in AD 829, Emperor Wenzong ordered governors to lessen the rate. "The foreigners in the South Sea are here because of their admiration for Chinese culture, and they expect to be treated with kindness. However, they hear rumors of senior officials demanding more taxes, and it has spread among the people … As for the foreigners in Lingnan, Fujian, and Yangzhou, the governor should appoint a supervisor to watch over them, allowing them to come and go freely and engage in their own trade without imposing additional taxes, other than the import tax, market tax, and tribute."[24]

Islam was also brought to China in the Tang era. It was recorded that four Islamic saints came to China to preach the religion. One of the saints resided in Guangzhou, one in Yangzhou, and the other two in Quanzhou.[25] It was proved that the Islamic tombs in Quanzhou were built in the Song Dynasty. As there were many Arabs living in Yangzhou and Guangzhou in the Tang, Islam must have been brought to China in the same era. Persian merchant Suleiman also wrote in his journals in AD 851 about the daily lives of Arabs in Guangzhou:

---

22. "Biography of Lu Jun," in *Old Book of Tang*, vol. 177, book 14, 4591.
23. "Biography of Wei Gao," in *New Book of Tang*, vol. 158, book 16, 4937.
24. "Benevolent Proclamation of Recovery in the Third Year of Dahe," in *Collection of Tang Imperial Decrees*, vol. 10 (Beijing: Zhonghua Book Company), 65.
25. He Qiaoyuan, "Lingshan," *Book of Min*, vol. 7, in *The Collected Series of Siku Quanshu*, vol. 204 (Section of History) (Jinan: Qilu Press, 1997), 131 (below).

The Arab merchants in China gather in a trading city called Kangfu. There is one Islamic priest and one mosque there. Most of the houses in the city are built with wood and bamboo mats, so there are often fires. When foreign merchant ships arrive at the port, officials collect their goods and impose a 30% customs tax. Once all the ships have entered the port for the season, the goods are returned to the original owners to sell. If the king likes a particular item, he will pay the highest price for it in cash. Many Islamic merchants gather in Guangfu, and the Chinese emperor appoints an Islamic judge to govern the Muslim population according to Islamic customs. The judge prays and reads religious teachings with the Muslims several days a week and blesses the Islamic Sultan at the end of the prayers. The judge is fair and just, and all actions are based on the teachings of the *Quran* and Islamic customs. As a result, Iraqi merchants who come here praise the place.[26]

Guangzhou hosted the tomb of Sa'd ibn Abi Waqqas, who was said to be the uncle of Muhammad, founder of the religion. The former escorted the Koran to China and reached the capital, Chang'an, in AD 632. Emperor Taizong allowed him to create a mosque there, and later he built mosques in Jiangning and Guangzhou.[27]

The Arabs made up a large percentage of the foreigners residing in Guangzhou. It was said the foreign population there once reached 120,000. Compounds of Arabic communities were then called "Fan Fang" (蕃坊). "The Fan Chief is in charge, leading the market and ships, registering its name and goods, accepting ships' feet, and forbidding rare and exotic items. Foreign merchants who cheat will be imprisoned."[28] The Fan Fang is located outside the city of Guangzhou and has street names such as Chaotian Street, Manao Lane, and Tianshui Lane, which are derived from Arabic meanings or names. During the Song Dynasty, historical records clearly recorded that there was a Fan Chief in the Guangzhou Fan Fang, who was appointed by a foreign national and responsible for managing public

---

26. Zhang Xinglang, *Compilation of Historical Materials on Sino-Western Communication*, book 2 (Beijing: Zhonghua Book Company), 201.
27. Shen Fuwei, *History of Cultural Communications between China and the West* (Shanghai, Shanghai People's Press, 1985), 172.
28. (Tang Dynasty) Li Zhao, "Supplement to the History of the Tang Dynasty (Part Three)," in *Siku Quanshu* version, book 1035, 449 (upper).

affairs within the Fan Fang, attracting foreign merchant ships. The Fan Fang has Arab-style buildings such as Fan Houses, Fan Markets, Fan Schools, and Fan Warehouses, which are exclusively for foreign merchants and their families to live, trade, and study.

3. Xuanzang Goes to India for Buddhist Texts

Journey to the West was one of China's most famous ancient novels. The novel depicted Xuanzang's trip to India for Buddhist texts and made Xuanzang a household name in China.

Xuanzang, whose surname was Chen and given name was Yi, was respectfully known as the "Tripitaka Master." He was from Guoshi (near present-day Chenhe Village, Yanshi County, Henan Province) and was born in the second year of Emperor Wen of Sui's Reign of Benevolence (AD 602 or AD 600). When Xuanzang was ten years old, his family encountered misfortune, and he went to the Jingtu Temple in Luoyang to study Buddhist scriptures along with his already-ordained elder brother, Chen Su. Under the Sui Dynasty's system, one had to go through the state's selection and complete the "ordination" procedure before a Buddhist believer could become a monk. In the 10th year of Emperor Yang's Reign of Grand Enterprise (AD 614), the Minister of State, Zheng Shanguo, came to Luoyang for "ordination." At that time, there were hundreds of candidates, but 13-year-old Xuanzang was not eligible to participate in the selection. However, he was exceptional in appearance and ambition, which caught Zheng Shanguo's attention, and he was specially permitted to ordain as a monk.

Xuanzang became a monk and lived in the Jingtu Temple in Luoyang. During the late Sui and early Tang dynasties, warlords were in control, and only Sichuan had a relatively stable situation, so monks from all over the country flocked to Sichuan. In Sichuan, Xuanzang spent several years reading Buddhist scriptures. During this time, he also traveled to Jingzhou (Jiangling in Hubei), Xiangzhou (Anyang in Henan), and Zhaozhou (Zhao County in Hebei). In the last years of the Wude era, with the stability of the national situation, Xuanzang returned to Chang'an. As his knowledge increased, Xuanzang's doubts and confusion also grew, and the Chinese Buddhist scriptures and high monks could not answer these questions. So, Xuanzang decided to go to the birthplace of Buddhism,

India, to seek the Dharma. Just at this time, an Indian senior monk named Popo Mituoluo came to China. After meeting with him, Xuanzang became even more determined in his decision to travel.

Xuanzang set out from Chang'an and passed through Qinzhou (in the north of Tianshui, Gansu), Lanzhou, and finally reached Liangzhou. When he arrived in Guazhou (southeast of Anxi, Gansu), spies from Chang'an who were pursuing him caught up with him: "There is a monk named Xuanzang who wants to enter Western Regions. The county where he is located should be tightly guarded and captured." Thus, Xuanzang not only had to face the harsh natural conditions but also had to constantly avoid official pursuit.

Xuanzang ventured through the dangerous passes alone and almost died when he was shot by an arrow at a frontier checkpoint. He finally managed to pass through the fourth pass and entered the vast and boundless Moheyan Qi to the southeast of Yiwu (Hami in Xinjiang). The Moheyan Qi is over 800 *li* long, with no flying birds or walking animals above or water and grass below. At night, the cold wind is like a knife, and during the day, the hot wind is like fire. One day, when Xuanzang took off his water bag to have a drink, he accidentally dropped it due to its weight and spilled the water. In the desert, no water means no life. Xuanzang "had not a drop of moisture for four nights and five days, his mouth and stomach were dry, and he was about to die." However, Xuanzang had a strong will and resolutely moved forward, never taking a step back to the east. On the half of the fifth night, he felt a little relieved because of the cool wind. The next day, his horse suddenly went down a fork in the road and refused to go straight. Miraculously, Xuanzang found "a few *mu* of green grass" and, after not going far, he also saw a pool of water with a sweet smell. He drank the water, and both he and his horse regained their strength. Xuanzang survived death and finally walked out of the desert, reaching the gateway to the Western Regions, the country of Yiwu.

In Yiwu, Xuanzang met the envoy of the Kingdom of Gaochang (Turpan, Xinjiang). The envoy reported Xuanzang's message to King Quwen Tai. Quwen Tai was a devout Buddhist and, upon hearing the news, instructed the king of Yiwu to send Xuanzang to Gaochang, and immediately sent people to welcome him and asked him to change his western route and first come to Gaochang. Originally, Xuanzang was planning to travel west along the northern edge of the Tianshan from Khokhan-Bulak (Jimusaer, Xinjiang), but he could not refuse and had to go. On the night of his arrival, King Quwen Tai and the queen personally greeted Xuanzang with candles and welcomed him into the precious tent in the back courtyard of the palace. Quwen Tai was very respectful of the Buddhist monk Xuanzang and allowed him to preach in the temple next to the palace. He wanted Xuanzang to stay in Gaochang for the rest of his life. However, Xuanzang was determined to go west and swore never to stay, not eating or drinking for four days before he was allowed to leave. When he left, Quwen Tai and the ministers, monks, and people came out of the city to bid farewell. They also sent five Buddhist monks, 20 followers, 30 horses, and gifts of gold, silver, silk, and clothing to accompany Xuanzang. Special letters were written and sent to each country along the way, each letter accompanied by a gift of a large silk scarf, and two carts of fruit were prepared to be sent to the protector of the West Turks, Yehu Khan (the son-in-law of the Khan of the Western Turks), to take care of Xuanzang's journey. Xuanzang referred to Quwen Tai's hospitality as "more than the waters of the river Jiao and considering the weight of the Congling Mountains is not too much."

Thanks to the support of the King of Gaochang, Xuanzang's travel conditions greatly improved. Xuanzang and his entourage traveled along the southern foot of Tianshan Mountain via the Silver Mountain route to reach the Aqini kingdom (today's Yanqi in Xinjiang) and stayed for a night. Perhaps due to the kingdom's lack of enthusiasm, they departed the next day. Later, they crossed the Peacock River and the Wei River, arriving at the Quzhi kingdom (today's Kuche in Xinjiang). Xuanzang observed towering Buddha statues standing on either side of the main road outside the western gate of the Quzhi kingdom, where a major Buddhist assembly was held every five years. Every autumn, monks, and devotees from the kingdom would gather, and even the royals and commoners would put aside their mundane tasks to practice strict discipline and listen to the scriptures. Every temple decorated its Buddha statues with treasures and took them out in splendid processions. This event was much grander than the one in the Tian Kingdom and lasted 15 days, concluding with the grand Bathing Buddha Festival.

After a two-month stay in Quzhi, Xuanzang set out westward, passing through Baluka (possibly near Aksu or Baicheng), following the Aksu River and Kumalik River, and finally reaching the Ling Mountain pass at the southern foot of the Tianshan. The pass was a crucial gateway across the Tianshan, known for its dangers and hardships. Often, traversing this passage came at the cost of life. "Valleys filled with snow, which even in spring and summer freezes. The route was perilous, with harsh, cold winds and rampant dragons which posed threats to travelers. Violation of any rules, like wearing red clothing or shouting loudly, could lead to visible disasters. Fierce storms would stir up flying sand and rain down stones, endangering those who encountered them."[29] "Congling Mountains, situated in the middle of the Sambu continent, connects to the great Snow mountains in the south, leads to the Hot Sea and Thousand Springs in the north, extends to the Huo country in the west, and reaches the Wuqiao country in the east, spanning thousands of miles in all directions. The cliffs are layered hundreds of times over, the valleys are perilous, always covered in snow and ice, and the cold wind blows fiercely. All of these are descriptions of the Congling Mountains, highlighting the harsh climate of the plateau."[30] This description highlights the harsh plateau climate of the Congling Mountains (Pamir Mountains). After crossing the Snow Mountains, they reached Daqingchi (also known as Issyk-Kul Lake in Kyrgyzstan). Heading north from the lake, they arrived at Suye City (or Suiye, eight kilometers southwest of today's Tokmok City in Kyrgyzstan). Here, Xuanzang met the Western Turkic Khagan, Ye Hu Khan. As Xuanzang approached the Khan's tent, Ye Hu Khan came out to greet him from a distance. The Khan also sent envoys with letters to various affiliated states, notifying them of Xuanzang's passage. Passing through notable Central Asian cities like Zheshi (present-day Tashkent in Uzbekistan), Xuanzang eventually reached India, where the monks were amazed by his dedication and took the initiative to show him various Buddhist sites.

Xuanzang spent five years at the famous Nalanda Monastery in Magadha, where he studied Buddhist scriptures and Brahmanical classics while also learning Sanskrit and many dialects of India. He soon became a scholar of Indian Buddhism and established a prominent status within the Buddhist community. King Jieri of Kānyakubja held a grand ceremony in the city of Qu'nü, attended by kings, officials, and monks from 18 Indian countries. For this grand event, a special Baotai Traveling Palace was constructed, and the scene was quite luxurious: "The king first built a large monastery in the west of the river. The monastery started from the east of the Baotai, rising more than a hundred feet high, with a golden

---

29. *Records of the Western Regions of the Tang Dynasty*, vol. 1 (Beijing: Zhonghua Book Company, 2000), 67.
30. *Records of the Western Regions of the Tang Dynasty*, vol. 12, 964.

Buddha statue in the middle that was as tall as the king himself. To the south of the platform, there was a precious altar built for the purpose of bathing the Buddha statue. About fourteen to fifteen *li* to the northeast from there, a separate traveling palace was constructed."[31] Xuanzang, as the main debater, proposed the "Evil Perception Theory" as the topic of discussion. He promoted Mahayana Buddhism and refuted opposing views, impressing the attendees with his profound knowledge and eloquence. Later, his *Tri-kāya Doctrine* spread across India, earning him the title "Mahayana Deva." Clearly, Xuanzang's era differed from that of Faxian. Apart from seeking scriptures, he was also able to discuss Buddhist studies with Indian monks on an equal footing.

In AD 643, Xuanzang declined offers from Nalanda Monastery and set off for China. He took 650 Buddhist texts, statues, flowers, and fruit seeds. Going via modern Pakistan, Afghanistan, the Pamir Mountains, Hetian, and Qiemo in Xinjiang, he finally reached Chang'an in AD 645.

4. JIANZHEN BRINGS BUDDHISM TO JAPAN

During the Sui-Tang Dynasty, Japan was referred to as the "Wa Kingdom" (Wakoku), and it was said to be located "in the southeast sea of Silla, residing by a mountain island. It travels for five months in the east and west and three months in the north and south. It communicates with China ... and has some writing, and people respect Buddhism."[32]

Before the Sui Dynasty, Japan had already been communicating with China along the Yellow Sea route. In the third year of the Sui Dynasty's Daye (AD 607), a delegation from Japan led by Ono no Imoko made its first visit. During their audience with Emperor Yang, the Japanese envoys stated, "We heard that the Bodhisattva Emperor in the west (referring to the Sui emperor) is promoting Buddhism, so we sent envoys to pay our respects and brought several monks to learn Buddhism." However, a phrase in the letter from Japan to the Sui court, which read, "The sun-rising place emperor sends a letter to the sun-setting place emperor," displeased Emperor Yang. The following year, Emperor Yang of

---

31. *Records of the Western Regions of the Tang Dynasty*, vol. 5, 440.
32. "Records of the Eastern Barbarians," in *Old Book of Tang*, vol. 199, book 16, 5340.

Sui sent Pei Shiqing, holding the title of Wenlin Lang, as an envoy to visit Japan in return. Pei Shiqing and his team set out from Wendeng in Shandong. They "passed through Baekje (a kingdom in Korea) and arrived at Takeshima (located southwest of Jeollanam-do's Jindo), from where they looked south toward Danluo Kingdom (Jeju Island). They then passed through Dusima Country (Tsushima), which is isolated in the vast ocean. They further traveled east to Yizhi Country (Iki) and then to Zhusi Country (Tsukushi). After that, they reached the Qin King's region (the western area of the Shanyang Road where the Qin clan resided). The people there were similar to those of the Central Plains (China) but were considered to be of the barbarian islands, and it was doubtful if they could be clearly understood. After passing through more than ten regions, they reached the coastline. All the regions east of Zhushi were tributary to Wa (ancient name for Japan)."[33] Pei traveled from Wendeng across the sea to the Baekje region of the Korean Peninsula. From there, he headed south through Tsushima Island and Iki Island, crossed the Korea Strait, and arrived at northern Kyushu in Japan. He then crossed the Seto Inland Sea and finally reached Osaka Bay. Subsequent mutual visits between the two sides indicate that the Sui Dynasty and Japan had close interactions.

In the Tang, there were two major sea routes between China and Japan. The northern sea route went via the Korean Peninsula to Busan and then crossed Tsushima Island reaching Kyushu Island in Japan.

> There are two sea routes from China to Japan, the northern and southern routes along the coast of the Korean Peninsula. The northern route passes through the northeast of Dongzhou (now Penglai, Shandong) and across Daxie Island, Guixin Island (Tuoji Island), Mo Island (big and small Qin Island), and Wuhu Island (Nanhuangcheng Island), among others, for a distance of 300 *li*. Crossing the north to the Wuhu Sea (Laotie Mountain Waterway) to the Mashi Mountain (Laotie Mountain in Dalian, Liaoning) is 200 *li* (approximately 100 kilometers) east of the Duli Town (Lüshun). The route goes along the east coast and passes through Qingni Pu (Dalian), Taohua Pu (Jinzhou), Xinghua Pu (Zhuanghe), Shirenwang (Shicheng Island), Tuotuo Bay (Dayang River), and Wugu River (Dandong) for 800 *li*.

---

33. "Account of the Wa Kingdom," in *Book of Sui*, vol. 81, book 6, 1827.

Portrait of Jianzhen

After entering the Korean territory, it goes down the Korean Peninsula to Busan. Then, it passes through Tsushima Island and Yki Island to reach northern Kyushu in Japan. This route is also known as the northern route of the Yellow Sea. The southern route, also known as the southern route of the Yellow Sea, was taken by the monk Yuanren when he returned to Japan during the Tang Dynasty and was a shorter route. Both routes mainly sail along the coast, which is relatively safe, but political and military changes on the Korean Peninsula may affect the smoothness of the route. During the mid-Tang Dynasty, due to the unification of Silla on the Korean Peninsula, Japan's relationship with Silla was tense and had to take a detour to the East Sea route and go south to Mingzhou (Ningbo) and Yuezhou (Shaoxing). The East Sea route is divided into two, the southern route, starting from the port of Mingzhou or Yuezhou, crosses the East Sea and arrives near the Amami Ōshima in southern Japan, then goes north through Tokharoi, Yejiu, and Duomi, crossing the Osumi-kaikyo Strait, arriving at the southwest of Kyushu, in Satsuma. Zhenzhen went east, following this route. The northern route departs from ports such as Chuzhou (Huai'an), Yangzhou, Mingzhou, and

Wenzhou, among others, crosses the East Sea, and arrives in Japan near the islands of Shikoku and Honshu.

Monk Jianzhen was previously surnamed Chunyu. He was born in AD 688 in Yangzhou. His father was a Buddhist believer. At the age of 16, Jianzhen practiced monkhood at Dayun Temple in Yangzhou. In the third year of Chang'an, during the reign of Wu Zetian (AD 703), a 16-year-old Jianzhen entered the Dayun Temple to become a novice monk under the guidance of the renowned "Master of Ordination" Dao'an. Two years later, he received Buddhist ordination as a novice monk. In the first year of the Jinglong era (AD 707), he traveled to the eastern capital of Luoyang to study. The following year, he went to the capital Chang'an to continue his studies and was ordained as a full monk by the famous master of the Vinaya school, Hongjing, who presided over the South Spring Temple. In the following five years, Jianzhen devoted himself to the study of Buddhism in Luoyang and Chang'an, gradually becoming a learned and scholarly monk. At 26, Jianzhen came back to Yangzhou to preach Buddhism.

Around this time in Japan, Buddhism became very popular. However, regulation and good practice was lax. This has two negative consequences: first, the court is unable to protect its financial revenue and maintain social stability, and second, it cannot ensure the quality of the monks, as some morally suspect individuals are able to mix in. In the 5th year of the Japanese Tempyō era (7th year of the Kaiyuan era in Tang, AD 733), monks such as Rōshu and Fuchō accompanied the Japanese envoy to China to study and seek to recruit high-level monks to Japan to teach the discipline. In the capital city of Luoyang, they invited Dafu Temple's Abbot Dao-xuan to Japan to teach the discipline. In the 24th year of the Kaiyuan era (AD 736), Dao-xuan and the Japanese deputy envoy, Nagao, arrived in Japan together. As qualified monks for the ordination need to meet the standard of "three teachers and seven evidences," only a few abbots like Dao-xuan were invited, and it was not possible to establish a platform for ordination. Therefore, Rōshu and Fuchō thought of inviting Abbot Jianzhen to Japan to teach discipline and ordain.

In October of the first year of Tianbao (AD 742), Rōshu and Fuchō arrived in Yangzhou with a letter of introduction from Li Linfu's brother Li Linzong, the Prime Minister, and asked Li Cou, the military commander of Yangzhou's granary, to build a large ship and prepare food and other supplies to send Rongrui and others back to Japan. Rōshu and Fuchō then went to Daming Temple and

A Japanese ship of delegates to the Tang Empire

asked Jianzhen to go to Japan to teach Buddhism: "The Buddhist law has flowed to the country of Japan, although there is its law, there is no one to transmit it. In our country, there was a prince of saintly virtue who said: 'Two hundred years later, the sacred teaching will flourish in Japan.' Now is the time I wish to travel east to promote civilization."[34] At that time, Jianzhen was teaching monastic rules to the monks, and upon hearing the news, he replied: "The king of the country of Japan, Nagaya, reveres the Buddhist law and has made a thousand robes to bestow on the great virtue and the many monks of this country. The robes are embroidered with four sentences on edge: 'The mountains and rivers are different regions, the wind and moon are the same sky, sent to all Buddhist disciples, to jointly establish this connection.' With this in mind, it is truly the flourishing of Buddhist law and a country with fate." Jianzhen, who was teaching monastic rules to the monks, asked if there was anyone willing to go to the country of Japan to transmit the law. The monks were silent for a moment, and after a while, the monk Xiangyan replied:

---

34. Zhenren Kaiyuan, *Records of the Tang Dynasty's Eastward Expeditions,* annotated by Wang Xiangrong, 40.

"That country is too far away, life is difficult to survive, the sea is vast and endless, with nothing to rely on. The human body is difficult to obtain, and birth in China is difficult; without preparation for progress, the outcome has not been reached. Therefore, all the monks are silent and have no response." Jianzhen, who believed in the Mahayana doctrine of "universal salvation," upon hearing Xiangyan's reply, said decisively: "This is a matter of the law, why should I be afraid of losing my life? If others do not go, I will."[35] Upon hearing Jianzhen's words, 21 monks expressed their willingness to go to Japan together.

Jianzhen's journey to Japan faced many challenges. This might be due to the Tang Dynasty's strict policy prohibiting monks from traveling abroad without authorization or because of the treacherous natural conditions and rough seas. After enduring numerous hardships, it was only on the sixth attempt that he finally succeeded.

The first time: With the introduction letter from Li Linzong, Li Cou, the chief of the warehouse in Yangzhou, was very cooperative and prepared everything as required, including building a new ship and preparing food. In April of the second year of the Tianbao era (AD 743), due to internal conflicts among the monks, a monk named Hai went to the government office in Yangzhou to report that a group of monks from Kaiyuan Temple and Daming Temple were secretly communicating with pirates. At that time, the coastal areas of Taizhou, Wenzhou, and Mingzhou (Ningbo in Zhejiang) had sea bandits looting, and the imperial court was implementing a sea ban. When the envoy from the Huaihai Road, Ban Jingqian, heard about this, he was shocked and immediately ordered the arrest of all the monks. When the monks produced Li Linzong's introduction letter, Ban Jingqian simply confiscated the ship and released all the monks, returning their belongings. As a result, Jianzhen's first attempt to travel east was thwarted.

The second time: After Rōshu and Fuchō were released in August of the second year of the Tianbao era, they discussed the matter of traveling east with Jianzhen again. Moved by their spirit, Jianzhen took out 80 strings of coins and bought a used military ship from the envoy of the Lingnan Road, Liu Julin, and recruited 18 boat workers and 85 craftsmen, with 17 other monks accompanying him. They set off from Yangzhou in December. When the ship sailed along the

---

35. Zhenren Kaiyuan, *Records of the Tang Dynasty's Eastward Expeditions*, annotated by Wang Xiangrong, 40–42.

Yangtze River to Langgoupu (near the mouth of the Liuchang River in Taicang, Jiangsu), it was suddenly hit by a storm, and the old ship was damaged. Everyone had to go ashore. "The tide came, the water reached my waist; some people were on the reeds, and others were in the water. Winter was cold, the wind was strong, and it was very difficult."[36] Reeds are a type of bulrush.

After the craftsmen quickly repaired the ship, it sailed to the Zhoushan Islands. Jianzhen's attempt to travel east was once again declared a failure.

The third time: A month later, after the old ship was repaired, they set off again. They planned to sail directly to Japan from Sang Mountain (the area around Daquan Mountain north of the Zhoushan Islands). They encountered another storm on the way, and the old ship ran aground. Jianzhen and his team climbed onto the island.

Jianzhen's journey to Japan was full of hardships, whether due to the Tang Dynasty's strict policy against private travel by monks or the harsh natural environment of storms and dangers. It was only until the sixth time that he was successful.

Three days later, nearby fishermen sent aid in the form of water and rice. After another five days, the Tang Dynasty's naval patrol discovered them and brought them back to the mainland, reporting to the governor of Mingzhou. The governor placed them in the Ayuwang Temple in Mao County (Ningbo, Zhejiang).

The fourth time: during the third year of the Tianbao era (AD 744), monasteries from Yuezhou (today's Shaoxing, Zhejiang), Hangzhou, Huzhou, Xuanzhou (Xuancheng, Anhui), etc., came to request Master Jianzhen to teach the Buddhist scriptures. After teaching in these places, Jianzhen returned to the Ayuwang Temple. At this time, Japanese monks Rōshu and Fuchō, despite facing many disasters in their quest for Buddhist teachings, still did not regret it. Jianzhen was moved by their spirit and managed to buy a ship in Fuzhou, preparing food, water, and other supplies. He led more than 30 people, including Xiaoyan, and set out from Mingzhou, with plans to go from Taizhou, Wenzhou, to Fuzhou. One morning, when Jianzhen's group set out from Chanlin Temple in Huangyan County, they suddenly heard that the soldiers were coming. It turned out that Lingyou, one of Jianzhen's disciples who stayed in Yangzhou, and the

---

36. Zhenren Kaiyuan, *Records of the Tang Dynasty's Eastward Expeditions*, annotated by Wang Xiangrong, 51.

other monks couldn't bear the thought of their teacher "climbing mountains and crossing seas, facing difficulties for several years, traversing thousands of miles of rough waters, with an uncertain future of life and death,"[37] and reported to the Yangzhou government. The provincial governor of Jiangdong sent someone to bring Jianzhen's group back to the Daming Temple in Yangzhou. The fourth attempt to go east ended in failure again.

The fifth time: In the spring of the 7th year of Tianbao (AD 748), Rong Rui and Pu Zhao arrived in Yangzhou from Tong'an County (Qianshan, Anhui) and visited Jianzhen at Chongfu Temple. The three discussed the methods of going to Japan and decided to prepare the materials for shipbuilding according to the methods of the 2nd year of Tianbao. On June 27th, Jianzhen and his disciples, sailors, and 35 others set off from Chongfu Temple and traveled east along the Yangtze River to the mouth of the Yangzhou Canal. They stopped at Santa Mountain in Yuezhou (now Xiaoyangshan, Zhejiang) for a month, waiting for a favorable wind. When the wind was favorable, they sailed to the Shufengshan (Zhoushan Archipelago) area, where they waited for another month. On October 16th, Jianzhen and his party set sail again, heading east. Suddenly, the wind was strong, and the waves were high; the ship was sometimes like a high mountain and sometimes like a deep valley. Everyone was powerless and only constantly prayed to Guanyin. After a few days, the wind and waves were still high on the sea, and there was no fresh water on the ship, and they could not cook rice, so they could only chew raw rice and drink salty water. "It was a hard life; what could be worse than this?" After a few days, it rained, and everyone took out their bowls to catch the rain. After two days of rain, the drinking water problem was finally solved. After drifting in the sea for 14 days, the ship finally stopped in a place with blooming flowers and lush trees and bamboo, and it was already November in winter. Originally, Jianzhen and others had lost their way and arrived at the southernmost part of Hainan Island. They met four enthusiastic merchants who led them to Zhenzhou (Hainan, Yaxian). They lived in Daling Temple in Zhenzhou for more than a year, and Jianzhen and other monks built a Buddha hall and did Buddhist activities. Later, they followed the east coast of Hainan Island to the north of Wan'an Prefecture (Lingshui, Hainan). They then took a boat to

---

37. Zhenren Kaiyuan, *Records of the Tang Dynasty's Eastward Expeditions*, annotated by Wang Xiangrong, 60.

the northern end of Hainan Island, Yuezhou (southeast of Haikou). After living here for a while, they set out from Chengmai (west of Haikou) and crossed the Qiongzhou Strait to reach Leizhou (Haikong, Guangdong), then north through Luozhou (north of Lianjiang, Guangdong), Baizhou (Bobai, Guangxi), Wuzhou to Guizhou Shijian County (Guilin). Jianzhen lived in Guizhou for one year. The Guangzhou governor, Lu Han, learned about this and welcomed Jianzhen and his team to Guangzhou. Jianzhen and his team set out from Guizhou and traveled along the water route via Wuzhou to Duanzhou (Gao'ao in Guangdong). At Longxing Temple in Duanzhou, Rongru "gracefully migrated," and Jianzhen was very sad. The climate in the Lingnan region was hot, and Jianzhen, unfortunately, contracted an eye disease. Although treated by Arabs, he still lost his sight in both eyes. After leaving Guangzhou, Jianzhen and others traveled north via Dayu Mountain and passed through Qianzhou (Jianjiang in Jiangxi), Jizhou (Ji'an in Jiangxi) to Jiangzhou (Jiujiang in Jiangxi). Within Jizhou, Xiangyan died. As the most famous master of giving vows at the time, Jianzhen taught the scriptures and gave the law along the way. He then followed the Yangtze River to Runzhou Jiangning County (Nanjing in Jiangsu). When his disciple Lingyou heard the news, he welcomed Jianzhen to Longxing Temple in Yangzhou.

On the fifteenth day of October in the twelfth year of Tianbao (AD 753), Japan's tenth mission to Tang, led by Ambassador Fujiwara Kiyokawa and his subordinates, as well as the famous Japanese student Abe no Nakamaro, arrived at Yanguang Temple to pay respects to Jianzhen. Kiyokawa informed Jianzhen that the request made by the Japanese mission to Tang Emperor Xuanzong had been rejected and asked for Jianzhen's opinion. Despite being 66 years old and blind, Jianzhen agreed to Japan's request. After news of Jianzhen's departure to Japan spread, Longxing Temple took strict precautions. At this time, Abbot Rengan was passing through Kunzhou (Jinhua in Zhejiang), and upon learning that Jianzhen was leaving, he prepared a ship and waited at the riverhead. On the 19th of October, Jianzhen and 24 of his disciples set off from Longxing Temple and reached the riverhead, where they boarded a ship and headed for Huangshipu (Changshu in Jiangsu) to meet with the Japanese mission. On the fifteenth of November, the four ships set out together. On the 21st, the fleet arrived at Arinna-jima (Okinawa in Japan). On the 6th of December, they passed through Manyo-jima, and the following day they reached Yiku-jima. On the 20th, Jianzhen and his party arrived in Akatugun, Satsuma Province. On the

26th, Japanese Monk Yinquing led Jianzhen to Tai Zu's palace. In the sixth year of Shengbao (the thirteenth year of Tianbao, AD 754), Jianzhen arrived at Namba on the 1st of February. On the 4th, he entered the capital and stayed at Dong Temple. The fourth ship, which had traveled with Jianzhen, was blown off course on the sixteenth of November, and its whereabouts are unknown. The first ship ran aground on the 6th of December and was unable to proceed. After repairs, it was blown off course again by a northerly storm and drifted to Annan (modern-day Vietnam), where all 180 passengers were lost except for Kiyokawa and ten or so others, who eventually made their way to Chang'an but were unable to return to Japan.

During his ten years in Japan, Jianzhen founded the Ritsu sect in Japan, known as "Tō Ritsu Shōtai" (Tōshōdai-ji Temple). Even though he was blind, he could still help proofread the translations of Buddhist scripture and distinguish herbal medicines by smell. Among his fellow travelers, there were sculptors, painters, architects, and hand-craftsmen. They also contributed greatly in introducing Chinese culture to Japan. Along with him were a group of craftspeople, such as jade workers, painters, sculptors of Buddha statues, carvers, engravers, embroiderers, repairmen of text, and engravers of inscriptions, among others, 85 people in total who accompanied him during his second journey to the East. In AD 763, Jianzhen passed away. In AD 763, Jianzhen died there. In AD 779, the famous Japanese writer Zhenren Yuankai, commissioned by Zhenren's son Situo and others, wrote the famous book *The Record of the Great Tang Dynasty's Expedition to the East*.

5. Japanese Monk Ennin (圓仁) Visited the Tang Empire

Ennin was a Japanese monk born in AD 794. He became a monk at the age of nine, and was a disciple of Jianzhen's first generation. In AD 836, Ennin, then 43 and already a famous monk in Japan, decided to join the 18th Japanese delegates in visiting China. According to Japanese seafaring experience, each time the Japanese sent an embassy to China, it was usually composed of four ships in a fleet to help each other. This was the last embassy sent by Japan, and the head of the embassy was Fujiwara no Tsunetsugu, with a deputy named Ono no Hyoe. There were about 650 people in total. When the fleet set sail for the first time from Hakata, they encountered a storm, and the third ship was damaged, with only 20 or so of the 140 people on board surviving. After this accident, the Japanese Shingon Buddhism monk, Zhenji, who was on board this ship, never set foot on a ship again. The second attempt also failed. Finally, on July 8, AD 838, the fleet set off for the third time. This time, the first and fourth ships set off first, and the second ship set off later. Ennin was on the first ship carrying the Chinese embassy. On the way, the two ships lost contact. When they entered the Yangzhou Sea area, the ship was hit by a strong wind again, and many places were broken. When the tide receded, the ship sank into the sand and could not move. People had to insert the oars vertically around the ship into the sand and then use ropes to tie the oars and ship together to prevent the ship from breaking apart. Eventually, the team arrived in Hailing County (present-day Taizhou, Jiangsu) on July 30, AD 838.

In February of the fourth year of Emperor Kaicheng (AD 839), Ennin left Yangzhou and arrived in Chuzhou (Huai'an, Jiangsu), where he met with the embassy. Since he was unable to go to Taizhou to worship at Tiantai Mountain, he devised a plan to leave the embassy and not return to China with the Tang envoy. On June 7th, Ennin's party traveled from Chuzhou to Dengzhou (Penglai, Shandong) and arrived at the Fahua Monastery in Qingning Village, Chishan Village, Wending County (Wending, Shandong). The Fahua Monastery was established by Zhang Baogao from Goryeo, so it was also known as the Goryeo Monastery. On February 19th of the fifth year of Emperor Kaicheng (AD 840), Ennin set out from the Goryeo Monastery in Chishan Village and went west through Dengzhou, Qingzhou, Beizhou, Zhaozhou, and Zhenzhou, arriving at Wutai Mountain, another sacred place of the Tiantai sect, on April 28th to worship. On July 1st of the same year, he started from Bingzhou, Fenzhou, Jinzhou, Puzhou, and Tongzhou and arrived in Chang'an on August 20th. During his time in Chang'an, Ennin received the Diamond Realm Great Law from Yuan Zheng, practiced the True Meaning of the Embryonic Essence, and studied the Embryonic Essence with Su Xidi. He also received the Embryonic Essence from Fahua and learned Siddhaṃ script from the Southern Indian monk Baoyue. He collected many Buddhist scriptures and paintings. Ennin lived in Chang'an, the Western Capital of the Tang Dynasty, for four years and ten months. However, due to the "Huichang Anti-Buddhist Persecution" incident during the reign of Emperor Wuzong, on May 16th of the fifth year of Huichang (AD 845), Ennin covered his head and disguised himself to escape from Chang'an. He traveled through Luoyang, Zhengzhou, Bianzhou, Sizhou, and Yangzhou to arrive in

Chuzhou. However, the officials in Chuzhou did not allow him to return to Japan from there, so he had to come back to Dengzhou, a thousand *li* away. In the first year of the Dazhong era (the 14th year of the Japanese Emperor Showa, AD 847), he left Dengzhou on a Goryeo sea vessel and returned to Japan in September. During his stay, he visited over 20 commanderies and over 60 counties, including Jiangsu, Anhui, Shandong, Hebei, Shanxi, Shaanxi, and Henan provinces. He stayed in China the longest of all Japanese monks who visited in the late Tang Dynasty. And his experience was the most complicated.

After Ennin returned to Japan, he completed a book entitled *Ennin's Diary: The Record of a Pilgrimage to China in Search of the Law* in AD 847. The book was composed of four volumes. He recorded what he experienced in China, including political affairs in the eras of Emperor Wenzong and Emperor Wuzong, communications, weather, markets, and Buddhist temples.

Ennin wrote the book in Chinese. When the earliest copy of it was discovered in AD 1883 in Kyoto's Tō-ji (East Temple), it was immediately regarded as a treasure. The book provides the most detailed and comprehensive account of the author's observations and experiences of Buddhism along the way, such as the conduct of high-ranking monks, the size, duties, and daily life of monasteries, the rituals of fasting, chanting sutras, offering incense and preaching, Buddhist holidays, the imperial policy on Buddhism and the major events that arose from it, particularly the destruction of Buddhism by Emperor Wuzong of the Tang Dynasty and its aftermath. These records are crucial in supplementing the scarce information on Chinese Buddhist history and have extremely high historical value. Other social customs such as holidays, sacrifices, diets, taboos, and the local population, production, prices, transportation routes, post stations, the activities of maritime merchants from Silla, and the settlement of Silla people are also important historical materials for understanding the society of the Tang Dynasty. It was regarded as one of the three most important journals of Eastern culture. The other two were *The Western Regions in the Tang Dynasty* and *The Travels of Marco Polo*.

CHAPTER FIVE

TRANSPORTATION DEVELOPMENT IN THE SONG AND YUAN DYNASTIES

The Song Dynasty only briefly expanded its territories. Most of the time, it maintained the status quo. As a result, land transportation networks in the Song only had limited development. In contrast, its sea transportation was advanced, in accordance with economic development and technological progress in ship building and seamanship.

The Yuan Dynasty was the largest in Chinese history. Consequently, post stations also developed greatly. Although, being nomadic tribes, Mongolians were also keen on water transportation. The proportion of post stations on waterways was much higher than that of the later Ming and Qing dynasties. In fact, water transportation reached its peak in the Yuan Dynasty: it not only straightened up the Grand Canal connecting the capital of Beijing with Hangzhou but also developed water transport along the coasts for grain as well as overseas communications.

1. In Alliance with Goryeo

On May 19, AD 1123, a fleet of two divine ships and six passenger ships, slowly moored in front of Zhaobao Mountain, has arrived at the Yinjiang Estuary in Dinghai County, Mingzhou (now Zhenhai District, Ningbo, Zhejiang). At this time, the grand Daoist ceremony was taking place at the headquarters of the temple located only ten steps away from Zhaobao Mountain. The eunuch Wugong Dafu Rong Peng was making offerings to the gods and praying for the fleet. Suddenly, "a divine object appeared, in the form of a lizard, in reality, the Lord of the East Sea Dragon." The Daoist ceremony lasted for seven days. On the morning of the 24th day, the fleet set sail, with the sound of gold drums ringing and colorful flags fluttering. On the top of Zhaobao Mountain, eunuch Guan Bi was burning incense, looking out to the ocean, and bowing again. It's a fleet led by Ceremonial Secretary Lu Yundi and Secretariat Drafter Fu Moqing set out from Dinghai County of Mingzhou (present-day Zhenhai District in Ningbo, Zhejiang). Their destination was Goryeo's capital.

After the division of the Five Dynasties, although the Northern Song Dynasty unified the Central Plains, the geopolitical situation had changed greatly compared to the Tang Dynasty. At that time in China, the neighboring political powers such as the Liao, Western Xia, Tibet, Dali, etc., surrounded the north and west sides of the Northern Song Dynasty. The Liao kingdom in the north was powerful, with its territory extending from the sea in the east to the Jin Mountains in the west, from the flowing sands in the east to the Luqu River in the north and the Baigou in the south, covering an area of 10,000 *li*.[1] Although the Western Xia and the Tibetans had some conflicts with the Northern Song government, the power of the Northern Song was strong enough to withstand them. Only the Khitan (Liao Dynasty) in the north was powerful, "only the northern enemy is strong, ten times stronger than the Qiang people," "having great power and being the only rival country in the Central Plains, and often having a desire to take advantage."[2] The Khitan and the Northern Song Dynasty became two equal neighboring countries and were often in a state of hostility. Therefore, the Northern Song Dynasty wanted to unite with the Western Xia and Goryeo kingdoms to jointly resist the Khitan. The Khitan also had the idea of joining forces with Western Xia and Goryeo to jointly deal with the Northern Song Dynasty: "I will join with Yuan

---

1. "Geography (Part One)," in *History of Liao*, vol. 37, book 2 (Beijing: Zhonghua Book Company, 1974), 438.
2. Li Tao, *Extended Continuation to Zizhi Tongjian*, vol. 150, book 11 (Beijing: Zhonghua Book Company,1979), 3650–3652.

Hao and Goryeo to attack the Central Plains. Yuan Hao will take Guandong, and Goryeo will take Deng, Lai, Yi, and Mi states." "Goryeo is separated by the sea, and it may not be able to occupy these states for a long time, but if the soldiers go to raid Shandong for government and private wealth, I will take the army of thirty-six states in Hedong as the boundary."[3]

Goryeo, which is adjacent to the Liao Dynasty, was deeply influenced by the culture of the Tang Dynasty, and the culture of reading and etiquette was no less than that of China. Unlike the nomadic people of the Khitan, their language was different, and there was a lack of a sense of identity. The land communication between Goryeo and the Northern Song was blocked by the Liao Dynasty and could no longer pass. The Northern Song and Goryeo faced each other across the sea and had envoys who communicated through sea routes, mainly the northern route and the southern route.

The northern route started from Dengzhou in the northeast of the Shandong Peninsula and landed at Wenjin on the west coast of the Korean Peninsula. In February of the fourth year of Chunhua (AD 993), Chen Jing, Secretary of the Secretariat, and Liu Shi went to Goryeo as envoys and took the northern route. Starting from Mouping County in Donzhou, they went through Backe Sea Port (Eight-Corners of Fushan) and Zhi Island (Zhifu Mountain in Yantai), rode the wind and sailed the sea, and landed at Wenzhou Port (Wenzhou in South Korea) and arrived at Haizhou, 160 *li* away, then passed 100 *li* to Yanzhou (Yan'an in Korea), and 40 *li* to Baizhou (Baichuan in Korea), and finally 40 *li* to the capital Kaicheng.

But, the boundary between the Northern Song and Liao was the Damao Mountain and Baigou, and the area north of the Bohai Bay belonged to the Liao. "When climbing to the top of the state, it is close to the northern barbarian, known as the extreme edge, and the mountain and rivers in the middle of the barbarian are vaguely visible, and the wind is one sail, and arrives at the city gate. Since the national dynasty, there has always been a concentration of troops, teaching water

---

3. Li Tao, *Extended Continuation to Zizhi Tongjian*, vol. 150, book 11 (Beijing: Zhonghua Book Company,1979), 3652.

wars, and transmitting beacon from day to night, in order to alert."[4] Therefore, the route from Deng Zhou to and from Goryeo is easily disturbed by the Liao army. On the other hand, after the end of the Heavenly Holy period, due to the pressure from the Liao kingdom, Goryeo temporarily stopped its contact with the Northern Song, and this northern route stopped.

During the reign of Emperor Xining of the Song Dynasty, in order to change the humiliating situation of poverty and weakness in the mid-term of the Song Dynasty and to get rid of the passive situation brought by the alliance of Liao and Xia to the Song Dynasty, he decided to adopt an active attack strategy: "Wang Shao took Xixia's right arm by taking the Xi River and wanted to take Lingwu to cut off Liao's right arm, and then Goryeo raised its troops, intending to capture Liao."[5] The strategic intention was to tighten contact with Goryeo on the east side and attack Xixia urgently on the west side, so that the Liao Dynasty would have a rear concern and could not fully deal with the Song Dynasty and finally achieve the goal of recapturing the 16 states of Yan Yun. For this reason, Emperor Xining of the Song Dynasty specially issued an edict: "Goryeo's customs are still civilized, its country master is quite knowledgeable about etiquette, although far away at sea, respectful of the central dynasty, never slack, and the court gives gifts and privileges, all on the right of all countries."[6] The connection between the Song and Goryeo was restored and strengthened.

In order to avoid the harassment of the Liao army, the landing port for Goryeo's ambassadors or merchants was changed to the southern port of Mingzhou (Ningbo, Zhejiang): "Before the Heavenly Saint, the envoys entered from Dengzhou; since Xining, all from Mingzhou, saying that the Dengzhou road has sand and rock, cannot be traveled." In AD 1122, the King of Goryeo died. Emperor Huizong chose to send a delegate, led by Lu Yundi and Fu Moqing, to mourn the king. On March 14, AD 1123, Emperor Huizong opened a banquet before the fleet that had set out from Kaifeng. After 50 days, the fleet finally reached Mingzhou, where they changed to eight other ships. Two of the ships were made specially for this occasion.

---

4. Su Dongpo, "Proposal on the Recall of the Naval Forces in Dengzhou," in *Complete Works of Su Dongpo*, vol. 4 (Zhuhai: Zhuhai Press, 1996), 563.
5. Shao Bowen, *Shao's Record of Observations and Hearings*, vol. 5 (Beijing: Zhonghua Book Company, 1983), 41.
6. Li Tao, *Extended Continuation to Zizhi Tongjian*, vol. 323, book 22, 7786.

Transportation Development in the Song and Yuan Dynasties | 103

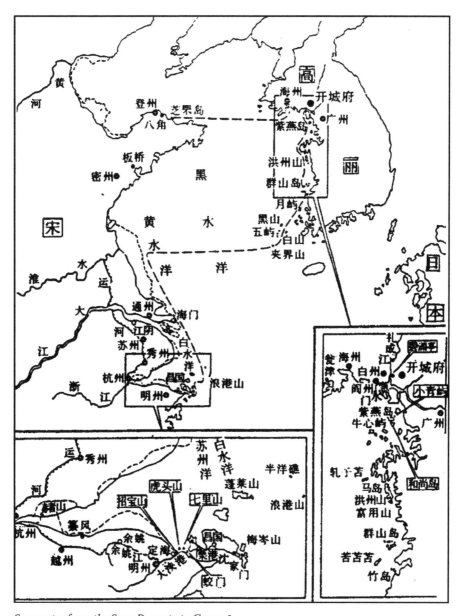

Sea routes from the Song Dynasty to Goryeo[7]

---

7. Xin Yuan'ou, *Shanghai Sand Ship* (Shanghai: Shanghai Bookstore Press, 2004), 49.

On May 24th, the fleet left Zhaobao Mountain. On the 25th, the fleet arrived at Shenjiamen (Putuo, Zhoushan, Zhejiang). In general, when two mountains face each other with a navigable channel between them, it is called a "door" (*jiamen*) and is an ideal anchorage for boats. Shenjiamen is surrounded by four mountains and is open on two sides, with a more favorable situation, and is, therefore, a major transportation route in Zhejiang to Korea and Japan, where ships stop to rest. At that time, there were "ten or so families of fishermen and woodcutters" on the island, and the Shen family was the local surname. That night, sailors held a worship ceremony on the island: "That night, the mountain opened the curtains, swept the ground and worshipped, the boat people called it 'shrine sand,' it is actually the god who governs the river, and there are many offerings. Each boat has a wooden plank as a small boat, carrying Buddhist scriptures, grain, and food, and the names of the people recorded in the book are included and thrown into the sea to eliminate the evil spirits."

The next day, because the wind was not right, the fleet stopped at Meicen (Putuo Mountain).[8] On the 28th, they set off, passing through Hailu Reef, Penglai Mountain (Daqu Mountain), and Banyang Reef (Southeast Banyang Reef of Huanglong Mountain). From the 29th, they passed through Baishui Ocean, Huangshui Ocean, and Heishui Ocean. The Song people already had a scientific understanding of the color differences in the sea area. The first reason for the different colors of seawater is due to the difference in depth, which affects the absorption of sunlight. The second reason is related to the content of sediment in the water. "After sailing through Penglai Mountain, the water was deep and blue-green like glass." This is because there is less sediment in the east Zhejiang Sea area, so the seawater is blue-green. From Shenjiamen to the nearshore area around Hangzhou Bay in the north, the seawater is shallow, and there is less sediment, so the surface of the sea is often blue-green. Hence it is called the Baishui Ocean. From the mouth of the Yangtze River to the north, it is influenced by the large amount of sediment brought by the Yellow River, and the water surface is yellow, so it is called Huangshui Ocean: "Huangshui Ocean, or Sha Wei, its water is turbid and shallow. The boat people said that its sand comes from

---

8. The following interpretations of place names are based on Wang Wenchu, "A Preliminary Exploration of the Maritime Routes between the Two Song Dynasties and Goryeo," in *Collected Studies on Ancient Transportation Geography* (Beijing: Zhonghua Book Company, 1996), 31–45.

the southwest and spans thousands of miles across the ocean, which is the place where the Yellow River enters the sea." In the northern part of the Yellow Water Ocean, the fleet turned east and sailed into the Black Water Ocean: "Black Water Ocean, that is, the North Ocean also. Its color is as dark as ink. When I saw it suddenly, I felt my heart and guts lost. The angry waves are thin, standing like ten thousand mountains. At night, the waves glisten, and the light is like fire. When his boat rises on the wave, he does not feel that there is a sea, but he sees the sky is bright and fast." The sea here is far from the mainland shoreline, and it is already a deep sea area, so it has a dark blue color similar to black.

On June 2, the fleet arrived at Jijie Mountain (Xiaoheishan Island), which may be the boundary between Song and Goryeo. The fleet thus entered the territory of Goryeo. On the third day, the convoy passed through Wuyu (five small islands southwest of Daegyeoldo), Paekdo, Baekseong (Buckwheat Island), Hyeonseong (Hyeonseong Island northwest of Jeju Island), Woldo (in the middle of the sea in Hindri, North Jeolla Province, Joseon), Rinsan Island, Baekjeong Island, and Kneeling Tomak. Whenever a convoy of Chinese ambassadors enters, fires and flames are lit at night on the top of Mount Heungheung to guide the direction of the convoy, and each mountain in the north corresponds with the other until the King's Castle.

On June 4, the boat passed through Chuncho Tomak, passed through Penang Reef, and Bosa Tomak, and arrived at Takeshima (northwest of Mojang, west of Heungdeok, and southwest of Gufu, Joseon). "The boat arrived at Takeshima and anchored. There were several mountains and lush forests. There are also people living on it, and the people are also long. In front of the mountain, there were hundreds of white rocks of different sizes, like piles of jade." When the fleet completed its mission and returned to China, they spent the mid-autumn night in Takeshima: the night was quiet, "the bright sun reflected the band, the slanting light was a thousand *zhang*, the mountains, the forests, the ravines, the boats, and the objects were all golden." On this golden night, the whole delegation danced and danced, drank wine, and played flutes, leaving the dangers of the ocean behind. On the fifth day, the fleet sailed from Takeshima to Tomakomak (Hedgehog Island in Fuan). On the sixth day, the fleet arrived at Qunshan Island (ancient Qunshan Islands), where the fleet dropped anchor, and the Goryeo officials greeted the mission. On the seventh, they arrived at Yokoyo.

On the 8th of June, the ship departed from Yokoyo and passed through

Buryong Mountain (Wonsan Island), Hongju Mountain (Seungnyan-ri on Anmyeon Island), Jaemae Island (near Jaeil Island in Anheungsi), and Majima Island (Anheung in Taeansi). The official horses were kept here when there was no business in Goryeo because of the abundant water and grass. On June 9, they passed Nine-Head Mountain, Tangren Island, Twin Women Reef (north of Anxing waters), and in the afternoon passed Monk Island (Da Wuyi Island), Ox Heart Island (Longyou Island), Nie Gong Island, Xiao Qing Island (a small island south of Yongzong Island), and anchored at Ziyan Island (Yongzong Island to the west of Incheon). At Ziyan Island, local officials sent people to offer food and fresh water. There were more than ten types of food, mainly wheat-based, which they continued to provide for three days. If the ship could not set sail due to winds, the offerings would cease after three days. Since the divine ship did not berth at the shore, the food and water gifts from Goryeo were transferred by small boats. The delegation in return offered tea and rice.

On June 10, they set sail from Ziyan Island and by the afternoon reached Jishuimen (the mouth of the Licheng River in the Yellow Sea of Korea) and anchored at Ge Ku (the anchorage of Jishuimen). On June 11, they passed the watershed and reached Longgu (the anchorage of the Licheng River mouth) to anchor again. On June 12, AD 1123, the fleet reached Licheng Port (礼成港) near Goryeo's capital of Kaicheng. The Goryeo government sent a guard of honor to welcome the Chinese fleet and thousands of locals also joined the ceremony. Licheng Port was famous because whenever Goryeo government officials were sent to China, they would always set out from this port. After reaching Licheng, the Song delegates traveled by land. And on June 13, they reached the capital of Goryeo. Having completed their mission, they set out on July 15 for China. However, as the winds were not favorable, the fleet didn't reach Dinghai County until August 27.

The ships, with which Lu Yundi traveled, reflected the high level of building technique in the Song Dynasty. When Zhang Xue was the governor of Zhizhou, he "once wanted to build a large boat. His aides could not calculate its dimensions, so Wei taught them to construct a small boat, measure its dimensions, and then multiply them by ten." Technicians at that time had already invented a method of building ships according to models, which was similar to modern techniques.

The largest capacity of ship built in the Song measured up to 5,000 *hu* (斛, one *hu* = 51.8 liters). "Sea merchant ship, size varies, the large 5,000 *liao* (one *liao*

= 150 kg), can carry five or six hundred people; medium 2,000 to 1,000 *liao*, can also carry two or three hundred people; the rest is called 'drill wind,' small and large eight yards or six yards, each ship can carry more than a hundred people."[9] The "magic ship" that Lu Yundi took on his mission was "a magic ship of Dingxin Lishe Huaiyuan Kangji and a magic ship of following the flow of the river. It is as lofty as a mountain, floating on the wave, the prow of the sail, yielding to the flood dragon. Therefore, with its shining and prominent imperial elegance, it intimidates overseas lands and surpasses both past and present." These two "magic ships" were the big boats specially built by Emperor Huizong of Song to show off his powerful and technologically advanced country, in an attempt to give the Goryeo people a deterrent. The six-passenger boats of the same trip were rented by the court in Fujian and decorated by Mingzhou according to the style of a "magic ship." The size of the passenger boats was "more than ten feet long, three feet deep, and two feet five feet wide, and could carry two thousand *hu*. The system: all of them are made of giant squares of wood, and they are mixed and made, and the top is as flat as a balance, and the bottom side is as a blade so that it can break the waves and travel." Both *hu* and material were the weight units of ships in the Tang and Song dynasties, and they were basically equal. The passenger boat could carry 2,000 *liao*, which means it was only a medium-sized sea vessel. Or "magic ship" was a large sea vessel that could carry 5,000 *liao*.

The ship's sturdiness and stability were improved. "In order to ensure the longitudinal strength of the ship, the keel was often made of full wood of cedar pine to ensure the sturdiness of the ship. In order to reduce the swaying of the ship and increase the stability, and on both sides of the belly of the boat tied the large bamboo for the wooden instrument to resist the waves." The ship was divided into three cabins: the front, middle and rear. The fore cabin was between the headmast and the mainmast, the bottom floor was a cooking room with a water closet, and the spare space was the soldiers' accommodation. The middle compartment was divided into four rooms. The rear bunker was called a house, "more than ten feet long, with windows on all four walls, just like a house. The upper railing was painted and decorated with a canopy." The rooms were assigned in order of the status of the officials of the mission.

---

9. "Biography of Zhang Xue," in *History of Song*, vol. 379, book 33 (Beijing: Zhonghua Book Company), 11696.

The equipment on the ship was increased. In order to increase the power of the ship, the ship's sail boom was tall and numerous, making full use of the wind as power: "The big boom was ten feet high, the head boom was eight feet high, and the wind was right to open the cloth fifty, a little deviated from the use of sharp canopy, left and right wing open, so that the wind. At the top of the main mast, an additional ten small sails are added, called wild foxes. They are used when the wind is calm." In order to make it easier to maneuver the ship in the ocean, three sets of rudders were set up at the stern of the ship: "The back of the ship has two sizes of the rudder, which are easy to change according to the depth and shallowness of the water. After that, two hawsers were inserted from the top, which was called the three pairs of hawsers, but it was used when entering the ocean."

Two factors contributed to the improvement of sea skills in the Song Dynasty. One was that sea maps became available. When Zhao Rushi wrote *Zhu Fan Zhi* (*Records of Foreign People*), he often read illustrations of various tribes. The second was the application of compasses. Previously, sailors normally had to depend on the weather to determine their locations. When days were clear, they could judge by the sun, the moon, and the stars above. But when the weather was bad, it would be very difficult to tell which direction one was heading in. "That night, one couldn't stay in the open sea, so they navigated forward by observing the constellations. If it was dark and cloudy, they would use a floating compass to determine the north and south directions." Most of the merchants who conducted maritime trade at that time mentioned the importance of the water-floating compass: "When faced with stormy weather and darkness, they relied solely on the compass for navigation. The compass was handled with utmost care, not daring to make even the slightest error, for the lives of everyone on the boat depended on it."

The Song people went to Goryeo in May and June and returned home in July and August to take advantage of the monsoon. China's mainland, Japan, Korea, and nearby sea areas are typical monsoon areas. The east coast of China and the west coast of the Korean Peninsula both run north-south, and the wind direction of the southeast monsoon and the northwest monsoon is very similar, so the Song people went to Goryeo mostly in summer, using the southeast monsoon, and returned home, using the northwest monsoon, mostly in autumn. "When the ambassadors traveled, the south wind was used on the day of departure and the

Illustration of the Ningbo Ship

north wind on the day of return."[10] If everything goes smoothly, it takes only five or six days for a sea voyage to or from the country. In general, the one-way journey time is more than ten days. If there was a hurricane, the voyage was long, and there was a danger of capsizing: "When the sea route was used for the mission to Goryeo, the sea was full of water, the islands were dangerous, and when there was a black wind, the boats would be defeated when they touched the reef."[11] It was in the middle of July, in early autumn, when the northwest monsoon and southeast monsoon alternated, and the wind direction changed from time to time. First, there was no wind, and on July 24, the mission anchored at Qunshan Gate and waited for the wind until August 8, when the northeast wind started, and the tide entered the ocean. On the morning of the ninth, we passed the Takeshima and saw the island of Black Mountain. At this time, the hurricane came, "suddenly the storm in the southeast, and again encountered the sea movement, the side of the boat is about to tilt, people are afraid. The boat was about to tumble, and people were afraid. They had to return to Takeshima to escape the wind. On the

---

10. Xu Jing, *Illustrated Account of the Imperial Envoy to Goryeo during the Xuanhe Period*, vol. 39, in *Zhi Bu Zu Zhai Collection* version, photocopy ed. (Beijing: Zhonghua Book Company).
11. "Biography of Goryeo," in *History of Song*, vol. 487, book 40, 14052.

second day, the hurricane was approaching, and the wind was stronger, so it was still dangerous to take shelter at Takeshima." After waiting for another six days at Qunshan Island, the ship set sail again at *shen* on the 16th. After that, the fleet stopped and traveled due to the wind direction, and returned to Dinghai County only at the end of August, sailing for 42 days.

From the late Tang Dynasty onwards, the Central Plains was cut off from the rest of the world by vassalage and the rise of the neighboring Khitan and Nanzhao states, which blocked the Central Plains' access to its neighbors. This was followed by the division of the Five Dynasties and Ten Kingdoms. After the establishment of the Northern Song Dynasty, little was known about the military, history, geography, politics, economy, and customs of the surrounding areas. Therefore, the Song Dynasty stipulated that whenever an official went on a mission to a foreign country, the envoy had to pay attention to the various conditions of the country he visited and compile them into a "trip record," "trip record," "mission record," etc., after returning home. For example, during the Dazhongxiangfu period, Lu Zhen went to Khitan and wrote *Light Carriage Record*; in AD 1013, Wang Zeng went to Khitan and wrote *Shang Khitan Matters*; in AD 1075, in the eighth year of Xining, Shen Kuo, a right-justified scholar and a bachelor of the Hanlin Academy, served as a messenger to Liao and wrote *Xining's Mission to Khitan*. These writings were mostly in the form of diaries, recording what the ambassadors saw and heard along the way, and were reported to the Privy Council, the highest military organ of the state, for reference.

Among the delegates that went to Goryeo in AD 1123, there was one man who excelled in calligraphy. His name was Xu Jing. He was chosen because the Goryeo government had expressed their wish to meet a calligraphy master. Xu Jing not only fulfilled his mission, but also collected a great amount of information and made detailed illustrations of Goryeo society. His journals were compiled into 40 volumes, entitled *Goryeo Book of Diagrams*.

It was very difficult for Xu to collect materials for his journals within the short time span of one month. This was exasperated by the fact he could not move around by himself—he had no free will. The hotels where the delegates resided were heavily guarded by Goryeo soldiers. Xu Jing was only allowed to leave his hotel six times in total. Xu Jing was a thoughtful person, and he watched and asked many questions on the way and during the banquet. During the time the mission was in Korea, Goryeo sent Yoon Eun-sik, the Minister of Justice, and

Kim Boo-sil, the Minister of Rites, as "receiving companions," and Kim In-kyu, the Minister of Privy Council, and Lee Ji-mi, the Minister of War, as "pavilion companions." Kim Bushi was a very good writer and knew a lot about history, so Xu Ge should have learned a lot about the country of Goryeo from him. In addition, before going abroad, Xu Jing carefully read Wang Yun's *Jilin Zhi*, made in Chongning. Jilin is Goryeo. The book consisted of 30 volumes, which was not small, but there were no maps. Xu Jing knew that "it is especially difficult to make a book of diagrams," therefore, when he made the *Goryeo Book of Diagrams*, he "diagramed the shape of things and said things for it."

It contains 28 categories, including the founding of the kingdom of Goryeo, the lineage of the royal family, the fiefdom, the city, the gate, the royal palace, the official costume, the bureaucratic figures, the ceremonial objects, the guards, the weapons, the flags, the chariots and horses, the government offices, the shrines, the Taoism, the costumes of the people and women and the sofas, the customs, the festivals, the imperial edicts, the *yanli*, the pavilions, the tents and vessels for the ambassadors, the oars, the sea routes between Song and Goryeo, and so on. In addition to the history of the founding of the kingdom and the lineage, all the other contents were seen by Xu Jie at the time. For example, in the item "Oar," Xu Jing recorded several types of Goryeo boats that he saw with his own eyes: patrol boats, official boats, Song boats, and Maku boats. The patrol boat was "a boom in the middle, no scaffolding on it, but only a sculling beam." There were many of them, and when the delegation sailed into Qunshan Gate, thousands of patrol boats were there to meet them. The official boats were "covered with thatched roofs, with windows and windows underneath, and surrounded by rails and thresholds, with horizontal timbers running through them, and raised out as shelters, with their faces wide at the bottom. The reed was not used throughout the body, but the whole wood was used to make the reed and nail it. In the front, there is a mechanical wheel, on which a large boom with fifteen sails is applied, and a fifth of the sails are spread out and not closed, fearing that they will be opposed to the wind." Pine boat is a boat especially for the head of the mission, more gorgeous, "the head and tail are straight, in the boat house for five rooms, covered with thatch. There were two small rooms in front and back, with couches and curtains. In the middle, there were two open rooms with brocade mattresses, which were the most splendid." The boat was a boat for the ordinary officials of the mission, and "the house was made of green cloth, with a long pole instead of a pillar underneath, and each of the four sides was tied with a vermilion rope." Before the mission, Xu Jing thought that since Goryeo was in the middle of the sea, the shipbuilding technology should be very advanced. The actual ships he saw were very simple, and Xu Jing could not understand this phenomenon: "Are they accustomed to the water because they are comfortable with it?" The actual ships were very rudimentary, and Xu Jing could not understand this phenomenon: "Is it because they were accustomed to it because they were comfortable in the water?"[12] When the Chinese mission's magic ship entered the harbor, the people of Korea came in droves, and "the spectators were like a wall," opening their eyes to the world.

Except for seven or eight volumes on the founding of the kingdom and the lineage, which are not illustrated, all the other volumes are illustrated by Xu Jing. The maps include maps of the territory and neighboring countries, the capital city, the distribution of the palace, and the sea route. Unfortunately, all these maps were lost during the rebellion of Jingkang. Thus, the present *Illustrated Account of the Imperial Envoy to Goryeo during the Xuanhe Period* has only text but no map. What is more unfortunate is that Emperor Huizong of the Song Dynasty sent Lu Yundi's mission to Goryeo in order to "unite with Korea to control Liao" in diplomacy. However, before and after the mission, Emperor Huizong set the policy of "uniting with Jin to destroy Liao." The Liao Dynasty was destroyed, but the bad luck of the Northern Song Dynasty also came. In AD 1126, the Kingdom of Jin invaded the Song and captured Emperor Qinzong and his father Huizong. Unfortunately, all illustrations made by Xu were lost during the invasion.

2. Western Expedition by Taoist Priest Changchun

In the early 13th century, in the vast Mongolian steppe, a group of people were marching, and there was a 70-year-old man in the group who stood out. He was the master of the Quanzhen Sect, Qiu Chuji. The purpose of his trip was to visit Genghis Khan, who was called "a generation of heavenly pride" by later generations.

Qiu Chuji, the word Tongmi, the Taoist name Changchunzi, the customary

---

12. Xu Jing, *Illustrated Account of the Imperial Envoy to Goryeo during the Xuanhe Period*, vol. 33.

name of Changchun real person, Dengzhou Qixia people. He was born in the eighth year of the Golden Emperor's reign (AD 1148) and began to study Taoism at the age of 19, studying under Wang Chongyang, the first generation of Quanzhen Taoist masters. In his later years, he lived in an era of war and turmoil, when the Jin, Southern Song, Western Xia, Western Liao, and Mongolian regimes were in existence, and the Mongolian regime, under the leadership of Genghis Khan, was the most powerful as it continued to fight. In the third year of Jin Xingding (AD 1219), Jin and Southern Song dynasties were invited by envoys, but Qiu declined. In the winter of the same year, Liu Zhonglu, an envoy sent by Genghis Khan from the north of the desert, arrived in Laizhou and invited Qiu to go west. Qiu accepted Genghis Khan's invitation, firstly to preach and secondly to reduce the suffering of the people caused by the war, and a poem he wrote at Longyang Guan is a reflection of his state of mind: "Ten years of war and fire, ten thousand people are worried, there is no one or two out of ten million left. Last year, I was fortunate to have been given the edict of mercy, and this spring, I have to travel in the cold. I am still thinking of the 200 states in Shandong, even though I have to go 3,000 *li* north of the mountains. I'm still thinking about the 200 states in Shandong."[13] These poems express Qiu's opposition to war and his desire for peace.

On the 18th day of the first month of the 15th year of the Mongolian Emperor Taizu (Xingding 4th years in Jin, Southern Song Jiading 13 years, AD 1220), Qiu Chuji, 74 years old, led 18 of his disciples to depart from Laizhou. He arrived at Yanjing in February, arrived at Dexing (Zhuolu, Hebei) in May, and arrived at Xuandezhou (Xuanhua, Hebei) in August. In February of the following year, he went out of the fortress and passed through Yehu Ridge (Ehu Ridge northwest of Zhangjiakou) and Fuzhou (Zhangbei, Hebei). In March, he arrived at Yuerpo (Daliepo). In June, he arrived at Woliduo (Helin), and on July 25, he arrived at Abkhan Mountain. There were thousands of Han Chinese living in the mountains. All of them were artisans captured by the Mongolian army when they conquered Yanjing and other parts of the Central Plains. Since it was not suitable to travel by car, Qiu left his disciples, Song Daoan and Li Zhichang, to stay there. Qiu led Zhao Jiugu and nine others to continue their journey westward and crossed Jinshan (Altai Mountain) in mid-autumn. This section of the mountain road is

---

13. Li Zhichang, *The Journey to the West of the Changchun Zhenren*, in *Collection of Books* version (Beijing: Zhonghua Book Company, 1985), 5.

very steep; individual places to go over the mountain, the vehicle cannot pass, it is hundreds of accompanying with ropes will be Qiu vehicle hanging pull up the mountain and then put the rope to the mountain. After that, he crossed the ancient battlefield of Baidian, followed the northern foot of the Yin Mountain (Tianshan) to the west, passed through the large city of Biesima (around Jimsar, Xinjiang) and Luntai (in Fukang, Xinjiang), and arrived at the city of Arima (west of Huocheng, Xinjiang) in September. On November 5, his disciple Zhao Jiugu died of illness. After that, he traveled southwest and crossed the Huochan River. On November 18, he arrived at Samarkand, the capital of the Uzbek Republic, which was the largest city in Central Asia at that time.

On March 15 of the following year (AD 1222), Qiu left his disciple Yin Zhiping at the evil Mishkan and led five or six disciples to go to visit Genghis Khan. They crossed Iron Gate Pass, Jieshi City (Kash), crossed Amu Dangjia (Amu River), and arrived at the residence of Genghis Khan on April 5. Genghis Khan was very happy that Qiu Chuji had traveled 10,000 *li* to answer the summons and asked if there was any medicine for longevity that he could contribute, but Qiu Chuji answered truthfully, "There is the way of hygiene, but no medicine for longevity."[14] Genghis Khan did not show any dissatisfaction with this frank answer and called Qiu Chuji, a "divine immortal." Qiu Chuji was going to give a formal sermon on April 14, but due to the change in the military situation, Genghis Khan had to go on a personal expedition, so the sermon was changed to October, and Qiu Chuji went back to the Samarkand to wait.

As Genghis Khan had to pursue his military mission, Qiu Chuji postponed his preaching. It wasn't until mid-October that Qiu Chuji finally had the opportunity to preach his beliefs to the Khan in his palace—the modern Hindu Kush in Afghanistan. There were three talks between Qiu and Genghis Khan. The latter listened with all ears and even asked his assistants to take notes of Qiu's words. The notes were kept confidential.

Qiu Chuji returned to Samarkand afterward. On February 7, AD 1223, Qiu told Genghis Khan that he wanted to return to China. At first, the latter refused Qiu's request but finally agreed after he insisted. The next day, the Khan went hunting. When chasing after a boar, his horse lost control. He fell off the horse, but fortunately the boar did not attack him; it ran off when assistants came to

---

14. Li Zhichang, *The Journey to the West of the Changchun Zhenren*, 16.

the rescue. After Qiu heard about the incident, he told the Khan to stop hunting, because the boar was a warning from heaven. Genghis Khan replied that Qiu's words had their merits; he didn't hunt for the next two months.

On March 10 in the same year, Qiu Chuji bid farewell to Genghis Khan. Qiu and his pupils went via Xinjiang and Mongolia and finally reached Xuande Commandery in August. This was the end of his expedition.

Portrait of Genghis Khan

In February AD 1224, Qiu returned to Yanjing (modern Beijing) and resided in Changchun Temple (the modern Baiyun Temple). Taoism developed with great momentum under his influence. In July AD 1227, Qiu Chuji died at the age of 80.

After Qiu's death, one of his pupils, Li Zhichang complied his expedition to the west in a book entitled *The Travels of Taoist Priest Changchun*. The journal was of great importance in studying early Yuan history established by the Mongolians. It also recorded in detail the culture and customs of Samarkand (Uzbekistan), including their gardens, food, coins, costumes, and Islamic religion.

3. ZHANCHI (POST STATIONS) AND LAND AND WATER TRANSPORTATION IN THE YUAN

The Yuan Dynasty was one of the most extensive dynasties in China's history. How to achieve better transportation of people, information, and materials became the main concern of the court to maintain its rule. Therefore, the Yuan Dynasty set up a large number of post stations in various places: "Our country's frontier was so large that it was gradually spread out in the east and west, and in the south of Shuo, and all the countries under our jurisdiction were set up with post stations, so that all the people could arrive at dawn and arrive at night and be heard."[15] According to the explanation of the Ming Dynasty people, the meaning of "post station" was the meaning of the Chinese postal transmission book. The number of stations in each province was as follows:

> 175 land stations, 12,298 horses, 1,619 carts, 1,982 oxen, and 4,980 donkeys. There were 21 water stations, with 950 boats, 266 horses, 200 cattle, 394 donkeys, and 500 sheep. There were two cattle stations, with three hundred and six cattle and sixty carts. There are one hundred and seventy-nine stations under the jurisdiction of the provincial government in Henan and Jiangbei, including one hundred and ninety-six stations: one hundred and six land stations, with 3,928 horses, 217 carts, 192 cows, and 534 donkeys. There were 90 water stations with 1,512 boats. The total number of stations under the jurisdiction of Liaoyang and other provinces was 120: 150 land stations, 6,515 horses, 2,621 carts, and 5,259 cattle. There were 15 dog stations, with 300 stations and 3,000 dogs in Yuan, but afterward, except for the extinction and death, there were 289 stations and 218 dogs. Jiangsu, Zhejiang, and other places under the jurisdiction of the Central Secretariat, a total of 262: horse stations 134, 5,123 horses. There were 35 palanquin stations, with 148 palanquins. There were 11 step stations, with 3,332 transporters. There were 82 water stations, with 1,627 boats. There were 85 horse stations with 2,165 horses and 25 sedan chairs. There are 69 water stations and 568 boats. Hunan and other places under the jurisdiction of the Central Secretariat, a total of 173: 100 land stations, 2,555 horses, 70 carts, 545 cattle, 175 sedan chairs, and

---

15. *Yongle Encyclopedia*, vol. 19416, book 8 (Beijing: Zhonghua Book Company, 1986), 7192 (upper).

30 sedan chairs. There were seventy-three water stations and five hundred and eighty boats. Shaanxi Province had 81 stations: 80 land stations with 7,629 horses. There is one water station with six boats.

Sichuan Province: 48 land stations, 986 horses, and 150 cattle. There were 84 water stations, 664 boats, and 76 cattle. There were seventy-eight stations under the jurisdiction of the Yunnan provinces: seventy-four horse stations, with 2,345 horses and 30 cattle. There were four water stations and twenty-four boats. The three provinces in Gansu: six horse stations with 491 horses, 149 cattle, 171 donkeys, and 650 sheep.[16]

How to manage communications and transportation over such vast territory became vital for the Yuan administrators. Therefore, a huge number of Zhanchi sprouted in the country. Zhanchi was Mongolian for post stations.

According to the *Yongle Encyclopedia*, there were all kinds of Zhanchi in the Yuan Dynasty. For example, there were post stations by rivers. Most mail was carried by horses and only some went by carriage or even dogs.

Post station equipment varied according to the importance of their geographic locations. For example, those located on transportation hubs would usually have better equipment. Take the Zhenjiangfu Route for example, it had three post stations with both land and water transportation facilities.

Danyang Post Station in Dantu County had a total of 109 rooms. Customers travelling by land would be accommodated in the western wings of the post station; while those travelling by water would reside in the eastern wings. There were 45 stables for horses. Yunyang station in Danyang County had 27 rooms and 41 stables, and Lücheng station had 29 rooms and 41 stables. The three post stations had 40 horses and 30 ships on average. A total of 120 postmen, 900 sailors, and 80 hotel personnel worked in those three post stations.[17] Anyone who wanted to use these services had to present royal documents. When there were urgent military documents, characters in the documents would be written in the colors of gold or silver.

---

16. "Treatises of Army," in *History of Yuan*, vol. 101, book 9 (Beijing: Zhonghua Book Company, 1976), 2591–2594.
17. Zhishun, *Annals of Zhenjiang*, vol. 13, book 3 (Beijing: Zhonghua Book Company, 1990), 2803, 2804, and 2810.

Numerous post stations formed a transportation network centering on Dadu (Beijing) and spreading all over the country: "The holy dynasty has pacified the Song Dynasty, and the place is far and wide, and the large cities and small cities are covered by the sky. The announcement of the government and the movement of merchants, the floating of water and land, and the boat of Liangji were not far away from the remote areas."[18] Within each province, a network of transportation was formed, centering on the provincial headquarters and the major cities. Take Henan Province as an example. The northern and southern part of Henan Province in the Yuan Dynasty was basically bounded by the Yellow River and Yangtze River, reaching the sea in the east and Pingli in Shaanxi in the west, forming a transportation network centered on Bianliang Road, Henan Province Road, Xuzhou, and Xiangyang Road. Bianliang, now Kaifeng, Henan Province, was the political center and transportation center of Henan Province, and there were four post roads leading to various places. The first route goes west to Henan Prefecture Road; the second one passes through Zhuxian Town to the southwest, passing through Weichuan (Weishi County's Weichuan Town), Nanyang Prefecture, and reaches Xiangyang Road; the third route goes from Zhuxian Town south through Yanling, Shangcai, Ruyang (Runan), Zhenyang (Zhenyang), Luoshan, Jinzhu Station (northwest of Hong'an), Huangpi, Huangzhou Road (Huanggang) to Qizhou Road (Qichun), then enters Jiangxi Province; the fourth route goes east passing Qixian, Taikang, Chenzhou (Huaiyang), Taihe, Yingzhou (Fuyang), Shouchun (Shouxian), Luzhou (Hefei), Liuzhang Station (west of Quanjiao), Shuikou Station (east of Chuzhou City), Liuhe, and finally arrives at Zhenzhou (Yizheng). Henan Prefecture is a major transportation hub in the northwest of Henan Province, with three postal routes branching from here: the first goes southeast to Yexian, connecting with the postal route from Bianliang to Xiangyang; the second goes west through Mianchi, Shanzhou (Shan County), and Wanxiang (an old county town west of Lingbao) into Shaanxi territory, reaching Huayin; the third goes northeast into the Zhongshu Province, passing Mengzhou (Meng County) to Huaiqing Road (Qinyang, Shanxi). Xuzhou is the transportation hub of the eastern part of Henan Province. The first postal route

---

18. Xu Youran, "Record of the Construction of the Whaleback Bridge on the Zhangde Route," in *Notes from Zhu Tang,* vol. 7, in *Siku Quanshu* version, photocopy ed., vol. 1211 (Taipei: Taiwan Commercial Press, 1983), 625 (bottom).

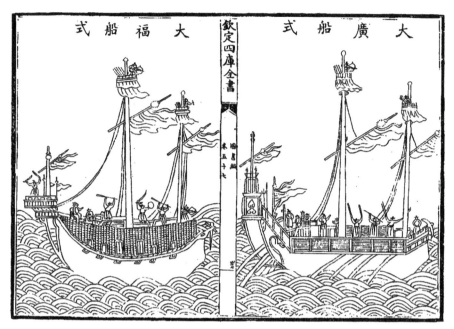

Illustrations of ships from the "Siku Quanshu"

is a waterway, going southeast through Peizhou (north of Suining), Suqian, Daqingkou (east of Huai'an Huaiyin District), Huaian, Baoying, and Gaoyou to Shaobo (northwest of Jiangdu's Shaobo Town), reaching Yangzhou and Tongzhou respectively; another route also goes southeast, but overland south through Lingbi (Lingbi), Qingyang (north of Sihong's Qingyang Town), Linhuai (Sihong's Linhuai Town), and Ganquan (Yangzhou Hanjiang District's Ganquan Town) to Yangzhou. Xiangyang is located on the upper reaches of the Han River and is a major transportation hub for the southwest region of Henan Province. Going south, it passes through Anlu Prefecture's Changshou County (Zhongxiang), Jiukou Station (south of Zhongxiang's Jiukou Town), and enters Huguang Province to reach Wuchang Road; another route goes south through Liyang Station, Jingmen Prefecture's Changlin County (Jingmen) to reach Zhongxing Road in Jiangling County, then south across Dongting Lake to reach Yuezhou.

One of the striking features of transportation networks in the Yuan Dynasty was the high proportion of its water post stations. As early as AD 1261, Kublai Khan ordered land post stations to be replaced by water post stations. Non-urgent documents would go via waterway. In the seventeenth year of the reign of

Emperor Zhongyuan (AD 1280), the Ministry of the Central Secretariat established a water station every 80 *li* in the territory of the Jianghuai Province, and all official business was conducted by water. Only a small number of horses were kept at the original horse stations for emergency use: "Except for ambassadors and military emergencies, the rest were allowed to travel by boat, starting from the water station in Jizhou."[19] Jizhou was located in present-day Jining City, Shandong Province, which required the use of water stations in the area around Jizhou. There were also water stations in the central and western regions. In the 15th year of the Yuan Dynasty (AD 1278), the Yuan army pacified Sichuan and established a water station from Xuzhou to Jingnan Province (Jiangling, Hubei).

In AD 1278, the Yuan armies conquered Shu (modern day Sichuan). Ever since, water post stations were set up on the route from Xuzhou to Jinnanfu (present-day Jiangling in Hubei). Until AD 1281, there were 19 water post stations on this route with 2,100 postal families and 212 ships for postal services.[20] According to the *Yongle Encyclopedia*, there were 132 post stations in Shu, of which 48 were on land, and 84 were water post stations.

Apart from building post stations on the rivers, Yuan administrations also set up water post stations in coastal areas. Quanzhou in Fujian was the largest port for foreign trade; imported goods from Quanzhou Port would then be transported to Dadu, the capital of Yuan.

Previously the goods were transported by land to Hangzhou and then via canal to Dadu. There were mountain ranges along the route, and the zigzagging roads and unfavorable weather conditions caused the deaths of many horses. In AD 1289, the Yuan administrations ordered 15 water post stations to be built along the coast from Quanzhou to Hangzhou. Each had 5 postal ships and 200 sailors, responsible for transporting only imported goods from foreign countries and rarities from merchants.

However, the number of foreign ships to Quanzhou was limited. And the sea route was only open to navigation in June and July when winds favored ships going north. As a result, costal post stations were abolished after two years. A more economic method was adopted. When foreign ships arrived in Quanzhou, a ship would then transport goods to Hangzhou. There were also post stations

---

19. *Yongle Encyclopedia*, vol. 19417, book 8, 7202 (upper).
20. "Shizu (Eight)," in *Book of Yuan*, vol. 1, 230.

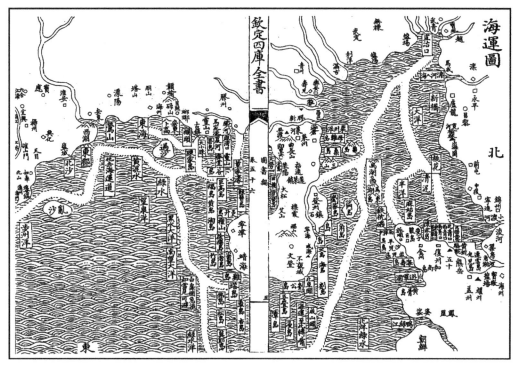

Illustrations of sea routes (north) from the "Siku Quanshu"

along northern coasts. There were 11 from Danluo to the Yalu River near the Korean Peninsula.

More important is the straightening of the Beijing–Hangzhou Grand Canal. The Sui Dynasty opened the North–South Grand Canal, which was centered on Luoyang and ran northeast to Ji County in Zhuo County, which was the capital of the Yuan Dynasty, and southeast to Hangzhou via Jingkou (Zhenjiang). During the Song and Jin dynasties, the Yellow River was broken, and the lower reaches of the Yellow River were changed to enter the sea from the lower reaches of the Huai River, after which the north-south confrontation led to the abandonment of this route. In the Yuan Dynasty, the first transport route was along the Huai River to the Yellow River, going against the water, disembarking at the Zhongluan dry station in the southwest of Fengqiu County, Henan Province, and transporting 180 *li* by land to the town of Qimen on the south bank of the Imperial River (Wei River), and then by water from the Imperial River to Zhigu (Tianjin) and on to Dadu. This route was tortuous and inconvenient for land and water transportation. So, a shorter north–south canal route was sought. In AD 1275, Guo Shoujing thought that the two waterways of Wen and Si could be used for transporting goods. So, a new canal was dug in the western part of present-day Shandong Province, and the project to straighten the North–South Grand Canal was started. First, in AD 1281, the Jizhou River was dug, using the Wen and Si waters as the source of water, from Jizhou (Jining, Shandong) northwest to Anshan (southwest of Dongping) in Shucheng, about 150 *li* long. From there, the canal was from the Huai River to the Si Water (Central Canal), from the Economic State River to Anshan, from the Daqing River to the sea via Dong'a and Lijin, and then from the sea to Zhigu, and then to Dadu by land. Later, it was changed to the land route from Dong'a to Linqing and then northward to the Imperial River. Next was the Huitong River, which was dug in the 26th year of the Yuan Dynasty (AD 1289). It started from the southwest of Anshan and drew the water from the Liangshanpo to flow northward through the northwest of Shouzhang to Dongchang (Liaocheng) and then northwest through Linqing into the Yu River, with a total length of 250 *li*. In the 28th year of the Yuan Dynasty (AD 1291), the Tonghui River was opened again. Guo Shoujing led Changping County Baifu village Shenshan spring and then led a *mu*, Yuquan each water to the capital and the righteous gate (Xizhimen) into the city, converging into the pool (Shichahai), and southeast out of the civilization door (Chongwenmen), to Tongzhou Gaolizhuang into the White River, the total length of more than 160 *li*. Since then, Jiangnan canal ships can directly transport grain into the metropolitan area.

Cereals transported by canals were called river canals, while those transported by sea were called sea canals. After the initial completion of the Beijing–Hangzhou Grand Canal, since the Huitong and Tonghui Rivers had not yet been dug, it was still not convenient to transport food northward, and the cost of transportation was high. Previously, when Boyan defeated the Southern Song, he ordered Zhang Xuan and Zhu Qing to send the archives of the Southern Song court from Chongming to the capital by sea. In AD 1282, Boyan envisioned transporting grain from Jiangnan to the capital by sea. In that year, he ordered Zhu Qing, Zhang Xuan, and others to build 60 flat-bottomed sea vessels, loaded with more than 46,000 *dan* of grain, from the sea. For safety reasons, the fleet sailed north along the coastline, and because of the unfavorable winds, it did not arrive in Zhigu until the following year. Although it took a little longer, it was generally more convenient than river transport, so two ten thousand households

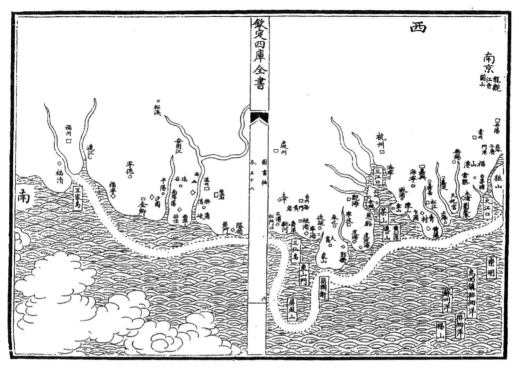

Illustrations of sea routes (south) from the "Siku Quanshu"

were set up to take charge of the sea transport, and Zhu Qing was appointed as a middle ten thousand household and Zhang Xuan as a thousand household. As a result, Jiangnan grain was transported by the canal and the sea road two ways to the north at the same time. Twenty-eight years (AD 1291), the government also set up the two canals Wanhufu, Zhu Qing and Zhang Xuan were in charge. In the beginning, the transportation of goods from Jiankang Prefecture (Nanjing), Chizhou (Guichi, Anhui), and Raozhou (Poyang, Jiangxi) was also carried by sea vessels upstream along the Yangtze River. Since the Yangtze River is very fast, there are many rocky islands in the river, and dark sand flows under the water, it is not suitable for flat-bottomed sea vessels to navigate, and some grain ships are damaged in the Yangtze River every year. Therefore, the grain from the Yangtze Delta region was sent by sea instead, and the loss was thus reduced. The route of the sea route was changed from time to time. In the beginning, the route was from Liujiagang in Pingjiang Province (Suzhou) to the sea, through Huanglian Shatou and Wanli Changtan in Haimen County, Tongzhou, Yangzhou Road, and into the ocean, then along the mountain plain on the mainland, through Yancheng County, Huaian Road, Haining Prefecture (Lianyungang West), Mizhou (Zhucheng), Jiaozhou (Jiao County), and then northeastward around the Shandong Peninsula. The distance from Shanghai to Yangcun Marina (in present-day Tianjin) was 13,350 *li*. In AD 1292, Zhu Qing and others suggested opening a new route, starting from Liujiagang, heading east, passing Chengjiaosha, Sansha, Biandansha, and Dahong, then venturing into the open sea, passing through Qingshuiyang, Heishuiyang, Chengshan, Liu Island, Zhifu Island, Shamen Island, and then the vast ocean north of Laizhou, arriving directly at the Jie River estuary. As this route traversed the open sea, the navigation path was more direct, and the distance was shortened. The following year, Qianhu Yin Minglüe pioneered another route, departing from Liujiagang to the sea, reaching the open ocean from Sansha in Chongmingzhou, heading east from the north of Heishuiyang, reaching Chengshan, and then turning west straight to the Jie River. This route was the shortest, only taking about ten days to reach its destination. The downside was that it traveled through the vast ocean, and during times of strong winds and fierce waves, grain ships often got damaged, a scenario that occurred every year. However, compared to river transportation, it was still more efficient and cost-effective.

CHAPTER SIX

PROSPEROUS TOURISM AND COMMUNICATIONS IN THE MING DYNASTY

In AD 1367, after Zhu Yuanzhang had conquered most of South China, he turned his focus to the north. He sent Generals Xu Da and Chang Yuchun with 250,000 soldiers to fight for the land. In February of AD 1368, Zhu established the Ming Dynasty, with its capital in Nanjing. In August, the northern expedition army conquered capital city Dadu, putting it to an end. In June of the ninth year of Hongwu (AD 1376), the Central Secretariat was reorganized as the Department of the Propaganda and Administration. In AD 1399, Zhu Di, the fourth son of Zhu Yuanzhang, overthrew Emperor Jianwen, the grandson of Zhu Yuanzhang and the former became Emperor Yongle. In AD 1421, Emperor Yongle moved to Beijing, therefore two capitals existed simultaneously. In AD 1428, the administrative divisions of Ming included two capitals and 13 provinces.

On the one hand, Ming administrators adopted centralization policies. On the other hand, they also encourage development of agriculture and tax reforms. Prosperity of handcrafts had provided ample products, while exchange and commercial development brought about an advanced communications system. Many new routes were constructed and as a side affair tourism became very popular; people's understanding of Chinese geography deepened.

1. Postal Routes and Post Stations in the Ming

Zhu Yuanzhang attached great importance to postal stations after establishing the Ming Empire. He ordered the Ministry of War to assume the responsibility of all post stations. "The postal service is used to transmit orders and reach the government of the four directions, so although there are different places and regions, it is not possible to do without it." It was stated that stations in vital transportation hubs had to equip 80, 60, or 30 horses according to the importance of their locations. Post stations situated in less important places were to equip 20, 10, or 5 horses, with donkeys as supplements. In the Yuan Dynasty, the cost of running a post station was assumed by postal families and farmers in the area. Zhu Yuanzhang was previously a farmer himself, so he understood exactly how heavy the burdens could be. Therefore, he reformed the postal system to reduce these.

First of all, he ordered that horses in postal stations could only be used to carry important and urgent documents, or military supplies. It was reported that once a marquis named Lu Zhongheng rode a postal horse home. When Zhu Yuanzhang heard the news, he was furious. "Angrily rebuked said: the Central Plains after the war, the people began to resume work, the registration of households to buy horses is very difficult. Make all follow your example, although the people sell all the children, buy horses to go delivery, cannot be given."[1] After that, it was clearly stipulated: "Whenever a public official, a marquis, or a harnessed horse was ordered to go on a mission, his servants and the ambassadors of the feudal lords were not allowed to take the postal boats without a certificate, and those who violated it were punished."[2] The Ministry of Military Affairs was instructed to announce this rule in all parts of the country.

Secondly, Zhu Yuanzhang asked the farm rent of postal families to be reduced according to their workload. "From the capital's Huitong Station to Suzhou, the 13th stage, south to the capital, west out of Qin and Jin, north to Yan and Ji, the most laborious, the field rent should be exempted. From Baishan Road to Zhengzhou, when Shaanxi and Shanxi two roads, its labor is the second, should

---

1. *The Official Chronicles of Emperor Taizu of Ming,* vol. 129, the 13th year of the Hongwu reign, on the Jia Wu day of the first month, in *The Actual Records of the Ming Dynasty,* book 3, 2044.
2. *The Official Chronicles of Emperor Taizu of Ming,* vol. 186, the 20th year of the Hongwu reign, October, on the Ding Si day, in *The Actual Records of the Ming Dynasty,* book 4, 2787.

be exempted from two-thirds. From Xingyang to Shaanxi, Shanxi, and Beiping, it was one hundred and twenty-one for the post, and the labor was second to none, so it was appropriate to waive one-third."³ Since the post road from the capital (Yingtianfu) to Suzhou passed through here, and the military center of gravity was also in the north at that time, the use of post stations was particularly high, and the people spent a lot of money on buying post-horses, and the labor was heavy, so they were exempted from all field rent.

The largest post station in the Ming Empire was Huitong Station located in the capital. In AD 1441, Beijing Huitong Station was divided into two. The one in north Beijing had 376 rooms and the one in the south had 387 rooms. The number of personnel in the northern branch exceeded 300 and that in the southern branch 100. They were hired for services such as cooking.

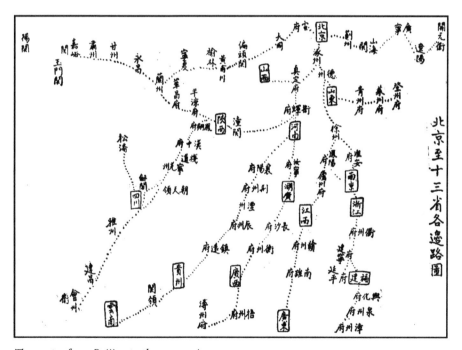

The routes from Beijing to the 13 provinces

---

3. *The Official Chronicles of Emperor Taizu of Ming*, vol. 98, the 8th year of the Hongwu reign, March, on the Yi You day, in *The Actual Records of the Ming Dynasty*, book 3, 1677.

Huitong Station also accommodated minority chieftains and foreign delegates. These chiefs were escorted by post stations along the way to Beijing. When they reached the capital, officers from the Bureau of Ceremonies would receive and accompany them to the station. Chiefs from Liaodong, Tulufan, Yunnan, Guizhou, etc., would reside in the northern branch. Foreign delegates from such countries as Korea, Japan, and Annan would reside in the southern branch. On the second day, delegates would either wear Ming clothes or their national attire to pay respect to the Emperor in the Forbidden Palace. Ming regulations also stated that foreign delegates and tribe chiefs must go to a specified market for business. If they were found trading in common local markets, escorts from Huitong Station would be punished.

There were 60 interpreters in Huitong Station responsible for translations. Responsible for interpreting when envoys or leaders from the following countries and ethnic minorities come to the capital: seven from Nüzhen, seven from Tatar (Mongolia), seven from Huihui, six from Yunnan Baiyi (such as the Dai ethnic group), five from Xixia (Tibet), five from Korea, four from Japan, three from Siam (Thailand), three from Champa (central Vietnam), two from Annam (Vietnam), two from Java, two from Ryukyu Kingdom, two from Uyghur, one from Myanmar, one from Zhenla (Cambodia), one from Hexi (Tangut), one from Sumatra, and one from Malacca Sultanate. The two branches altogether had 171 horses and 173 donkeys, serving as transportation for the delegates. When it fell short of horses, post stations nearby would lend their horses as a makeshift.

The number of post stations reached its peak between AD 1426 and AD 1435. There were 1,357 post stations in the country altogether. The total route length was around 90,000 *li*, with a post station every 60 or 80 *li*. Post stations in the Ming Dynasty fell into two categories: horse and water. All were set up on major routes and transportation hubs. The number of horses and ships equipped for post stations varied according to how busy the services were.

Only one or two post roads passed through, or the post stations beside the branch roads in the province were 20, 10, and 5 horses, respectively. The horses were divided into upper, middle, and lower classes according to their breeds, and each of them was hung with a small plate, stating the class, and they were handled by the plate. Each station's manpower, and funding quotas are determined by the number of horses. In Fujian and Guangxi, due to the limitation of natural conditions, horses were not easy to survive, so they were delivered by human

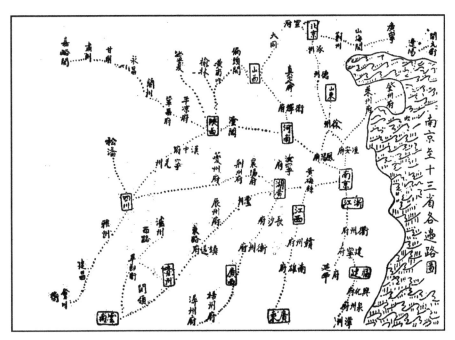

The routes from Nanjing to the 13 provinces

power instead. The boats prepared by the water stage are also more prepared by the main roads, 20, 15, 10, etc., and 7 or 5 for the secondary roads. Each boat had 10 sailors. In the case of military affairs, the ships are equipped with many oars and fast boats. The post had brass bells, and when there was an urgent official document, the brass bells would be hung on the horses and transmitted by flying horses. When the post station in front heard the bell, it would prepare immediately. As soon as the post horse arrived, the postman at this station would take the official documents and ride on his horse. The official documents were thus sent to the capital one stop after another.

Emperor Zhu Yuanzhang not only attached great importance to the construction of post stations but also paid much attention to their names. In the Yuan era, names of post stations were often adopted from local slang. Emperor Zhu asked his scholars to rename these post stations with more elegant names. For example, Yangzhoufu was renamed Guangling Post, and Zhenjiangfu was renamed Jingkou Post. It was thought that a total of 232 post stations were renamed.[4]

---

4. See *Annals of Ming Taizu*, vol. 105, in *Book of Ming*, book 3, 1757.

In addition, Emperor Zhu Yuanzhang asked his scholars to compile a book on post stations. In AD 1394, the book entitled *Thoroughfares of the Universe* was finally completed.

> The book *Thoroughfares of the Universe* was completed. At that time, the upper government thought that a wide area of public opinion could not be recorded without a book, so it ordered the Hanlin scholars and court officials to compile the number of roads and *li* in the world into a book. There were eight categories of directions: from the east to the Liaodong capital, there were 3,944 land *li*, 64 horse stages, 3,450 water and land *li*, and 40 stages; from the northeast of Liaodong to Sanwanwei, there were 4 horse stages, making 360 *li*; from the west to Songpan in Sichuan, there were 5,560 land *li*, 92 horse stages, 8,300 water and land *li*, and 100 stages; and from the southwest to Jinga in Yunnan, there were 6,444 land *li* and 100 horse stages. In the southwest, it is 6,414 *li* by land, 100 horse stages, 8,375 *li* by both land and water, and 113 stages; in the south, it is 6,655 *li* by both land and water, and 78 stages; in the southeast, it is 3,525 *li* by both land and water, and 54 stages; in the north, it is 3,614 *li* by horse stages, 53 horse stages, 4,245 *li* by both land and water and 61 stages; and in the northwest, it is 5,000 *li* by Gansu, Shaanxi Province. To Shaanxi and Gansu, it was 5,500 *li*, 81 horses and land, 6,720 *li*, and 96 stages. The Chief Secretary had thirteen chief posts: one for each of Zhejiang, Fujian, Jiangxi, and Guangdong: thirteen water posts in Zhejiang for 948 *li*; forty-one water and horse posts in Fujian for 2,845 *li*; fifteen water posts in Jiangxi for 1,520 *li*; and forty-five water and horse posts in Guangdong for 4,390 *li*. Henan, Shaanxi, Shandong, Shanxi, Beiping, Huguang, Guangxi, and Yunnan, each with two ways: Henan Water Stage 31, for 2,845 *li*, and Horse Stage 22, for 1,175 *li*; Shaanxi Water Stage 51, for 4,100 *li*, and Horse Stage 42, for 2,430 *li*; Shandong Water Stage 29, for 1,915 *li*; Horse Stage 26, for 1,484 *li*; and Shanxi Water Stage 50, for 4,000 *li*. The water and horse stages in Shanxi are 50, for 4,300 *li*, and the horse stages are 41, for 2,380 *li*; the water and horse stages in Beiping are 47, for 3,445 *li*, and the horse stages are 39, for 2,364 *li*; the water stages in Huguang are 18, for 1,730 *li*; the horse stages are 26, for 1,535 *li*; the water stages in Guangxi are 53, for 4,460 *li*, and the water and horse stages are 64, for 4,265 *li*; and the water and horse stages in Yunnan are 96, for 1,000 *li*. In Yunnan, the water and horse stages were 96, with 7,200 *li*,

and the horse stages were 83, with 5,275 *li*. In Sichuan, there were three ways: the water stage was 94, with 7,265 *li*, the horse stage was 82, with 4,795 *li*, and the water and horse stage was 70, with 5,900 *li*. At that time, the world's roads were 19,000 *li* in length and 11,750 *li* in width. This is the major strategy, but the four barbarians were not involved.[5]

In the original text of the *Thoroughfares of the Universe*, the phrase "and from northeast Liaodong to Sanwanwei, there are four horse stages, which are 360 *li*" is "There are two roads from northeast to Kaiyuan: sixty-eight horse stages, which are 4,340 *li*, and 44 water stages, which are 3,450 *li*," Sanwanwei is Kaiyuan, and the distance is the same.

It recorded all postal routes in the country and could not be found in any other book of the same era. For example, the book recorded postal routes setting out from Yingtianfu (Nanjing) to all other protectorates and prefectures under direct governance. The details were as below:

a. There were two routes from Nanjing to Zhenjiang. One was by water with two stops, measuring a total length of 210 *li*. The other was by land with three stops, measuring 190 *li*.
b. There were five stops from Nanjing to Changzhou by water, measuring a total length of 410 *li*. There were seven stops from Nanjing to Suzhou by water, measuring a total of 590 *li*.
c. There were ten stops from Nanjing to Songjiang by water, measuring 800 *li*.
d. There were three stops from Nanjing to Yangzhou by water, measuring 220 *li*.
e. There were eight stops from Nanjing to Huai'an by water, measuring 540 *li*.
f. There were two routes from Nanjing to Xuzhou. One was by water with 17 stops, measuring 1,100 *li*. The other was by land with 15 stops, measuring 750 *li*.

---

5. *The Official Chronicles of Emperor Taizu of Ming*, vol. 234, the 27th year of the Hongwu reign, the ninth month, on the day of Geng Shen, in *The Actual Records of the Ming Dynasty*, book 5, 3423–3426.

g. There were two routes from Nanjing to Taipingfu. One was by water with two stops, measuring 150 *li*. The other was by land with two stops, measuring 120 *li*.
h. There were two routes from Nanjing to Hezhou. One was by water with three stops, measuring 240 *li*. The other was by land with four stops, measuring 185 *li*.
i. There were two routes from Nanjing to Luzhou. One was by water with five stops, measuring 510 *li*. The other was by land with nine stops, measuring 495 *li*.
j. There were six stops from Nanjing to Chizhou by water, measuring 600 *li*.
k. There were eight stops from Nanjing to Anqing by water, measuring 740 *li*.
l. There were four stops from Nanjing to Ninguofu by water, measuring 420 *li*.
m. There were five stops from Nanjing to Huizhou by water, measuring 720 *li*.
n. There were five stops from Nanjing to Guangde by water, measuring 600 *li*.

After Emperor Zhu Di moved the capital to Beijing, it gradually became the center of the national transportation network. Consequently, the importance of Nanjing diminished. Many routes from Nanjing to other provinces were abolished.

2. Travels by Merchants

The Ming Dynasty was a dynasty in which China's handicraft industry and commerce were extremely developed. For example, Shengze Town in Wujiang County was a silk distribution center at that time, "all the products in the euphemism, are gathered in Shengze Town, the world's clothing and more rely on it. The wealthy merchants came to buy it with thousands of miles of carriages and thousands of golds, and they were like a metropolis."[6] The merchants traveled from south to north and became the most active people in social interactions at that time. The famous merchant gangs of the Ming Dynasty included the Jin merchants in the north, the Hui merchants in the south, and to a lesser extent, the Longyou merchants in Zhejiang and the Dongting merchants in Southern Zhili.

---

6. Qianlong, "Natural Resources," in *The Wujiang County Annals*, vol. 5.

The Ming man Wang Shixing revealed the secret of the richness of Jin merchants: "Pingyang, Ze, and Lu's magnificent merchants, not hundreds of thousands of people are not called rich, and the method of their residence is good. Their people are high in their conduct, and their partners and businessmen are called fellows. One person pays the capital, and all the partners share the business, although they do not swear and have no private stash. The grandfather or the children's interest beggar loan to people and the road died, the lending industry gave up the decades, the children and grandchildren are born and know, more anxious to work hard to pay back its loan, then he has a large accumulation of people, and want to get this person to be a partner, that they do not forget the death of life. Then the person loses a small interest in the front and gets big profits in the back, so there is no capital salty can be living."[7] Thus, it can be seen that partnership and good faith are the two basic rules of businessmen.

With the prosperity of business, the traffic guide for merchants and business guidebooks were published, which became the basic material for future generations to understand the business route of Ming merchants. In AD 1570, Anhui merchant Huang Bian complied a book entitled *Land and Water Ways in China*. It recorded details on business routes in all aspects, including post stations, mountains, rivers, ports, accommodation, products, security status, business associations, transportation prices, and risks on the road.

From volume one to volume four, Huang's book recorded the routes from the capital of Beijing to the other 13 provinces, as well as those to the borders and neighboring the Great Wall. The content of these four volumes is excerpted from the official postal route distances of the time, with some additions. For example, the route from Beijing to Daliang Post in Xiangfu County, Kaifeng Prefecture, where the Henan Provincial Administration is located:

> Shuntiafu. 40 *li* to Lugouqiao. 30 *li* from Liangxiang County. 60 *li* Zhuozhou. 15 *li* Lousang Village. 30 *li* Dingxing County. 10 *li* Baigou River. 60 *li* Ansu County. 15 *li* to the Ducao River. 35 *li* to Baoding Prefecture (*Fu*). 45 *li* to Xingyang Post. 45 *li* to Qingdu County. 60 *li* to Dingzhou. 50 *li* Xinle County. 90 *li* from Zhending Prefecture. 60 *li* Luancheng County. 40 *li* Zhaozhou. 5 *li*

---

7. Wang Shixing, *Guang Zhi Yi*, vol. 3, in *Three Geographical Works of Wang Shixing*, Zhou Zhenhe ed. (Shanghai: Shanghai Classics Publishing House, 1993), 313.

Xiaoheqiao. 60 *li* to Baoxiang County. 33 *li* to Du Yincun River. 28 *li* Neiqiu County. Jindi Village. 45 *li* to Shunde Prefecture. 35 *li* Shahe County. 32 *li* to Duming River. 27 *li* Lüweng Shrine. 20 *li* Handan County. 20 *li* Zhaowangcheng. 20 *li* Taichengang. 30 *li* of Cizhou. 20 *li* to the city of Jiangwucheng. 40 *li* to Zhangde Prefecture. 50 *li* to Tangyin County. 60 *li* Qi County. 50 *li* to Weihui Prefecture. West to Shaanxi and Sichuan. Southwest from Zhengzhou to Yunnan and Guizhou. 20 *li* south to Shamen. 50 *li* to Yanjin County. 25 *li* Qiyi. 40 *li* to Dingdian. 30 *li* to Daliang post, Xiangfu County, Kaifeng Prefecture, Henan Province.

Since the *Ming Canon* only records the names of the post stations in the Wanli period but not the distance of the post route, it is possible to fill in the gaps. The same journey was recorded in the official post route of the Qing Dynasty:

(Beijing Shuntianfu) to Kaifengfu, Henan Province. 605 *li* to Hengshan post in Zhengding County. 60 *li* to Guancheng post in Luancheng County. 40 *li* to the Haocheng post of Zhaozhou. 60 *li* to Huaishui post, Baoxiang County 60 *li* to Zhongqiu post, Neqiu County 60 *li* Xingtai County Long Gang stage. 70 *li* Linluan post, Yongnian County. 45 *li* Handan County Congtai Stage. 70 *li* magnetism state Busyang stage (into the border of Henan). 70 *li* Yecheng post of Anyang County. 70 *li* Tangyin County Yigou stage. 60 *li* to Qimen post, Qi County 50 *li* to Weiyuan post of Ji County. 70 *li* to the Linyan post in Yanjin County. 90 *li* to Daliang post, Xiangfu County, Kaifengfu.

In the Qing Dynasty, Zhengding County was the Ming Dynasty's Zhending County, Xingtai County was the capital of Shunde Prefecture, Anyang County was the capital of Changde Prefecture, and Ji County was the capital of Weihui Prefecture. This shows that the distance from Beijing to Kaifeng was exactly the same in the Ming and Qing dynasties. Huang's book was very popular among merchants. It could be compared to an old type of the *Lonely Planet*, because it had all the helpful information to merchants on the road, who had to arrange everything themselves. Government officials, on the contrary, could be easily accommodated in hotels provided by post stations.

From volume five to eight, Huang recorded waterways and roads less traveled. For example, he recorded 15 different waterways from Suzhoufu to Songjiangfu.

This *fu*. Wujiang County, 50 *li*. 40 *li* Pingwang Post. 30 *li* Wangjiangjing. 30 *li* Wangjiangjing Prefecture. 10 *li* to Dongzhakou. 60 *li* south to Pinghu County. East 3 *li* to Qiliqiao. 24 *li* to Jiashan County. That is, Weitang. 6 *li* Zhangjinghui. There are kilns. 12 *li* to Fengjing. 18 *li* of Mao Bridge. A five-hole building. 9 *li* Zhujing. Xietangqiao, 13 *li*. Two bridges with 6 holes. 14 *li* of Songjiangfu Kuatangqiao. 30 *li* Sijing. 20 *li* Qibao. Land Road. 30 *li* to Toukou. 24 *li* to Longhua Temple Pagoda. That is Huangpu. 12 *li* Shanghai County. This is the outer river. This is the outer river.[8]

The water route between Suzhou and Shanghai is not long but is described in detail, with towns, bridges, and kilns recorded one by one. There are 6 waterways from Suzhou to Songjiang, linking Songjiang, a textile center, and Suzhou, a printing and dyeing processing center, into a network of water and land routes. At that time, some merchants from all over the country sat in Suzhou City to make purchases, while others went to various market towns to buy. The rivers and beaches connected the villages and towns, and the towns were linked to Suzhou, Songjiang, and other large and medium-sized cities. A ship, full of merchants and cotton cloth, sailing to and from. The water towns of Jiangnan became one of the most economically prosperous regions in the Ming and Qing dynasties.

Apart from running business, merchants were also interested in visiting scenic resorts in their leisure time. Huang's guidebook also gave useful information in these respects. For example, the chapter, "From Pingqiang Town in Jiading Prefecture to Emei Mountain" not only recorded the routes in detail but also gave recommendations on the best seasons for climbing:

Pingqiang Town. Small boat. Forty *li* junction. Disembarkation. Eighty *li* to Huangjiegen. Eighty *li* to Dengjunpo. Ninety *li* to Laobaolou. Ten *li* to Emei County. Sixty *li* to Baishui Temple. Up the mountain. Dingxinpo. Xiaoshenkeng. Five *li* to Dashenkeng. Ten *li* to Changlaoping. Six *li* to the Shedaotui. Ten *li* to the Husunti. Ten *li* of Chuhuanxi. Fifteen *li* of Meizipo. Ten *li* of Thunder God Temple. Ten *li* eighty-four pan. The road has eighty-four twists and turns. The Huanxi Pavilion. Tianxian Bridge. Tianmen Stone. Three *li* in total. Guangxiang Temple. Jingang Tai.

---

8. Huang Bian, *Unified Journey Map Records*, vol. 7, in Yang Zhengtai, *A Study of Ming Dynasty Post Stations*, 204.

Puxian Temple. Puxian Temple in the top of the extreme, the wind is very big, tile with iron, and the light release miracle clear, only in April and May can climb. Its mountain after the pit snow, winter, and summer does not disappear, July and August snow closed cliff path, cannot go.[9]

Cheng Chunyu complied a book entitled the *Guidebook for Merchants* in AD 1626. It was composed of four volumes, with guidelines under numerous categories. Descriptions of routes only covered 1.5 volumes of the book. Cheng adopted a method of telling the names of post stations in the form of songs, so it would be easier to memorize:

> How many states does the water journey from Nanjing to Beijing pass through? There are 46 places in Huanghua, and the distance is three thousand three hundred and ten. From here, downstream on the Longjiang River, Longtan sends past Yizhenba; from Guangling to Shaobo, reaching Yucheng, Jieshou is near Anping and Huaiyin. As soon as you leave the Yellow River, it's Qingkou, and Taoyuan is right before the ancient city of Lin; Zhongwu straight river connects to Xiapi, Xin'an, and Fangcun await Pengcheng. There are Jiagou, Siting, and Shahe post stations; Luqiao is south of the city and matches with Fuma; Changgou is forty away from Kaihe, and Anshan Shuiyi is close to Zhangqiu. Chongwu sends off to Qingyang, Qingyuan water follows Weiheliu; Dukou connects with Jiamaying, Liangjiazhuang resides and proceeds to Ande. Liangdian connects to Xin Qiao, Zhuanhe post station, then leads to Qianning; Liuhe looks far to Fengxin on foot, Yangqing directly to Yangcun crossing. Hexi and Hehe return to Luhe, only separated from the capital by forty routes; Every station is sung in order, so travelers can recognize them without mistake.[10]

Other contents include the business motto *Rules for Businessmen*, *Ten Keys for Businessmen*, and *Mechanisms for Buying and Selling*, as well as *Choosing Auspicious Days for Travel* and *Four Times of the Year*. As businessmen need to know the geography of the country and deal with various officials, all the

---

9. Huang Bian, *Unified Journey Map Records*, vol. 7, in Yang Zhengtai, *A Study of Ming Dynasty Post Stations*, 200.
10. Cheng Chunyu, *Requirements for Scholars and Merchants*, vol. 1, in Yang Zhengtai, *A Study of Ming Dynasty Post Stations* (Shanghai: Shanghai Classics Publishing House, 1994), 259.

prefectures, counties, and guardhouses in the country are included, as well as the list of the royal families in each province. One of the features of the book is the inclusion of a large number of mottos on human life. The section of *The General Theory of the Foot of the Boat* is devoted to the rules of renting transportation tools—boats: "And the matter of hiring a boat; you must cast the teeth of the plan, ask them the truth, do not be greedy for small private hires, this is the first priority for customers. Although the locals are tricky people, it is still difficult to escape its art, not to mention the foreign lone guest." Although the price was more expensive, the broker knew the owner's details and could guarantee the safety of the boat. Although it is introduced by the intermediary, you must be careful everywhere: "If the boat is newly launched, newly repaired, and the pieces are not in order. Or if the size of the ship does not correspond to the size of the ship, it is a borrowed thing. And scruffy old ship lost in the oil wash; the personnel is indecent, must be less debt ship also. The method of looking at the ship must be to estimate the beam head, count the warehouse mouth, see the gray seam dry and wet, see the guy neat and tidy, before the transaction."[11] From inspecting the equipment of the ship's artifacts to paying attention to the temperament of the shipowner or shipwright, all is the experience.

When merchants were on the road, they should put safety before anything else. Cheng warned: "More haste, less speed." He wrote that ships should be anchored in the harbor as early as possible. To prevent any accidents from happening, one shouldn't try to speed up and sail at night. If one travels on land, one should rest at hotels as early as possible. And one should also be fully dressed when he went to bed. Should there be any emergencies, he could jump up and go.

Apart from attaching great importance to personal safety, Cheng warned that one should also keep an eye on their luggage. He wrote that one should pay attention to companions in the same ship too. If someone was well dressed but without much luggage or someone looked suspicious, then chances were high that they were thieves or swindlers. In Suzhou and Hangzhou, practices included luggage being placed under the planks. If one wasn't careful enough, luggage might be stolen.

Two poems by anonymous poets reflect the mood of Ming merchants on the

---

11. Cheng Chunyu, *Requirements for Scholars and Merchants*, vol. 2, in Yang Zhengtai, *A Study of Ming Dynasty Post Stations*, 294.

road. The poem "Land Road" reads: "The arcs and yarns of the pontiff's door are in all directions; life is hard to escape from the frontier of profit and fame. The heroes won the chess game, and the rich and famous returned to the scene. The years are weary of the water and the wind, and the long and the short are bitter. You know that you can walk slowly without being busy." "Poem on the Waterway": "Thousands of streams and thousands of schools are always in the past. The moon and the wind sit in the poetry scroll, and the rivers and mountains are invited to fall into the wine cup. I am worried about the return of the geese and the letters of the geese, and I do not cry that the dead sheep are poor. Merchants, scholars, and farmers are happy with their work, and the waves of grace are swelling the sea and the sky."[12]

3. Leisure Travel by Government Officials

Trips made by merchants were often essential to some extent for business survival and success. Compared with merchants, trips by government officials and scholars were usually made out of their own choice.

Between the years of AD 1368 and AD 1506, the Ming government issued strict rules on population movement. At the end of the Ming administration, eunuchs in fact controlled central power. Government officials and scholars were so depressed that they turned to nature for comfort. Their travels were usually made in leisure. They not only visited scenic resorts but also researched local customs and listened to local people for their joys and sorrows. Yuan Hongdao, a famous poet of the era, was one example. After he resigned from his post as the Chief of Wu County, he traveled to Jiangsu and Zhejiang for three months, covering a total length of over 2,000 *li*.

Additionally, the society in the late Ming Dynasty was in an era of "heaven collapsing and earth disintegrating." Wang Yangming's philosophy of the "Study of the Mind" broke through the constraints of the Cheng-Zhu School of Neo-Confucianism. Intellectuals began to pursue a normal human life, advocating "no need to be pretentious, no need to go against one's nature, no need to obscure

---

12. Cheng Chunyu, *Requirements for Scholars and Merchants*, vol. 2, in Yang Zhengtai, *A Study of Ming Dynasty Post Stations*, 291.

one's heart, no need to suppress one's ambition, and to act with an upright heart."[13] They went out into nature and into society. Yuan Hongdao said, "There are three great failures in the world, but not in a broken country or a dead family. If friends do not get together in the mountains and rivers, it is a failure; if friends are too busy to get together, it is a failure; if the time is not right to travel, or if the flowers fall and the mountains dry up, it is a failure."[14] In the season of travel, it became fashionable for the literati to travel with like-minded friends. The private trips of the literati can be called "private trips."

These officials and literati traveled in groups: "The travels of princes and lords were either to serve the imperial court, or to lead the envoys, or to station the troops in the emplacement, and to ask about the customs of the lower garments."[15] Or travel with only servants: "When I travel, I have a lot of inconveniences because I have a lot of servants and my bag is heavy, so I eliminated the lazy and weak from the children and slaves, eliminated the flashy from the clothes and footwear, eliminated the unhurried from the luggage, and eliminated the weary from the guests, and packed lightly."[16] The difference between eunuchs and private travelers determined the time and route of their trips, the way they traveled, and the food, lodging, and transportation during their trips.

As outstanding geographers and travelers of the Ming Dynasty, Wang Shixing and Xu Xiake were representatives of eunuch travel and private travel, respectively. The term of office of local middle officials in the Ming Dynasty was not long, and the transfer was frequent. Wang Shixing was appointed to the Sichuan Provincial School in October of the 16th year of the Wanli era, then to the Guangxi Provincial School in April of the following year, to the Yunnan Lancang Military Department in the 18th year of the Wanli era, to the Henan Provincial School in July of the 19th year of the Wanli era, to the Shandong

---

13. Li Zhi, "Three Poems on Misspeaking," *Burning the Books*, vol. 2, in *The Collected Works of Li Zhi* (Beijing: Social Sciences Literature Press, 2000), 76.
14. Yuan Hongdao, "With Wu Dunzhi," in *Annotations and Collation of Yuan Hongdao's Collection*, vol. 11 (Shanghai: Shanghai Ancient Books Publishing House, 2008), 506.
15. Chen Jiru, "Preface to Leisurely Travel to Qingfu," *Late Fragrance Hall Collection*, vol. 3, in *Collection of Books Banned or Destroyed by the Four Treasuries*, vol. 66 of Collection Section (Beijing: Beijing Publishing House, 1997), 581 (below).
16. Zou Diguang, "Travel Notes to Tiantai Mountain," *Initial Green Pavilion Manuscript*, vol. 15, in *Collection of Books Banned or Destroyed by the Four Treasuries*, vol. 103 of Collection Section, 338 (above).

Provincial Food Supervision Department in December of the 20th year of the Wanli era, and back to the capital in March of the 22nd year of the Wanli era as a junior secretary of the Imperial Household Department. In six years, he was an official in five provinces. Wang Shixing kept a diary during his trips to these provinces. The travels to Shu, Chu, Yunnan, and Guangdong in the *Travel Notes on the Five Mountains* are all about what he saw and heard on the way to his post. Since officials had to arrive at their destinations within the time limit set by the court, it was impossible for Wang to stop for a long time on the way and stay at a certain scenic spot. For example, when he was appointed to the Sichuan Provincial Academy in the 16th year of the Wanli reign and went to Chengdu, he entered Sichuan from Baoji in Shaanxi Province and took the postal route. He arrived at his destination in 29 days, hardly staying in the same place for more than two days. When he encountered bad weather and poor road conditions, he could not travel to the famous scenery near the stage road. "In the ninth year of the reign of the emperor, I had a meal in the yellow sand, traveled along the Han River, and was about to reach Shin, when I entered the temple of Confucius Ming. The tomb is in Dingjun Mountain, ten *li* south of the river. The wind and rain do not become a line. The next day, I went to Shin and had a meal on the frustrating water. Frustration into the Han, its water from Luyang, when the rain is a big injection, Daan River cannot be crossed, is then left in Qingyang."[17] It rained heavily all day, so Kongming's tomb could not be visited. The next day it rained heavily again, so I could not cross the Daan River. When I arrived at my destination, I could go to the nearby attractions as I thought. Wang Shixing was a provincial minister in Sichuan and Guangxi, so he had fewer political affairs compared with other provincial officials. In Chengdu, after the examinations, Wang Shixing visited all the places around Chengdu according to his own ideas.

Xu Xiake, on the other hand, was a representative of private travel, and his routes were designed to serve the purpose of his travel expeditions, so he did not always choose the nearest straight route, nor did he necessarily take the major roads, avoiding as much repetition as possible, so as to take full advantage of his travels to visit as many sites as possible within the limited time available. Sometimes you will choose to take a short detour. Once you arrive at a destination,

---

17. Wang Shixing, *Travel Notes on the Five Mountains*, vol. 5, in *Three Geographical Works of Wang Shixing*, Zhou Zhenhe ed. (Shanghai: Shanghai Ancient Books Publishing House, 1993), 107.

take a radial tour. When he was in Guangxi, he set out from Nanning, heading west, passing through Xinningzhou, Taipingfu, Anpingzhou, and Longyingzhou. Upon reaching Xialeizhou, he turned eastward, passing through Xiangwuzhou, Zhenyuanzhou, Jielunzhou, Doujiezhou, and Long'an, before returning to Nanning.

As a government officer on his way to his posts, Wang Shixing could take advantage of horses and ships provided by post stations on route. For example, on his way to Sichuan from Beijing, he mainly rode horses. From Sichuan to Guangxi, he traveled by ship from Chengdu to Jiangling along the Yangtze. However, sometimes, Wang paid for some private tours with his own money. He rented boats by himself to visit famous resorts like Poyang Lake and the Pavilion of Prince Teng in Nanchang.[18] And sometimes, Wang could even sit in a sedan chair when he traveled.

In contrast, Xu Xiake had a limited budget, though he preferred less traveled roads. Therefore, he covered most of his journeys on foot. Sometimes, he also traveled by ship, on horse, or in sedans, but that would account for less than half of his journeys.

In terms of accommodation and dining, Wang was much more privileged. As a government officer, he could stay at hotels provided by post stations for free. Ming administrations ruled that government officers who stayed at post stations overnight could have up to 5 *sheng* (升, one *sheng* = 107 milliliters) of rice per day. For those passing by (but not staying overnight), they could have up to 3 *sheng* of rice per day.[19] When on private trips, Wang would often reside in Buddhist temples.

Xu Xiake also resided in Buddhist temples and hotels regularly. That would account for 50% of his accommodation. On other occasions, he would stay at farmers' houses, on the ships, or at friends' places. As Xu often took roads less traveled, sometimes he couldn't find any houses nearby, so he had to sleep under the stars. When he stayed at farmers' houses, Xu and his servants would cook for themselves.

---

18. Wang Shixing, *Travel Notes on the Five Mountains*, vol. 6, in *Three Geographical Works of Wang Shixing*, Zhou Zhenhe ed., 129.
19. "Annals of Ming Taizu," vol. 29, in *Annals of Ming*, vol. 1, 500.

4. From Travelers to Geographers

In the Ming Dynasty, scholars would usually pack a Chinese calligraphic brush when they traveled. They recorded their journeys in journals. Some wrote about sceneries; some would record their observations of society and nature. In other words, they combined travel with research—Xu Xiake and Wang Shixing were two of the most well-known. Xu wrote *Journals of Xu Xiake* and Wang wrote *Guang Zhi Yi (The Trans-China Travel Journal)*. Both books were considered masterpieces that marked the beginning of Geography as an independent discipline in China. The writers were also considered the most famous geographers in Chinese history.

Wang Shixing, character Hengshu, called Yuanbai Daoist, also called Taichu, was born in the twenty-sixth year of Jiajing (AD 1547), and died in the twenty-sixth year of Wanli (AD 1598). A native of Linhai, Zhejiang. When he was a student, he had already traveled around Hangzhou and Yuezhong. In AD 1577, he became a scholar and served as a magistrate in Queshan County, Henan Province. Four years later, he left for the capital, where he visited Mt. After entering the capital, he served as a minister of rituals, but he was still fascinated by the landscape. In the thirteenth year of the Wanli reign (AD 1585), he returned home after his mother died of illness. During his two years at home, he traveled to Tiantai, Yandang, Qiantang, Taihu Lake, and other famous mountains and rivers. In the 16th year of Wanli (AD 1588), on his way back to Beijing, he visited Dongyue Tai Mountain. In the autumn of this year, Wang Shixing was ordered to take the examination in Sichuan visited Xiyue Huashan on the way, and lingered in Emei, Qingcheng, and other mountains. In April of the following year, he was transferred to Guangxi Tixuedao, passing through Hengyang, and visited Mount Hengshan. By now, he had traveled to all the five mountains. In the spring of the nineteenth year of the Wanli era (AD 1591), he was appointed as a military minister in Lancang, Yunnan Province, and visited such famous places as Kunming Pond, Duxiu Peak, Taihua Mountain, Ducang Mountain, and Jidu Mountain. In July of the same year, he was transferred to Henan Tixuedao. In the twentieth year of the Wanli era (AD 1592), he was transferred to Shandong in December to supervise the grain road. In March of AD 1594, Wang returned to Beijing and was appointed as the junior secretary of the Dalisi Temple in charge of the Beijing camp. In AD 1595, he resigned from the post of governor of Henan and was transferred to Nanjing as the Secretary of Honglu Temple. He died more than two years later. In his spare time for government, he traveled to the twelve provinces of the two capitals except Fujian Province and wrote many wonderful travelogues and poems, which were collected as *Travel Notes on the Five Mountains*. In his later years, he also wrote two books, *Guang You Zhi* and *Guang Zhi Yi*, to theoretically summarize the objects of his early travels and investigations.

Wang's observations of nature and society were made with a dynamic perspective. For example, the book of *Yu Gong* first proposed the "four rows" of Chinese mountains, which were arranged in four east-west rows from north to south. In the Tang Dynasty, Monk Dao proposed the "two precepts of mountains and rivers": Chinese mountains were arranged in two rows, east-west to north-south. Zhu Xi, a famous theorist in the Song Dynasty, put forward the idea of China's three great dragons: "Zhu Zi said: the world has three great waters, said the Yellow River, said the Yangtze River, said the Yalu River. Now to the map of the examination of the Yangtze River and the South China Sea, the South Dragon in the East China Sea, the Yellow River and the Yangtze River in the Dragon in the East China Sea, the Yellow River and the Yalu River in the North Dragon in the Liao River."[20] The problem is that the division is not accurate enough, for example, the Song Dynasty had a small territory, so the Song view did not include the mountains of the Yunnan–Guizhou plateau; secondly, he did not notice that the development process of the regions divided by each mountain system is early and late. Therefore, he believed that the following division should be made:

> Kunlun is located in the middle of the land, and the four mountain ranges are outside the great wilderness. The one that enters China is the southeastern branch. The left branch is divided into three branches: The left branch circles the Yin Mountain and Helan of the Chinese court, enters Shanxi, starts from Taihang for thousands of miles, comes out as the Medical Lodge ends at Liaohai, and becomes the North Dragon. The middle branch follows Xifan, enters Minshan, and follows the Min River. The right side of the river is wrapped around Xuzhou and stops; the left side of the river goes north to Guanzhong, and the pulse is connected to Dasan Pass, left Wei, and right

---

20. Zhang Huang, "Lun San Da Gan Long," in *Book Compilation*, vol. 30, *Siku Quanshu* version, book 969, 564 (upper).

Han. In the middle out of the end of the South, Taihua, under the Taiyue Song high, the right turn of the Jing Mountains holds Huai Shui, left to fall a thousand *li* of plains, from the Taishan into the sea, for the Dragon. The right expenditure of the west of the Tufan, under the Lijiang, to Yunnan, around the Jin Yi, Guizhu, and Guanling, and east to Yuanling. It is divided into one, from Wugang out of Xiangxi to Wuling; and another, from Guilin Haiyang Mountain, through Jiuyi, Hengshan, out of Xiangjiang, east to Kuanglu; and another, over Yu Ling, and the lawn, to Huangshan, Tianmu, three Wu stop; over Yu Ling, and divided into Xianxia Pass, to Min stop. The division of the quay for the Dabanshan, right down the Bracang, left to go to the Tiantai, Simeon to the sea stop, the end of the South Dragon.[21]

Wang himself suggested dividing the mountain ranges by rivers. Although not scientific enough, interestingly, the mountain ranges he mentioned were more or less the same as modern geography.

What's more, Wang held an open attitude toward territorial development.

The beauty of Jiangnan is incomparable even after a millennium. During the Tang Dynasty, China was divided into twelve circuits. One of them was the Jiangnan East Circuit, which covered the regions of Sheng, Run, Zhe, and Min. Another was Jiangnan West Circuit, covering the regions of Xuan, She, Yuzhang, Heng, and E. Isn't this because the land was vast and sparsely populated? By the late Tang period, when the Qian family established their state, and the five kings of Wuyue ruled in succession, the two Zhejiang provinces began to flourish. When Wang Shenzhi and Li Jing took power, the eight Fujian provinces started to prosper. It was only during the Song Dynasty, when China was divided into twenty-three routes, that Jiangnan occupied eight of them: the two Zhejiang, Fujian, Jiangnan East, Jiangnan West, Jinghu North, Jinghu South, Guangnan East, and Guangnan West. The four routes in the Sichuan region were not included. From the Zhao Song Dynasty to the present, a mere six to seven hundred years, it's the peak of its prosperity. It remains uncertain when the spotlight will shift to areas like Guizhou and Guangdong.[22]

---

21. Wang Shixing, *Guang You Zhi (Part One)*, in *Three Geographical Works of Wang Shixing*, 210.
22. Wang Shixing, *Guang Zhi Yi*, vol. 1, in *Three Geographical Works of Wang Shixing*, 240.

Wang wrote that Jiangnan districts started developing in the Five Dynasties era. By the Southern Song Dynasty, the districts had already become an economic center of the country. Wang predicted that remote regions such as Guizhou and Guangdong would develop sooner or later—it was only a matter of time. He also stated that the cultural center of a country would change according to its economic center.

As Wang's travels took him all over the twelve prefectural administrations of the two capitals and his many years of experience as an official in the capital, he was not just a tourist, so he saw and heard a great deal. In addition, he was good at thinking and analyzing the differences in geographical phenomena in each region from a national perspective. From the perspective of economic geography, he observed that there were great differences in the kinds of goods or commodities available in the major trading ports of the country: "The world's horse-heads are the places where things come out and gather. Su, Hangzhou's coins, Huaiyin's grain, Weiyang's salt, Linqing, Jining's goods, Xuzhou's car and mule, the capital's city gods, Dengshi's bone, Wuxi's rice, Jiangyang's book, Fuliang's porcelain, Ning, Taiwan's replica bags, Xiangshan's ship, Guangling's Ji, Wenzhou's lacquerware."[23] That is to say, the peak of Jiangnan's literary figures emerged from the Jiajing period of the Ming Dynasty. Wang Shixing further reveals that variations in natural and economic environments among regions also influence their cultural milieu: "The southeast is abundant in fish, salt, rice, and paddy; the central regions and Chu territory are rich in fish; the southwest has an abundance of gold, silver mines, precious stones, pearls, amber, cinnabar, and mercury; the south yields rhinoceros, elephants, pepper, camphor, and foreign currencies and silks; the north offers cattle, sheep, horses, donkeys, and woolen blankets; the southwest provinces like Sichuan, Guizhou, Yunnan, and Guangdong produce large timbers. Jiangnan has firewood and gets fire from wood; the northern part of the Yangtze River is rich in coal and derives heat from it. The northwest has high mountains suitable for travel by land without boats; the southeast has expansive marshlands, suitable for boat travel with few horse carriages. People in Hainan eat fish and shrimp, which the northerners find too fishy; those in the northern frontier consume dairy, which southerners find too strong. People in Hebei consume leeks, garlic, and shallots, which those in Jiangnan find too spicy."[24] Wang Shixing

---

23. Wang Shixing, *Guang Zhi Yi*, vol. 1, in *Three Geographical Works of Wang Shixing*, 244.
24. Wang Shixing, *Guang Zhi Yi*, vol. 1, in *Three Geographical Works of Wang Shixing*, 242.

vividly illustrates that due to varying natural environments in each region, there are significant differences in their produce, further causing regional differences in diet, transportation, and daily habits. General travelers can observe significant regional variations between places like Hainan and the northern frontier or Hebei and Jiangnan. Within a single region, different natural environments also influence the cultural landscape. Wang Shixing observes this meticulously in Zhejiang Province, "Hangzhou, Jiaxing, and Huzhou are plain water towns, home to the people of the marshlands; Jinhua, Quzhou, Yanzhou, and Chuzhou, with their hilly and rugged terrains, are inhabited by the people of the valleys; Ningbo, Shaoxing, Taizhou, and Wenzhou, nestled between mountains and the vast sea, are home to the coastal people. These three groups each have their own customs. The marshland people live on boats, gather a myriad of goods, and the urban areas are inclined toward wealth and luxury, with the gentry exuding grandeur while the common folk remains insignificant. The valley people, influenced by the ruggedness of the stone environment, are fierce and impulsive, often violating laws, preferring frugality. Yet, the affluent among them are defiant, forming cliques to challenge the gentry. The coastal people, exposed to the elements and facing life-threatening risks, derive a modest living from the sea's bounty, neither too poor due to its benefits nor too wealthy as they don't engage in trading. Urban areas and the gentry coexist peacefully, with officials and civilians finding a balance between the distinctions of high and low, with their customs lying between luxury and frugality."[25]

Chinese people advocate living and working in peace and happiness, but the objective conditions of some regions with less land and more people, force local people to go to other places: "Jiang, Zhejiang, Fujian, three places, dense people and narrow land, in short, not enough to be one of the provinces in the Central Plains, so the body does not have the skills is not paste, the foot does not go outside the skills are not sold."[26] Wang Shixing went on to tell what he had learned in Yunnan. When he was first appointed as the military governor of Lancang, he learned that fifty to sixty percent of the Han Chinese in Yunnan were from Fuzhou, Jiangxi Province. At first, Wang thought that these Fuzhou people were traders and lived only in the cities. When he went deeper into the counties,

---

25. Wang Shixing, *Guang Zhi Yi*, vol. 4, in *Three Geographical Works of Wang Shixing*, 324.
26. Wang Shixing, *Guang Zhi Yi*, vol. 1, in *Three Geographical Works of Wang Shixing*, 337.

he found that most of the people who worked in the villages where the ethnic minorities lived, such as the Tufu and Tuzhou, were also Fuzhou people. Wang thought that this was the case only in mainland Yunnan. When his men returned from Burma and reported the names of the leaders of the minority villages they passed, Wang was surprised to find that his second judgment was also wrong: most of the leaders of the minority groups in the border areas were also from Fuzhou. The road from Yongchang City, where the Lancang Military Security Road is located, to Maimang was 10,000 *li* long and took two months to complete, with different ethnic groups living along the way.

Xu Xiake was born in AD 1586 in Jiangyin County (Jiangsu) and died in AD 1641. His family status was going downhill when he was born. Xu gave up the idea of becoming a government official after he failed an examination held by the local government. Even when he was very young, he was very into non-mainstream or obsucre books. History and geography were among his favorite topics.

At the age of 22, Xu set out from home and visited famous sites like Tai Lake, Mount Tai, and Tiantai Mountain. His mother supported his travel plans. Almost every year, Xu would set out in the spring and return home in autumn. Xu accumulated experience from those short trips, which laid the foundation for his much longer journeys in future.

During his short trips, Xu started to question the geographic books he had read. For example, some books stated that the Yellow River was much longer than the Yangtze. However, according to what Xu had seen with his own eyes, the volume of the Yellow was less than one-third of the Yangtze. This might indicate the Yangtze had more water sources than the Yellow River. To satisfy his curiosity, Xu decided to travel further and find out the reality.

Between the ages of 28 and 48, Xu had visited many famous mountains, including Mount Song, Hua, Heng, Wutai, Lu, Yandang, Wuyi, and the Yellow Mountain. He wrote 17 journals regarding these trips.

Between the ages of 51 and 54, Xu took much longer journeys. His hometown of Jiangyin was located at the end of the Yangtze before it reached the ocean. Xu spent four years seeking the Yangtze starting point. He set out in September AD 1636 from his hometown, and went via provinces like Zhili, Zhejiang, Jiangxi, and Guizhou, before finally reaching Yunnan. He had planned to visit Myanmar but gave up after his friends persuaded him not to. Xu wrote 9 volumes of journals recording this long journey. After dozens of years of travel, Xu compiled this into a book entitled *Journals of Xu Xiake* with a total of 10 volumes.

Xu Xiake greatly advanced geographic studies in China. His first contribution was his detailed study of karst landforms in China. The hard limestone is very resistant to mechanical erosion and physical weathering but is easily eroded by rain and groundwater along the joints and divided into many steep peaks and caves. When he was young, Xu Xiake had already visited two famous caves in the southern part of China, namely, Yixing Zhanggong Cave and Shanjuan Cave, and had accumulated some experience in investigating karst landforms.

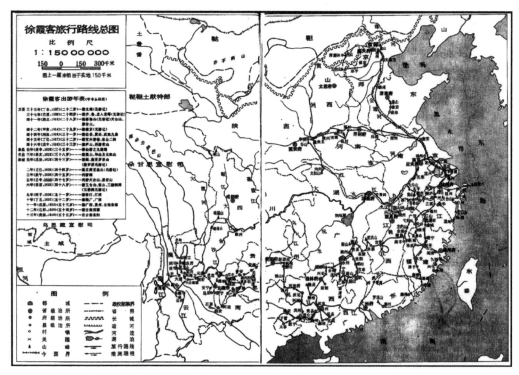

Map of the routes traveled by Xu Xiake[27]

During his western journey, he saw a large number of karst peaks in provinces such as Guangxi, Guizhou, and Yunnan, and each of these three provinces

---

27. Collected from Xu Hongzu, *Journals of Xu Xiake*, arranged by Zhu Shaotang and Wu Yingshou (Shanghai: Shanghai Ancient Books Publishing House, 1980).

was distinct. The mountain peaks in Guangxi are "pure stone, interspersed with rocks, each standing alone without mixing." Yunnan's peaks are "mostly made of soil, intertwined with occasional rocks, thus having many sinkholes." Guizhou, lying between Guangxi and Yunnan, is "notably precipitous and striking."[28] Within Guangxi Province, the karst landscape also varies regionally: The area from Guilin to Yangshuo within Guilin Prefecture has "isolated stone peaks," and the "mountains are solely made of rocks, leading to numerous water flows through caves, making the water clear." Hence, the landscape of Guilin is considered unparalleled in the world and has become a globally renowned scenic spot. To the west of Guilin Prefecture is Liuzhou Prefecture; the number of stone peaks along the Liujang Riverbanks has reduced. "The mountains, a mixture of soil and rock, sporadically display tens of rock peaks, standing tall in formations, appearing abruptly and prominently. What distinguishes this region from Yangshuo and Guilin is that while the latter is surrounded by rock peaks without any soil mountains, the former seems like spikes in a pouch, notably distinct and prominent."[29] Xunzhou Prefecture to the south of Liuzhou Prefecture has its Guixian County along the Yujang River where there are "sporadic stone mountains, looking like adorned snails." The limestone peaks here have been leveled to plains.

Another characteristic of karst topography is the development of caves. Xu Xiake visited a total of over 200 karst caves. He researched each cave, recording their locations, height, width, size, and depth of underground rivers within the caves.

Xu's second contribution was his research on river origins in China. Wherever he goes, he "first examines how the mountain ranges rise and fall, and how the waterways diverge and converge. Once he grasps the overall trend, he then delves into every hill and gully, meticulously scrutinizing each detail."[30] He paid great attention to the origins and flows of rivers and mountains. The most famous one is the *Origins of Rivers*. It corrected the mistaken belief since the book of *Yu Gong* that the main source of the Yangtze River is the Min River, and correctly proposed that "when tracing the source of the river, the Jinsha River must be regarded as the primary source." Xu pointed out the reason why it had been mistaken for the past

---

28. Xu Xiake, *Journals of Xu Xiake*, vol. 5 (Part One) (Shanghai: Shanghai Ancient Books Publishing House, 1982), 711.
29. Xu Xiake, *Journals of Xu Xiake*, vol. 3 (Part Two), 372.
30. Pan Lei, "Preface to Journals of Xu Xiake," in *Journals of Xu Xiake*, vol. 10 (Part Two), 1257.

2,000 years might be that Min was reachable by ships or canoes, but Jinsha was not. "The source of the river has repeatedly sought to discuss, so it began to get its far; the source of the river has never asked for, so only the near." "The Min River is navigable for boats and ships, while the Jinsha River winds through the valleys and gorges of the barbarians, where neither water nor land routes can be traced upstream." On the other hand, there was little communication between people in Sichuan and Yunnan, as the mountain paths were too difficult to travel. Therefore, "those in Xuzhou (Sichuan) only know its water out of Mahu, Wumeng, but do not know the upper stream from Yunnan Lijiang; those in Yunnan Lijiang know it as Jinsha River but do not know the lower stream out of Xuzhou as the source of the river."[31]

The volcanic hot springs are also described in detail in *Journals of Xu Xiake*. Xu Xiake in Chongzhen twelfth year (AD 1639) traveled to Yunnan Tengyue Prefecture (now Tengchong County) to explore Daying Mountain. The local people told him: "Thirty years ago, it was all big wood and giant bamboo, covered no gap, there is a dragon pool four, the depth cannot be measured, the sound of the foot to the wave and rise, no one dares to approach. Nearby shepherds, thunder and an earthquake killed five or six hundred sheep and shepherded several people. Even day and night fire, deep trees, and bamboo start with no remnants, and the pool is also into the land. Now there are water caves under the mountain, all from the root of the mountain to tease the cloud." The four dragon pools at the top of the mountain are the four crater lakes.[32] Due to the volcanic activity, there is gas emitted, so there are waves of lake water. After the volcanic eruption, the ejected lava formed pumice and closed the crater. Xu Xiake recorded in detail his observation of the current situation: "The stone at the top of the mountain, ochre red in color but light and floating in quality, like a beehive, is formed by floating foam, although it is large enough to hold, and two fingers can carry it, but its quality is still firm, really the remnants of the robbery ash." Due to the recent volcanic activity, there are many boiling springs and hot springs near Tengyue Prefecture, and Xu Xiake has recorded most of them. "And the south crossed the hill and went down, passed the Song Mountain and the various places, 20 *li* and entered the hot water pond Li Lao's house. The time is still afternoon. Look around. The

---

31. Xu Xiake, *Journals of Xu Xiake*, vol. 10, 1129.
32. *Journals of Xu Xiake*, vol. 8 (Part Two), 977.

hot water leaked; it's out very differently. Cover the small water in the dock from the East Gorge injection and the West cold springs. Around the small water, the spring hole out anywhere, it is as big as a tube, spraying orifices and up, as a drum boiling, a sound, jumping up the water surface of two or three inches. The heat is like boiling. There are several holes protruding from a person. There is a slanting spray from the stone, and the heat is particularly ... this cold spring south slope of the hot water also. The north leaning under the east slope, there are several places, or out of the sand hole, or out of the stone Guangzhou, which is also made before the round pool, and the heat is the same. Two pools look at each other, and the overflow hole is no less than a hundred."[33] This paragraph describes the Long Dome (now Yunnan Eryuan) and Heqing (now Yunnan Heqing) at the junction of the hot water pond hot springs.

Later generations spoke highly of the journals written by Xu. The scholars or officials in charge of the *Siku Quanshu* thought "(Xu) Hongzu had a passion for the unique and remote, and he intentionally traveled far and wide. His pace was sharp in search, and his writing was meticulous in recording. As a result, his travel notes are unparalleled in number. Although he documented his travels day by day, he never intended to craft literary pieces. However, based on his firsthand observations and experiences, his accounts are reliable. Especially regarding Guizhou and Yunnan, regions which are remote and where geographical records are sparse, this book provides a detailed analysis of the landscape and topography. It is indeed a unique complement to mountain studies and an external chapter to geographical records."[34] Liang Qichao, a famous scholar in the late Qing period, said Xu was more for adventures than for scenery. Ding Wenjiang believed that Xu Xiake made five major discoveries in geography. British scientist Joseph Needham said that Xu Xiake would qualify as a nature explorer in the 20th century.

---

33. *Journals of Xu Xiake*, vol. 8 (Part Two), 988.
34. *Siku Quanshu*, book 593, photocopy ed. (Taipei: Taiwan Commercial Press, 1983), 62 (above).

CHAPTER SEVEN

CANNONS, WESTERN STUDIES, AND DELEGATES

—Communications between China and Europe in the Ming and Qing Dynasties

In the Ming Dynasty, many European missionaries came to China preaching Christianity to locals in coastal provinces such as Guangdong. Matteo Ricci (利玛窦) was one of the most prominent missionaries in China. In order to win support from scholars and government officials, Ricci and many others opted to combine Christian preaching with Western studies. Priests therefore became the focal point of dialogue between China and Europe. In the era of the Kangxi Emperor, the government sent its first official delegates to visit Europe.

1. MATTEO RICCI AND HIS FELLOW MISSIONARIES IN CHINA

Christianity's spread in China can be categorized into three main periods. The first was during the Tang Dynasty with the arrival of Nestorianism (known as Jingjiao in Chinese). The second was during the Yuan Dynasty with the spread of the Church of the East (referred to as the Yelikewen Church). The third was in the mid-Ming Dynasty when Catholicism was introduced.

Roman Catholicism was introduced to China in the mid-Ming era as Matteo Ricci laid the foundation for Catholic teaching in China. He was born in AD 1552 in Italy, and became a member of the Society of Jesus when he was 19. In AD 1582, Ricci was sent by the Church to Macao, then a Portuguese colony. Whilst there, he received training on Chinese culture. The Society of Jesus was a scholarly religious congregation of the Catholic Church whose members were called Jesuits. The congregation ended in AD 1783. Jesuits were active for around 200 years in China, having experienced the transit from the Ming to the Qing era.

In AD 1583, Ricci and his fellow priest Michele Ruggieri (罗明坚) traveled to Guangzhou from Macao. They presented local officers with a world map and some other new gadgets which were met with amazement. When they realized it was difficult to preach Christianity in Guangzhou, they left for Zhaoqing, where they were welcomed by Prefect Wang Pan (王泮). In AD 1585, Ricci built the first Catholic church in China. It was called the Church of Flora (仙花寺), located near Xi River.

Matteo Ricci set up a library in the church where he displayed world maps, Western books, and astronomic instruments. Ricci explained everything in Cantonese, which amazed his audiences. The world maps he brought were an

Portrait of Matteo Ricci

eye-opener to the local people too, who had never heard of other countries before. There were many believers and doubters. Upon request from Prefect Wang Pan, Ricci translated the maps into Chinese. He put China at the center of the map and named it the *Complete Terrestrial Map* (山海輿地全图). This was the first world map in Chinese. Besides preaching, Ricci and Michele Ruggieri also composed a Sino-Portuguese dictionary—the first Chinese-foreign language dictionary in history. It was their invention to use Latin alphabets for the pronunciation of Chinese characters (later adopted in the creation of *pinyin*). Matteo Ricci also gave himself a Chinese name—Limadou.

In AD 1589, Limadou left Zhaoqing under pressure from local scholars who had turned against him. He then went to Shaozhou and built a second catholic church there. He translated *The Four Books* into Latin and introduced Chinese culture to the Europeans. *The Four Books* was a combination of four Chinese classics—*Great Learning, Doctrine of the Mean, Analects,* and *Mencius.* After six years in Shaozhou, Limadou set out for Beijing. However, China was at war with Japan at the time. Limadou reached as far as Nanjing and then finished in Nanchang.

In AD 1597, Limadou was promoted to Head of the Society of Jesus in the Greater China area, independent from the church in Macao. The Roman church asked him to go to Beijing and seek permission from the Emperor to preach Christianity in China Proper.

The following year, with the help from Wang Zhongming, then-administrator at the Ministry of Rites in Nanjing, Limadou set out for Beijing again. However, his visit was in vain: as the war continued, the authorities grew suspicious of foreigners. Limadou stayed in Beijing for two months. After learning that it was impossible to see the Emperor, he returned to Nanjing. During his stay, he tried his best to make friends with local scholars, including Xu Guangqi.

In AD 1601, Limadou made for Beijing a second time. This time he succeeded in giving the Emperor many presents from the West, including paintings of the Holy Mother, the Bible, two cuckoo clocks, a world map, and a piano. Apart from these, Limadou submitted a proposal to the Emperor, stating that he was willing to serve the Chinese Empire with his knowledge of the West and other matters; he did not mention Christianity. However, despite all his efforts, he didn't succeed in seeing the Emperor himself.

During his stay in Beijing, Limadou made friends with many scholars, including Xu Guangqi and Li Zhizao. These scholars were earnest in learning Western knowledge and technology from Limadou; together they translated many Western science books into Chinese. And in the end, they became Catholics themselves.

In AD 1605, it was recorded that more than 200 people converted to Catholicism. In AD 1610, Limadou died at the age of 59. Emperor Wanli granted a 20-*mu* (亩, one *mu* = 580 square meters) piece of land outside Fuchengmen in Beijing as a cemetery to host Limadou's tomb. The next year, the Emperor sent officers to attend Limadou's funeral.

The attitudes of the Catholic church toward traditional Chinese culture played a significant role in the fate of Christianity in China. During the Ming and Qing dynasties, Confucianism had become the mainstream of society, and the worship of ancestors and Confucius had long been the core of traditional Chinese culture, and traditional rituals were highly recognized by all levels of society. The Catholic doctrine was against idolatry, which created a serious confrontation with traditional Chinese culture. Limadou made a compromise in order to preach Christianity in China. First of all, he made friends with scholars and won their understanding. Second, he allowed Chinese scholars to worship their ancestors and Confucius. Third, he turned Western knowledge and technology into his "passport" in China before preaching Christianity to the locals. And most important of all, he opposed to preaching by force. It means that politically, one should support the rule of the Chinese emperor and the bureaucratic class; academically, one should have a high level of expertise; and in daily life, one should adapt flexibly to China's local customs and cultures.

2. Cannons from the West

The Chinese invented gun powder and fireworks, which spread to Europe in the 14th century via the Arabs. In the 16th century, improved Western firearms started to appear in China.

The earliest Europeans to have reached China's southeastern regions were the Portuguese and Spanish. Jesuit missionary Ai Rulüe recorded as "Folangcha" in the *Record of Foreign Lands*: "Folangcha is located in the northeast is Folangcha. It starts from 41 degrees to the south, goes up to 50 degrees to the north, starts from 15 degrees to the west, and reaches 31 degrees to the east, covering a total of 11,200 *li*. The land was divided into sixteen routes, with more than fifty states under it. Its capital city was called Balisi. The name of the capital city of the city was called "Folangji." ... Since the country was located in Eurasia, the Muslims generally called the Westerners Folangji, and the cannon also followed this name.[1] This shows that Folangji originally referred to the area of France today. The Arabs called all the Europeans or Western Christians Franks. The Ming Dynasty, influenced by the Arabs who came to do business with them, also used this name and called the Western artillery "Folangji."

In May AD 1517, the Portuguese entered the coastal areas of Guangdong Province in the name of paying tribute to the Emperor of Ming.

> In the beginning, the Folangji's ship was 10 feet long and 3 feet wide. There were more than 40 sculls on both sides, and 34 cannons were placed around. The bottom of the ship was pointed, and the two sides were flat, so that it was not afraid of the wind and waves. The place where people stood was defended by boards, so that they could not be afraid of the rocks. Each boat was manned by 200 men, and there were many sculls, so they could go fast even though there was no wind. When each cannon was raised and fired, the bullets fell like rain, and it was invincible, so the ship was called Centipede Ship. The cannon barrel was made of copper, the larger one was more than 1,000 pounds, the middle one was more than 500 pounds, and the smaller one was 150 pounds. For each cannon, four cannons were used, and the size of the cannon barrel was made of iron. The cannon shells were made of iron inside and boats outside and were eight pounds in size. The method of making gunpowder was different from that of China. The cannon could go more than a hundred feet away once it was raised and released, and wood and stone were broken.[2]

However, when their ships entered Dongguan County, they fired at locals. During this incident, Guangdong security defense officers realized their weapons were outdated and could not match Portuguese firepower.

---

1. Ai Rulüe, *Record of Foreign Lands*, annotated by Xie Fang, vol. 2 (Beijing: Zhonghua Book Company, 1996), 82.
2. Yan Congjian, *Records of Unusual Regions*, annotated by Yu Silai, vol. 9 (Beijing: Zhonghua Book Company, 1993), 321.

Chapter Seven

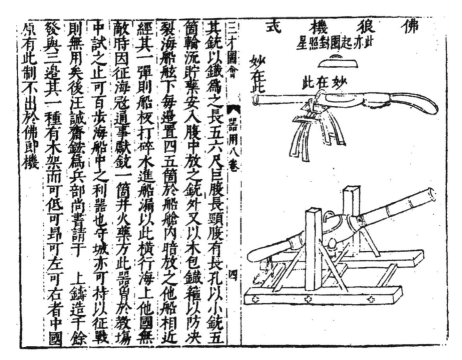

Portuguese cannons

The Chinese officers were determined to improve their equipment. When He Ru, Inspector of Dongguan, was collecting tax on the Portuguese ship, he met two Chinese. They were called Yang San and Dai Ming and had stayed with the Europeans long enough to understand the technology behind making cannons. This was reported to Provincial Inspector Wang Hong who planned a scheme to recruit Yang San and Dai Ming.

He Ru sent his man disguised as a wine peddler to approach the Portuguese ship. He got in touch with Yang San, who expressed a willingness to return to China. As planned, a small boat picked up Yang San and Dai Ming at midnight. And this was the beginning of cannon production in China.

In AD 1522, Ming armies defeated the Portuguese in Xinhui County, Guangdong. They confiscated the Portuguese warship as a trophy together with cannons loaded on the ship. This kind of cannon is "five or six *chi* long, with a huge belly and long neck. There are long holes in the belly, with five small cannons taking turns to store the medicine, and put it into the belly. Outside the cannon, it was wrapped in wood and iron to prevent it from breaking. Under the side of the ship, four or five of them were placed in the cabin of the ship, and they were placed secretly, so that if other ships were close to them, the shipboard would be broken, and the water would enter the ship. This is the way to travel the sea; other countries are invincible."[3] The Ming army put the Folangji machine into the schoolyard (military drill ground) for testing, and the effective range of this Folangji machine was about 100 paces. In April AD 1524, the Ming government started to build cannons in Nanjing. All the workers were recruited from Guangdong.[4] In AD 1530, the Ming armies started to copy the Portuguese warship. He Ru was placed in charge of production; he had been promoted to Magistrate of Shangyuan County in Nanjing.

He Ru's former boss, Wang Hong, had been promoted to the position of deputy chief of the Surveillance Bureau. Wang proposed to the Emperor that the Nine Garrisons on the northern borders should be equipped with cannons in order to guard against invasions from nomadic tribes:

> The state set up important towns along the northern border of the river, such as Gansu, Yansui, Ningxia, Datong, and Xuanfu, each of which had no less than 60,000 to 70,000 officers and troops, and set up dun and fortresses, which seemed to be well thought out for the purpose of defense. However, whenever the invaders entered, the soldiers could not defend themselves, and the damage to the official army moved by thousands. What is the reason for this? The first pier is not to contain the soldiers, only for the lookout place. And the fortress is not ready, and the weapons cannot reach far, so they are often defeated. For today's sake, we should use the cannons that I have imported. Small such as 20 tumbling below, far away from 600 paces, then use the pier, each pier a cannon, with three people to guard the. Large such as 70 tumbled above, far away from five or six *li*, it is used in the city fort, each fort with three cannons, with ten guards. Five *li* a pier, ten *li* a fort, small and large, near and far, corresponding, star array, there is no empty space, the thieves will have no room for enough, can be achieved without fighting.[5]

---

3. Hu Zongxian, *Planning of Maritime Charts*, vol. 13, in *Collection of Chinese Military Texts*, book 16 (PLA Publishing House and Liaoshen Publishing House, 1987), 1257–1258.
4. See "Records of Emperor Shizong of Ming," vol. 38, *History of Ming*, book 39, 974.
5. *Veritable Records of Emperor Shizong of Ming*, vol. 117, September of the Xin Mao month in the 9th year of the Jiajing reign, in *Ming Veritable Records*, vol. 41, 2763–2765.

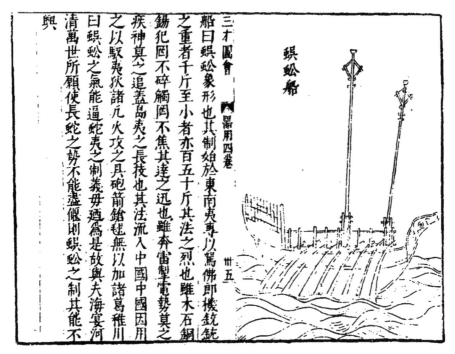

Portuguese ships

The officials of the Imperial Court could have left the issue of the army's weapons and equipment alone. The emperor appreciated Wang's petition and commended his loyalty in planning for the border, and ordered the two ministries of household and military affairs to further discuss the matter. Li Chengxun, the Minister of Military Affairs, agreed with this proposal and thought that "the Folangji cannon was really a powerful weapon in the army, so it was advisable to request the borders to repair the fortresses and allocate soldiers to be taught to guard the fortresses as suggested." Jiajing Emperor accepted the proposal of these two ministers and ordered: "the governors of the borders to make every effort to repair the fortress and not to mislead the borders with false stories." In September of the 15th year of Jiajing (AD 1536), 2,500 pairs of copper and iron cannons were distributed to the three sides of Shaanxi.[6]

---

6. *Veritable Records of Emperor Shizong of Ming*, vol. 191, September of the Xin Si month in the 15th year of the Jiajing reign, in *Ming Veritable Records*, vol. 42, 4041.

Ming armies continuously lost battles to Later Jin soldiers in the north. In March AD 1619, some 100,000 Ming soldiers fled after losing the battle in Liaoyang. The cannons discarded outside the fortress were taken away by the Later Jin soldiers. As a result, the total number of cannons possessed by Later Jin even surpassed the Ming Empire.

In October of the same year, Xu Guangqi, then in charge of training soldiers in Tongzhou near the capital, proposed buying Western cannons and recruiting Western soldiers to train the Chinese. However, all his proposals were tabled and didn't reach the Emperor. Therefore, Xu Guangqi sent his own men to Macao to buy four large iron cannons and invited four Portuguese artillery officers and six general officers. The Ming Dynasty called these Portuguese and British cannons with iron bullets "red foreign copper cannons" and "red foreign iron cannons." These cannons were "on *zhang* long, three or four *chi* in circumference, three inches in caliber, containing several liters of gunpowder, mixed with broken iron and lead, plus a large bullet of fine iron, also three inches in diameter and three or four *jin*. The bullet system is very ingenious, round in the middle of the cut, linked to a hundred steel bars, its length of more than a foot, the firebomb fly, the steel bar straight, sweeping and the front, 20 to 30 *li*, breaking giant wood, through the city, the attack is not destroyed."[7] Compared with the Folangji's gun, the red foreign cannon had a longer range, a higher hit rate, and greater lethality and was equipped with a sighting device.

In AD 1626, Nurhaci, founder of the Later Jin Dynasty, sent troops to attack Ningyuan. Ming armies were equipped with 11 cannons. Yuan Chonghuan, the general guarding Ningyuan, ordered soldiers to fire the cannons. Thousands of Later Jin soldiers were either killed or injured. It was the first time that Nurhaci was defeated. Emperor Tianqi of Ming was so pleased that he named these cannons as generals in defending his northern territory.

In AD 1631, Xu Guangqi proposed building an artillery based on cannons. "Each battalion used one hundred and twenty double-wheeled carts, one hundred and twenty artillery carts, and sixty grain carts, making a total of three hundred vehicles. If the enemy uses firearms, they will be defended by the law; if

---

7. "Li Zhizao's Petition on the Need for Western Cannons for Victory and Urgent Request for Aid" (1st year of Tianqi), in *Collected Works of Xu Guangqi*, vol. 1 (Shanghai: Shanghai Ancient Books Publishing House, 1984), 179.

the enemy is close, we will attack them with our infantry; if iron horsemen come, we will attack them with artillery, or we can attack them with our infantry." According to his plan, it should be composed of 15 integrated divisions with 60,000 soldiers in total. At that time, the Denglai Regional Inspector Sun Yuanhua had set up an artillery equipped with over 20 Folangji guns and over 300 cannons.

Unfortunately, one of Sun Yuanhua's subordinates, Kong Youde, led his division to support Liao. When Kong Youde's division reached Wuqiao County, he mutinied and returned to Shandong. In the next year, Kong Youde's rebels broke into Dengzhou and captured all the Western cannons in the city. In AD 1632, Kong surrendered to Later Jin, bringing with him the most advanced cannons of Ming.

In the same year, Xu Guangqi died. The task of building a modern artillery was then assumed by a German Jesuit called Johann Adam Schall von Bell (汤若望). After trial and error, Schall von Bell finally succeeded in building 40 cannons weighing over 20 kilograms each, as well as cannons of lesser weight. Later, he succeeded in making a long gun. In AD 1640, von Bell was rewarded by the Emperor for his contributions to building cannons. However, the Western-style cannons ultimately failed to save the Southern Ming regime.

After Later Jin soldiers were killed and injured by cannon fire from the Ming armies, Huang Taiji, Emperor of Later Jin, ordered his men to build cannons too. Its first batch were successfully built in AD 1631. It read: "Great General Assisted by Heavenly Blessings. Made in the auspicious dawn of spring in the fifth year of Tiancong. Overseen by the Chief Military Officer E'fu Tong Yangxing; monitored by the skirmishing officer Ding Qiming, prepared for the Emperor by Shuyin; cast by the metalworkers Wang Tianxiang and Dou Shouwei; and the blacksmith Liu Jiping." With the cannons brought by the rebel Ming officer, Kong Youde, Later Jin's strength was too much. In Chongde's first year (AD 1636, Chongzhen's nine years), Later Jin renamed Qing. In the first year of Shunzhi (AD 1644), the Qing army entered the country. In the siege, the Qing army's red cannons played a great role. Since the red-clad cannons played a great role in the siege, the rewards for the officers and soldiers were reduced accordingly: "Anyone who captures a government city with ladders will be rewarded with five men, the first with five hundred *liang* of silver, the second with three hundred and fifty *liang* ... Anyone who captures a city with red-clad cannons will be rewarded with three men, the first with two hundred *liang* of silver, the second with one hundred *liang*. The first man was rewarded with 200 *liang* of silver, the second with 100 *liang*, and the second with 50 *liang*."[8]

Although the Qing soldiers attached great importance to red foreign cannons, they also made mistakes in their daily management. On a summer day in the sixth year of Shunzhi (AD 1649), two women, Baichen's wife and Lai's wife, were herding geese in front of the Jinshui Bridge in Beijing. Out of sheer boredom, they sat on a pile of fuse cords for the red foreign cannons and started smoking. Unexpectedly, the sparks from the smoking ignited the fuse cords, leading to a massive fire. This fire consumed over 33,800 *jin* (a Chinese weight unit) of fuse cords stored there. Additionally, more than 200 artillery carts and over 120 warehouses nearby were also engulfed in flames, resulting in a total loss valued at more than 2,030 *liang* (a Chinese currency unit) of silver.[9] At that time, the expenses for a provincial government office, which included the salaries and various allowances for the seven official positions—Left and Right Governors, Manager, Examiner, Urban Officer, Chief Questioner, and Inspector—totaled just 2,841 *liang* of silver per year, covering salaries, administrative costs, and provisions for official attendants. Due to the gravity of the incident, the Ministry of Justice initially sentenced the two women responsible to be beheaded in their first trial. The Ministry of Works, starting from the top minister down to all the negligent officials, was fined from one hundred to fifty *liang* of silver and was held accountable for the losses. Emperor Shunzhi was comparatively lenient. He commuted the sentences: the woman from the Baichan's wife was sentenced to receive one hundred lashes, and the woman from the Lai family had thirty lashes. The other officials were penalized by docking their salaries for three to six months.

Qing armies improved their cannon making technology during the Kangxi Emperor's reign. In AD 1673, leaders of three southwestern provinces rebelled against the Qing government. They soon occupied the upper and mid reaches of the Yangtze. The Kangxi Emperor ordered Jesuit Ferdinand Verbiest (南怀仁) to make the cannons more transportable in the mountainous regions of South China. Ferdinand Verbiest had a Chinese name—Nan Huairen. He successfully

---

8. *Official Chronicles of Emperor Shizu of the Qing Dynasty*, vol. 54, Geng Wu on February of the 8th year of Shunzhi, in *Qing Chronicles*, book 3 (Beijing: Zhonghua Book Company, 1985), 431 (upper).
9. See *Official Chronicles of Emperor Shizu of the Qing Dynasty*, vol. 44, Yi Wei on June of the sixth year of the Shunzhi reign, in *Qing Chronicles*, book 3, 354 (below).

designed a light-weight cannon equipped with cannonballs weighing 1.5 kilos each. Altogether, 120 such cannons were built.

In AD 1680, the Kangxi Emperor ordered Nan Huairen to build more cannons. This time, Nan reduced the weight of the cannon body to around 150 kilos, which could be carried by horses and mules. In AD 1697, the Emperor reviewed a military parade near Yuquan Mountain in the suburbs of Beijing. Kangxi: "The country's military equipment cannot be the slack day, so every year must train the soldiers and practice test artillery. Your department that the eight banners, such as the President, prepare the military, I will personally read on the 18th." On the southwest side of Yuquan Mountain, the center of the flat land, hastily lined up with red-clad cannons. The horses, infantry, birdshot, and primus cade of the forward guard were lined up neatly on both flanks. Kangxi, dressed in armor, climbed to the top of Yuquan Mountain and took his seat in the yellow tent. The parade began with the sound of a conch and drums, and the troops marched together; sounding gold, the troops immediately stopped marching. This is done nine times. On the tenth occasion, the red foreign gun and other kinds of guns were practiced with live ammunition. "The army blew the conch, fired the

Portrait of the Kangxi Emperor

cannon, and fired the guns in succession, and the sound of the succession was incessant. The soldiers were also ordered to fire the red-clad cannons and other firearms, and all of them were fired at once, with a sound that shook the sky and the earth. When the cannon struck, all the trees and walls fell down in response to the sound."[10] Finally, the troops returned to their original positions. Throughout the entire drill process, the team unified, and the soldiers acted in unison. After the parade, Kangxi personally performed shooting, and five shots were hit. Then he ordered the princes, beile, and the eight banners' good shooters and 15 guards to perform hard bow shooting. Qinghai Taiji Zhashi Batuer and others also came to see the Eight Banners' military power impressed them.

3. Western Science and Technology in China

After missionaries had come to China, they participated in activities like remaking the calendar, producing cannons, and drawing maps. They enlightened Chinese scholars with contemporary science in many fields such as mathematics, astronomy, and topography. Meanwhile, they also translated Chinese classics into European languages and helped their fellow citizens better understand Chinese culture.

In this great cultural exchange between China and the West, the European geography introduced by the missionaries did not directly influence the military and political situation of the Ming and Qing dynasties like the artillery, nor did it improve China's agricultural water technology like the *Western Water Law*, but it impacted the Chinese scholars' understanding of China and the world and raised great doubts about the traditional view of China and Yi. Chinese scholars have always regarded Chinese civilization as the highest form of civilization between heaven and earth. "Those who live in the middle of heaven and earth are called China, those who live in the middle of heaven and earth are called the four barbarians, the four barbarians are outside, and China is inside."[11] China is the center of the world. The four barbarians are the "Eastern Yi," "Western Rong,"

---

10. *Imperial Instructions of the Benevolent Emperor*, vol. 16, in *Siku Quanshu*, book 411, 327 (below).
11. Shi Jie, "China Discourse," in *Collected Works of Cu Lai*, vol. 10, in *Siku Quanshu*, book 1090, 249 (below).

"Southern Man," and "Northern Di," which are in a backward state. From Zhang Qian's visit to the West in the Han Dynasty to Zheng He's seven voyages to the West in the early Ming Dynasty, the Chinese people's understanding of world geography progressed very slowly, so that the "world" consciousness centered on China within the four seas was constantly reinforced as an "illusory environment." "This is evident in the "Huayi Maps" and "Guangyu Maps" engraved in China over the ages.[12] On these maps, the area of China is located in the center of the map, and the area is very large, while the surrounding countries are blurred, and the ocean is artificially reduced.

When Limadou drew up the *Map of Mountains and Seas*, the blueprint was the European *Map of All Nations*, but in order to meet the mentality of Chinese scholars, he moved the zero-degree latitude and longitude line of Fukushima to the center of the map, and moved China to the middle of the map, with Europe, Africa, and North and South America on the two sides of the map. Wang Pan, the governor of Zhaoqing in Guangdong, printed this map and did not sell it publicly but gave it to the scholars. In AD 1585, in the *Book Compilation* compiled by Zhang Huang, volume 29 contains a full map of the mountains and seas and a map of the northern and southern hemispheres, which is probably based on Limadou's map. In AD 1602, when Li Zhizao reprinted the map, Limadou revised it according to the original map and other materials, corrected the errors of the old map, added customs and local products, enriched its content, and renamed it *Complete Map of the World*. The map was seven feet high and three feet wide and was divided into six panels in the shape of a screen. In the following year, Limadou again translated a new map, which was titled *Mystical Diagram of the Two Principles*, and had basically the same content as the previous map but with a slightly larger size.

Limadou's maps of the world were a great shock to the minds of Chinese scholars. Although China was still depicted in the center of the map, there were five continents on the map: Asia, Europe, Africa, North and South America, and Antarctica, and China was only a small part of the five continents. Although the concept of the continent of Magallanica is speculative and does not correspond to reality, the concept of the five continents, a product of the great geographic discoveries of the 16th century, was introduced into China for the first time. Thus,

---

12. See Wu Zhenhuan, *Western Geography in China during the Late Qing Dynasty* (Shanghai: Shanghai Ancient Books Publishing House, 2000), 40.

from a geographical point of view, Limadou's maps introduced a new world to the Chinese.

Limadou's map of the world introduced the concept of latitude and longitude in the West to China. In the middle of the 16th century, Europe was already using the planimetric projection method to draw maps. On the *Map of Mountains and Seas*, the lines of latitude and longitude were marked differently from the traditional Chinese square map: the latitude lines were parallel lines, while the longitude lines were curved lines. Limadou also introduced the role of latitude and longitude lines and how to divide them. He pointed out that lines of latitude and longitude should be drawn at every degree so that the location of countries or places in the world could be plotted on the map. The east-west latitude lines are parallel lines, which represent the length of the earth, with the equator as the starting line of latitude, and the north latitude is 90° up to the north pole. The north-south longitude lines are curved lines, which represent the width of the earth, and the circumference of the earth is 360° from Fukushima. The names of continents, seas, and places, such as Asia, Europa, the Mediterranean, the Nile, Romania, Rome, Cuba, Canada, the North and South Poles, the Earth, and the Atlantic Ocean, are still in use today.

The map of the world drawn up by Limadou, which also contains Chinese mapping results, is a product of the cultural exchange between East and West in the 16th century. In the preface to the map, Feng Yingjing said, "Even the teachings of the Chinese sages have never been heard of in the West, and the books of the saints of the Qian Dynasty have never been heard of by me. We have invented and benefited from each other, but it is a family of six, and our hearts are in harmony, so that the east and the west have been invigorated."[13] In the *Complete Map of the World Mystical* and *Diagram of the Two Principles*, there were many place names of China and Asia, which was not available in the Western world map before Limadou's time. In these two maps, the central part of Asia is marked with "Da Ming" and "Da Ming Hai," and the Yangtze River, the Yellow River and the Xing Su Hai, as well as the Great Wall, the Nunnery, and the Liaodong Nurgan. Therefore, Limadou's *Complete Map of the World Mystical* and *Diagram of the Two Principles* were the most complete maps of the world at that time.

---

13. Wang Mianhou, "On Limadou's 'The Complete Map of the World' and 'Mystical Diagram of the Two Principles' Inscriptions," in *Collection of Ancient Chinese Maps (Ming Dynasty)*, Cao Wanru et al. ed. (Beijing: Cultural Relics Publishing House, 1995), 109.

168 | Chapter Seven

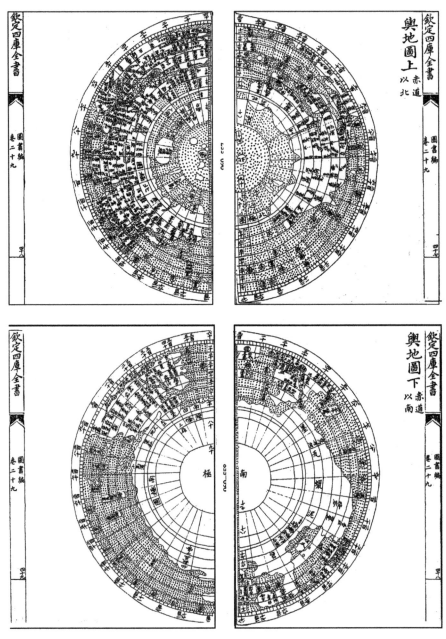

World maps drew by Limadou

Limadou not only introduced the Western world map to China, conversely, he also introduced Chinese maps to the Western world. In AD 1574, Limadou sent different kinds of Chinese maps he had collected during the years to Rome and in AD 1588, he translated a map of China into Latin.

Two other Jesuits, Giulio Aleni (艾儒略) and Nan Huairen, also significantly helped the passing of geographic knowledge to the Chinese. Like Nan Huairen, Giulio Aleni also gave himself a Chinese name—Ai Rulüe. In AD 1613, Ai Rulüe was preaching in Beijing. In AD 1623, he published a *Record of Foreign Lands*. It was China's first book on global geography. Ai Rulüe is an update on Pondy's work. The entire *Record of Foreign Lands* is in five volumes, and some editions have six.

In volume I, countries in Asia, including China and Korea, are introduced. Volume II was about Europe, introducing countries like Spain, France, and Italy. Ai Rulüe wrote in detail about European architecture, dress, food, marriage, religion, military, education, taxation, and laws. Volume III was devoted to Africa, introducing the geography and customs of Africa as well as Volume IV was for North and South America and for the first time the Chinese people introduced the process of the discovery of the American continent by the Gelong (Columbus). A part of the islands in the South Pacific and Antarctica, "their inhabitants, customs, mountains and rivers, livestock, and even birds, beasts, insects, and fish are all without legends or descriptions. As for the latitude of Antarctica, its distance, and how far or near it is, all remain unexplored and are not elaborated upon here, hoping that someone in the future might provide a detailed account."[14] Volume V is about the four seas, introducing the names of major seas, islands, marine animals, seafood, sea state, sea vessels, sea lanes, etc. The sea route introduces two routes from Europe to China: one is around the Cape of Good Hope at the southern tip of Africa, eastward through the Indian Ocean, and then northward through Southeast Asia; the other is through the Atlantic Ocean to America, and then westward through the Pacific Ocean.

In AD 1674, Nan Huairen published *Kunyu Tushuo* (*Universal Encyclopedia with Illustrations*). It was composed of two volumes. In the first, Nan explained the theory that Earth was round, and that the Earth had two poles. He also talked about earthquakes, movement of oceans, tides, and many other natural

---

14. Ai Rulüe, *Record of Foreign Lands*, annotated by Xie Fang, 142.

phenomena. The second volume was about the five continents, including their people and sceneries. In the appendix, there were maps of oceans and pictures of seafood. The first volume was taken mostly from the writings of Limadou, and the second volume mostly from Ai Rulüe. Nan Huairen added his own writings on natural phenomena to supplement the works of the two Jesuits.

Portrait of Nan Huairen

4. The Rites Controversy and Chinese Missionaries in Europe

When Limadou was preaching Christianity in China, he tried to avoid any cultural conflict by adopting a policy of accommodation. He recognized that it was Chinese custom to worship ancestors and Confucius, so he allowed Chinese converts to keep this tradition. However, many other missionaries in China disagreed with Limadou's practices. They opposed the expediency of Limadou and others, who forbade the worship of ancestors and honored Confucius. The controversy between the two schools continued from the late Ming Dynasty to the early Qing Dynasty. In Europe, the Holy See also issued several directives in this regard. However, these directives did not resolve the conflict between Chinese and Western cultures. During the era of the Kangxi Emperor, the disagreement on rites finally brought about an abrupt end to Christianity in China.[15]

In the course of the debate between the two factions of the missionaries, the Jesuits raised with the Kangxi Emperor the question of whether ancestor worship and Confucius worship were religious in nature. The Kangxi Emperor, who was described by the missionaries as "benevolent, wise, and curious," had issued an edict on March 22, AD 1692 (the thirty-first year of the Kangxi era), decreeing the protection of churches throughout the country and allowing people to practice their faith freely. Thus, missionaries were free to preach openly within the territory of the Qing Dynasty. However, Kangxi was also a cautious emperor, aware of the potential risks of a clash between two cultures, and therefore he specifically warned the missionaries to be careful in their missionary work and not to make local officials resentful and report them to the authorities. In response to the questions raised by the Jesuits, he officially replied on November 30, AD 1700, that the Chinese rite of honoring the ancestors was a rite of reverence for the ancestors and was not religious in nature. The opposition, formed mainly by non-Jesuits, seized on this incident and considered it a deviant act for the Jesuits to rely on the ruling of the emperor from outside the Church instead of asking the Holy See to solve internal problems of the Church. On November 20, AD 1704, Pope Clement XI ordered the Congregation for Divine Worship to issue seven prohibitions, which forbade the use of the name "Heaven" (天) for God, the hanging of plaques with the word "To Heaven" (敬天) in churches, the worship of Confucius and ancestors by Christians, and the keeping of tablets at home by the faithful. He also sent Charles-Thomas Maillard de Tournon to China to announce the prohibition. These regulations caused a conflict between the two cultures and challenged the authority of the Chinese emperor.

At first, the Kangxi Emperor kindly received the envoys sent by the Pope. However, after the Emperor had learned that the Pope had asked him to abolish Chinese rites among native Christians, he was offended and dismissed the mission. Immediately afterward, he issued an order that missionaries in China

---

15. See Shen Fuwei, *The History of Cultural Exchange between China and the West* (Shanghai: Shanghai People's Press, 1985), 381–385.

had to obey Chinese customs, and they must not preach without permission from the Qing government.

On January 25, AD 1707, Tournon publicized the Pope's decree in Nanjing, condemning Chinese rites and Confucian rituals. The Kangxi Emperor was furious and imprisoned Tournon in Macao. On March 17, the Emperor reiterated in Suzhou that all missionaries must obey the teachings of Limadou. Those who disobeyed would be deported.[16] On the other hand, the Emperor sent Fan Shouyi and Jesuit missionary Antonio Francesco Giuseppe Provana (艾若瑟) as his envoys to the Vatican City, hoping to make peace with the Pope.

Provana also had a Chinese name—Ai Ruose. He came to Macao in AD 1695 at the age of 33. When he was preaching in Shanxi, he converted Fan Shouyi, a local young man, into a believer. Since AD 1699, Ai Ruose was responsible for the parishes in Henan, Shaanxi, and Shanxi provinces. In AD 1702, he went to Beijing, became Head of the Jesuit Church there, and even won favor of the Emperor. Therefore, he was chosen as the Qing envoy to speak with the Pope.

Ai Ruose and Fan Shouyi set out in December AD 1707 from Macao. They traveled via Indonesia, the Indian Ocean, and Cape Hope in Africa, finally reaching Portugal in July AD 1708. It was February AD 1709 when they eventually arrived in the Vatican City. Ai Ruose explained to the Pope how the Kangxi Emperor saw worshiping ancestors and Confucius as rites rather than religion, and that the Emperor hoped the Pope could lift his ban on Chinese believers. Fan Shouyi recalled that the Pope felt so sorry over what had happened that he was even tearful and told them he had never asked Tournon to act in such way.[17]

It seemed that things would turn out well for the Chinese envoys. However, the Pope noticed that the papers submitted by Ai Ruose did not have any seals from the Qing government. He became suspicious and detained Ai Ruose in the Vatican for 32 months. After that, Ai Ruose stayed in Milan and Turin for another three years. In March AD 1709, the Pope stated that his ban on Chinese rites had to be observed closely. In March AD 1715, the Pope outlawed any further discussions. Missionaries should no longer appeal to the Vatican Church on the conflict of rites in China. In August AD 1716, the Pope's decree reached missionaries in Guangdong Province and all had to obey.

---

16. Shen Fuwei, *The History of Cultural Exchange between China and the West*, 384.
17. Yan Zonglin, *History of Communications between China and the West*, 116.

The Kangxi Emperor didn't believe any messages passed on to him regarding the Pope because he only trusted Ai Ruose, who never came back. "When I sent Ai Ruose to Rome, it was only after his return that I believed and made a decision." In September AD 1716, an open letter was written in Manchu, Chinese, and Latin, printed on wood, and stamped with the Guan Fang of the governor of Guangdong, which is commonly known as the "red ticket." At that time, 150 copies of this "red ticket" were printed and distributed to Westerners in Catholic churches and decent merchants who came to Guangzhou and Macau to do business, and they were to take them to Europe and convey them to the Papal. Upon hearing the new Papal decree, the Emperor made his own decision. He forbade Catholic missionaries to preach in China. In AD 1720, he escalated the ban to all foreigners.[18]

The letters from the Kangxi Emperor traveled slowly. They didn't reach the Pope until AD 1718. Realizing his mistake, the Pope set Ai Ruose free. However, Ruose was told that he shouldn't tell anyone that he was detained in the Vatican City. Instead, he should tell the Kangxi Emperor that he stayed in Europe because of illness.

Ai Ruose and Fan Shouyi went to Portugal where they were met with great hospitality. The King of Portugal not only sent a ship to escort them back to China but also prepared seven boxes of presents for the Kangxi Emperor. Unfortunately, less than one year after they had set out from Portugal, Ai Ruose died in February AD 1720 after they had passed Cape Hope. Fan Shouyi reached Guangzhou in June of the same year, but he didn't arrived in Beijing until September. Kangxi was in the summer palace in Rehe. Fan Shouyi rushed to Rehe on the fifth day of September, on September 11, kowtowing to Kangxi. Kangxi asked for a long time.

The Pope's delegates headed by Carlo Ambrogio Mezzabarba (嘉乐) met with the Kangxi Emperor in March AD 1721. Mezzabarba was also known to the Chinese as Jiale. In November, he proposed a more lenient eight rules for Chinese converts. This made the Kangxi Emperor furious since he perceived it as an offence to traditional Chinese rites. In June AD 1742, Pope Benedict XIV decreed the cancellation of the eight indulgences.

In January AD 1724, the Yongzheng Emperor, son of Kangxi, ordered all foreign missionaries to leave China within six months. "The faithful only know you

---

18. See Shen Fuwei, *The History of Cultural Exchange between China and the West*, 384.

(the priests, Baduomin, and others), and in case of trouble on the frontier, the people will follow your orders. Although we do not need to worry about this now, if thousands of warships come to our shores, there will be a great danger." All successive Emperors, including Qianlong, Jiaqing, and Daoguang, forbade Catholic preaching in China.[19]

At first, it was only controversial among different schools of the Catholic Church. Unfortunately, the disputes escalated to such an extent that the Qing Emperors forbade any preaching of Christianity in China because they felt that traditional Chinese culture was violated. It wasn't until December 8, 1939, that the Roman Church lifted the ban on Chinese converts, who after that could worship their ancestors and Confucius openly.

Fan Shouyi remained in Beijing after meeting the Kangxi Emperor. He was often asked by royal family members to talk about his trips to Europe. After talking more, Fan Shouyi thought of writing a travelogue—"Shenjian Lu" ("Witnessing Europe"). However, when he finished writing, none of the royal family members helped him publish it. Fan died in AD 1753. The original manuscript of his essay "Shenjian Lu" was taken to Rome, where it lies on the shelves of the library, enclosed in a book called *The Nomenclature*. In 1937, a Chinese man called Yan Zonglin discovered Fan's journals—they were tucked within a book in a Roman library. The journals, written 200 years ago, were eventually printed and published in 1941.[20] This travelogue, although slightly thin, and not detailed enough, recollections may be wrong, but this is after all the Kangxi years of Chinese people in Western Europe, living and studying perceptions.

The first European country Fan Shouyi visited was Portugal. He was amazed by its fountains, stone churches, and golden statues of the Holy Family. "When I landed at the Jesuit house, the monks were as attentive as ever, and they sent me silverware to settle down. The view was magnificent, and it was called a rich country, with everything. There were many springs and caves, and the houses were all three or four stories, and the mansions of princes and kings were even more beautiful. If the Church of God, the Church of Our Lady, and the Church of the Saints are purely made of stone, they are very strange and exceptional, and

---

19. See Shen Fuwei, *The History of Cultural Exchange between China and the West*, 385.
20. See Yan Zonglin, "Record of Personal Observations" annotations, in *History of Sino-Western Exchange*, 187–198.

all the carvings are made of gold and silver. There were many monasteries and hundreds of monks in each of them, and there were also schools of the fourth grade of elementary school, the second grade of secondary school, and the third grade of university. There were also several welfare institutions which were very large, and many rich gardens." These descriptions are very similar to the accounts of the first people to leave the country after the Opium War. The King of Portugal met with the Chinese Jesuits several times. Apart from being stunned by the grandeur of the royal palace, Fan also noticed some differences in the rites between the Chinese and the Portuguese royal courts. In China, government officials had to kowtow to the Emperor, while their Portuguese counterparts only had to bow to the King.

A few months later, Fan Shouyi came to Spagna (now Spain) via the Strait of Gibraltar. After living here for two months, he entered the border of Italy and began to travel overland, entering Rome via Pisa. As a cleric, Fan Shouyi recorded a large number of religious buildings: "When I arrived here (Rome) for two days, I met with the king and was given a favorable reception and ordered to see the palace, which had tens of thousands of houses inside and outside, and was so tall and strange that it was difficult to propose. There are many gardens, a large library, and a large kitchen, regardless of the number of scriptures they have, even the bookcases and boxes, it is difficult to mention. Since its opening, the history of all the nations of the world has been fully available." "The Catholic Church and the Church of Our Lady of the Angels are beautiful both inside and outside, and the altar is a sight to behold. The altar is probably made of stone, and the altar is made of precious stone. The offerings are all gold and silver. The Jesuits have ten houses and three churches. The vessels used in the churches, and the garments, were covered with jewels and gold." "There is a church of St. John of the Cross, near the palace of the ancient kings, which is deep and large, carved into the white stone of the Twelve Apostles, with a repository of sacred objects and iron doors on all sides."

The furnishings and clothing of the secular houses in Rome also attracted Fan Shouyi's attention: "In the houses of the princes, the walls were decorated with embroidered satin, the benches with gold flowers, the treasures were priceless, and the beds and tents were decorated with trillions of dollars. The carriages and saddles of the people in and out of the house were too beautiful to be compared. The ambassadors and servants, each with clothes and hats." "And where the ambassadors of various countries, they were very flashy, for the glory of the king. All the goods of the neighboring countries were provided. The handsome people of the neighboring countries gathered in the city."

The city's public gardens and ancient ruins were also imprinted into Fan Shouyi's mind one by one. "There are many scenes in the gardens inside and outside the city, repaired every year, spring and summer rest, set out the treasures." The merits of the city's public gardens are also well documented in the writings of people who have gone global in modern times. "People made a high beam, more than ninety *li* long, to draw water from the great springs of the distant mountains, flowing into the city, digging holes to get the springs, cross streets pile of ancient mountains, cut stone people, four sides of the bubbling water, the street paving stone, each family has water law." The "man-made a high beam" refers to the Claudia waterway, leading Sopiago water into the Roman city. Qianlong years to build the Yuanmingyuan, the garden has a large number of Western water law—fountains. "There is a non-palace non-temple, its room such as a tower, round, the upper and lower five connected, there are more than 10,000 rooms, around the windows, layer by layer can see, is the ancient lion place, now has collapsed half of it." This is the famous Roman Colosseum. It was only in modern times that the Chinese went global again, and through their travelogues, these landscapes became known to the Chinese.

"There were many welfare institutions in the city, including welfare institutions for military service, for transients, and for the poor and chronically ill, all benefited from it. The rich and noble families were supported by doctors from inside and outside the city, and there were special rooms for medicine, and the beds of the patients were clean and lovely." This gives us a glimpse of the perfection of public medical and charitable institutions in Europe in the early 18th century.

Some say it is not true: "There is a complete stone hollow tower, which can accommodate a thousand people." The tower is the Stonehenge of Anton, more than 92 meters high, composed of 28 stones, carved with Roman-Germanic war designs, and hollowed out in the middle so that people could spiral up to the top of the column. The phrase "a thousand people can be accommodated" is incorrect. At the end of the Ming Dynasty, the *Record of Foreign Lands* compiled by the missionary Ai Rulüe also recorded this stone tower: "In addition, there is a tall and full stone pillar, the outer circumference of which is painted with stories of ancient kings' images, which is very impressive. Inside, it is empty, allowing a few people to climb up and down, like a pagoda."[21] The same is recorded in Nan Huairan's *Illustrations of the World Map*.

5. TULICHEN AND HIS DELEGATES IN RUSSIA

In AD 1713, the Kangxi Emperor sent a delegation to visit the Torghut, a northern Mongolian tribe in close contact with the Qing Dynasty. The Torghut clan had migrated to the lower Volga River reaches in the 1630s, forming the core of the modern Kalmyks. In this sense, it was the Qing Dynasty's first official visit to Europe.

The Torghut tribe is a branch of West Mongolia in China, one of the four tribes of the Uuld Mongols. Originally, they were nomadic to the east of Lake Balkhash and to the north of the Jungar Basin, in Tarbgti (Tacheng in Xinjiang), and around the Irtysh River. Around the 1630s, the Jungar tribe, who lived north of the Tianshan Mountains and in the Ili River Basin, grew stronger, constantly swallowing up other tribes. To avoid conflict with the Jungar tribe, the Torghut tribe left their original pastures and traveled a long distance across the Kazakh grasslands. Around AD 1630, they migrated west to the grasslands between the Volga River and the Ural River. Although the Torghut tribe was far from their homeland, they still maintained their ethnic customs, religious beliefs, and lifestyles and had close ties with the Qing government. Their connection with the mainland generally went through Kazakhstan, Jungar, and Jiayu Pass. After AD 1698, due to the obstruction of the Jungar tribal leader Tsewang Rabtan, this road was cut off. In AD 1709, the Torghut tribal envoy Samutan had to go through Russia, passing through Siberia and entering from Kuren, and entered Beijing around AD 1710 or AD 1711 after walking for more than two years on the way. Emperor Kangxi decided to send a mission to visit.

The Qing Dynasty mission to the Torghut tribe consisted of 34 people, including Yin Zhana, a student of the Crown Prince, Nayan, a member of the Lifan Academy, Tulichen, a student of the Cabinet, 2 Uuld people, 3 accompanying military officers, 4 Torghut tribes, and 22 servants. At that time, the Tsewang Rabtan of the Jungar tribe still dominated the northwest region. The shorter

---

21. Ai Rulüe, *Record of Foreign Lands*, annotated by Xie Fang, 85.

northwest route to the Volga River basin was difficult to pass, so they had to follow the route taken by the Torghut tribal mission, passing through Russia.

On June 23, AD 1712, the mission set out from Beijing, headed north through Zhangjiakou, entered the territory of the Chahar in Inner Mongolia (east of Jining in Inner Mongolia), passed through Han Mountain (south of Ulaanbaatar in Mongolia), crossed the Tula River, headed north to the present-day Ergun River and Selenge River confluence, and reached the then Sino-Russian border. On August 24, they reached the Russian border of Chukubaixing (called Selengesk by Russia, which was abandoned in the 19th century. Baixing in Manchu means village or town). The mission stayed here for five months and three days, and it was not until February 8, AD 1713, that they received a reply from Russian Emperor Peter the Great agreeing to pass. Two days later, the mission set out, divided into more than 70 sleighs, passing through Wudibaixing (Ulan-Ude, southeast of Lake Baikal), along the south bank of Lake Baikal, and arrived at Erkou City (Irkutsk, southwest of Lake Baikal) on the 25th. The Russian side proposed that the mission should proceed by water due to the muddy roads. At that time, it was winter, and the Angara River was completely frozen. The mission was stuck here, waiting for the river to thaw while building boats. On May 27, the mission went up the Angara River to the northwest. On June 15, they arrived at the confluence of the Angara and Yenisei Rivers in Yeniseysk. They then switched to the land route, crossed the watershed of the Yenisei and Ob Rivers, and reached Makosko. They then went upstream along the Ket River by water, reached the confluence of the Ket and Ob Rivers in Nalimu Baixing, and followed the Ob River downstream, passing through Surgut and Samarsko (near the confluence of the Ob and Irtysh rivers) and then went up the Irtysh River, passing through Demyansk, and arrived at Tobolsk on August 24, where they negotiated with the Russian Siberian governor Gagarin.

Eight days later, the mission set out, went southwest along the Tobol River to Tyumen, then along the Tula River to Yabanqin, switched to the land route again, passed through Feyeer and Verkhoturye, and crossed the Ural Mountains. After passing through Solikamsk, they continued southwest, passing through Kazan and Symbirsk, and arrived near the Torghut tribe in Saratov on January 2, AD 1714. The winter grasslands of the Volga River were covered with vast snow, and the mission could only stay here for the winter. On June 27, AD 1714, after the river thawed, the mission set out again and crossed the Volga River. On July 12, they reached their destination, the residence of Ayuka Khan, Manuzhahai.

The journey through Russia's Siberian territories took the delegates three years to complete. They reached their destination on July 12, AD 1714 and delivered the Kangxi Emperor's messages to Ayuka Khan, chief of the Torghut. When the Chinese envoy returned to Beijing, it was already April AD 1715.

Before the departure of the mission, the Kangxi Emperor issued a very detailed decree, the content of which was mainly in six aspects: first, to express gratitude to the Torghut for sending the envoy Samudan to pay tribute; second, the issue of sending back the nephew of the Ayuka Arabszur was being negotiated with Russian merchants and Tsewang Rabtan; third, if the Ayuka proposed an alliance against Tsewang Rabtan, it should be politely declined; fourth, if the Russian tsar wanted to send an envoy to receive the mission, it could be agreed, and when receiving it, it should be emphasized that China "is based on loyalty, filial piety, benevolence, righteousness, and faith, and respect for the conduct, and governance of the country and the people are based on this fundamental." Fourthly, if the Russian Tsar sends an envoy to receive the mission, he may agree to do so, and when he does so, he should emphasize that China "is based on loyalty, filial piety, benevolence, righteousness, and faith, and respects its conduct, and that the country is governed by this principle, and that the people are at peace and love peace, and that Russia may transfer its border troops to the west as far as possible; fifthly, the mission personnel should behave in a non-condescending manner, and should not accept gifts, and their personal conduct should be strictly regulated; sixthly, the mission should investigate the Russian state during its journey. The mission had to investigate the Russian situation on the way, "the livelihood of the Russian people, the geographical situation, must also be noted."

Mission, it can be said that the strict implementation of Kangxi's instructions, completed the task. After returning to Beijing, Kangxi received the main members of the delegation and gave them an imperial meal to reward them. Tulichen will be seen and heard on this trip, with the Manchu and Chinese languages written *Record of Foreign Lands* presented to the Kangxi Emperor. The *Record of Foreign Lands* was published in the Yongzheng years, and soon, Europe had a French, Russian, English, and German translation. Since then, there are also a variety of translations of Japanese. Therefore, although Tulichen was only the second or third person in the mission, later people called the mission "Tulichen Mission."[22] Tulichen made several missions to the Russian border colony of Chukubashi in the early years of the Kangxi and Yongzheng dynasties. In the 22nd year of the Qianlong reign (AD 1757), the Qing army put down the Junggar rebellion. Twenty-four years (AD 1759), recovered the South Tianshan Road. So far, the territory of the Qing Dynasty included the North and South Tianshan Road. In AD 1770, the Torghut, who had been settled in the Volga River valley for 140 years, finally returned to the Ili region the following year under the leadership of Vorbashikhan, who was unable to withstand the Russian oppression and was properly settled by the Qing government.

The *Record of Foreign Lands* is a detailed account of what Tulichen and his party saw and heard in Russia, including all the settlements, mountains and rivers, landscapes, climate, flora and fauna, products, ethnic groups, population, customs, religions, transportation, and soldiers of the places they passed through, and is the first and most detailed geographical work on northern Eurasia in China. In particular, the map of northern Eurasia included at the beginning of the volume was evaluated by Europeans as being no less accurate than the maps of this region drawn by Western Europeans at the same time and sometimes even slightly more accurate.

The geography of northern Eurasia was already vaguely known in China in the pre-Qin period. In the Han Dynasty, Su Wu lived in the North Sea (Lake Baikal) for a long time. During the reign of Emperor Taizong of the Mongolian Yuan Dynasty, the Mongolian Heduan entered the Arctic Ocean region and set up the "North Sea" surveying station near 64°N in AD 1279, but these activities left only some place names and simple records. The *Record of Foreign Lands* records the area in considerable detail. Tulichen saw the phenomenon of extreme daylight in Yeniseysk. "This place is one month away from the North Sea Ocean, around the summer solstice, the night is not very dark, although the sunset and the night are deep, can still game, not a few moments, the East is the dawn and sunrise. The North Sea is the Arctic Ocean, Yeniseysk's geographical location is close to 60° north latitude, about 3,000 *li* from the Arctic Ocean, which is indeed a "January course." At sunset and late at night, people can still sit and play chess.

---

22. Zhao Yongfu, "Tulichen," in *Chinese Geographers through the Ages*, Tan Qixiang ed., vol. 3 (Shandong: Shandong Education Press, 1990), 44–58.

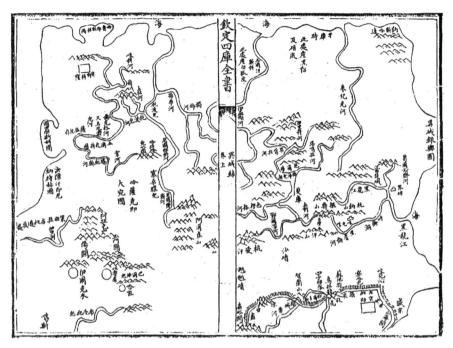

Map on the Front Page of "Record of Foreign Lands" by Tulichen

Tulichen vividly described the phenomenon of polar day with his own eyes. Another record about the animal, probably Tulichen from the Russian side of the inquiry: "the coldest in the north, there is a beast, walking in the ground, meet the Yang Qi will die. The body is large, weighing 10,000 pounds, and the bone is very white and moist, similar to ivory, soft, not much damage, every in the riverside soil to get it. In Russia, the bones are used to make bowls, plates, combs, and grates. The flesh is the coldest and can be eaten by people to get rid of fever. The Sanskrit name is Mamun Kubo, and the Chinese name is Shuoshu."[23] The "mammoth," also known as the woolly mammoth, is an ancient vertebrate that lived during the Quaternary glacial period. Because Siberia was covered in snow and ice all year round, individuals were often found intact in the permafrost, with flesh and skin as fresh as if they had just died. The mammoths were believed to have lived underground and to have died when they encountered sunlight. This is the earliest and most detailed record of the mammoth in the literature of

---

23. Tulichen, *Record of Foreign Lands* (Part One), in *Siku Quanshu* version, vol. 594, 808 (below).

various countries, according to some experts. It was a pity that the Emperor was more interested in descriptions of mammoths than what Tulichen wrote about the advanced military equipment of Russia.

The Qing Emperors were satisfied with the status quo, unaware that countries had made great progress in the industrial revolution. For example, the Qianlong Emperor, grandson of the Kangxi Emperor, also showed no interest in the cannons and rifles presented to him by the British government. The strength of the Qing armies continued to fall in the following generations. When the British fleets appeared in the South China Sea, the Qing Empire was completely unprepared for this modern form of warfare.

After writing the book *Record of Foreign Lands*, Tulichen presented it to the Kangxi Emperor. Future generations of historians as the "Shengshi wise master," "enlightened monarch" of Kangxi, in the sixtieth year of Kangxi, also with ministers relish: "now the Eros near the sea in the northern part of the rat such as elephants, cave to walk, see the wind and the sun is dead. Its bone like ivory, the natives to its bone bowl, plate, comb, grate, I personally saw its ware, then believe it to be true."[24] Words used, and the above quoted "foreign records" is very similar to the record. This shows that the twilight of Kangxi must have read this book carefully, and memory is still very strong, the polar day, mammoth, and other things are still very interesting. Tulichen's *Record of Foreign Lands* is not only a detailed account of Russian geographical phenomena, but also a record of some political and military conditions in Russia. In November AD 1714, when the mission stopped in Tobol on its way back to China, it had another long talk with the Russian governor of Siberia, Kagarin, about a wide range of topics, including the military situation of the two countries. "We replied that there were many types of firearms and cannons used in China, and all the items, such as bows, arrows, swords, and guns, were used. With the enemy, the degree of their sure hit, then the cannon; closer, before the gun shooting arrows." Kagarin said: "I also used to shoot arrows in Russia, but since the present Khan took office, it has been abandoned for more than 20 years."[25] From these words, it is reflected that the equipment of the Tsarist Russian army had been renewed by the time of Peter

---

24. *Chronicle of the Holy Ancestor of the Qing*, vol. 291, March of the 60th year of Emperor Kangxi's reign on the Ji Chou day, in *The Qing Chronicles*, book 6, 832.
25. Tulichen, *Record of Foreign Lands* (Part Two), in *Siku Quanshu* version, vol. 594, 838 (above).

the Great, and the difference between the armaments of the Russian and Chinese armies in terms of weapons and equipment had been more than 20 years, and the Qing soldiers had fallen behind in terms of weapons and equipment and battle formations.

It is difficult to understand whether Kangxi, the "Great Emperor of the Qing Dynasty," when reading the *Record of Foreign Lands*, besides being interested in the mammoth, paid attention to the words of Kagarin and was alerted to the difference in equipment between the Russian and Chinese armies. Kagarin's words do not seem to have attracted the attention of Kangxi. The Qing army construction and weaponry remained in the original state and no significant changes in the initiative. Qianlong was Kangxi's favorite grandson, and in AD 1793, the British government sent a Macartney mission to China. The British government prepared a large number of gifts for Qianlong, including Mauser guns, repeating guns, brass cannons, howitzers, and other advanced light and heavy weapons and models of warships in the world. In his later years, Qianlong was so complacent about the "Ten Perfect Martial Arts" that he did not care about the "tributes" from the Western "barbarians," and after watching the demonstration, he sent all these weapons and models to the Yuanmingyuan warehouse. After watching the demonstration, all these weapons and models were sent to the Yuanmingyuan warehouse and sealed up. Once again, the Qing government lost the opportunity to learn about the West. On the other hand, the quality of training of Qing soldiers was declining. In the late Qianlong period, when the emperor and the emperor's son, Jiaqing, were reviewing the battalions in Hangzhou, archery was still an important competition for the Qing soldiers. In the presence of the emperor and the emperor's son, the Qing soldiers performed "shooting arrows in vain, and the galloping horses fell to the ground." This sign of decline in the Qing army was particularly memorable to Yan, who mentioned it to his ministers after his accession to the throne as the Jiaqing Emperor. However, Jiaqing was already powerless to change the decline of the Qing army with his ability. During the Daoguang period, more than 120 years after the late Kangxi years, when the world's most advanced and well-trained British naval fleet appeared in the Chinese sea, the Qing army's equipment still had not improved a bit, and its combat ability was not the same as before.

CHAPTER EIGHT

TRAINS, RAILWAYS, AND CONTEMPORARY CHINESE POLITICS

In AD 1840, fighting broke out between China and developed Western nations. It was known to the Chinese as the First Opium War. The British fired cannons at China's southern islands and open the closed doors of the Qing Dynasty. Western civilization, accompanied by cannons, changed China profoundly. Such imported goods and services as telegraphs, steamships, railways, post offices, airplanes, and automobiles, altered the lives of millions of Chinese. Among all these, railways had the greatest impact on China's society; they not only improved transportation systems but also influenced China's political and social status quo.

1. **WUSONG RAILWAYS AND CULTURAL CLASHES BETWEEN EAST AND WEST**

Trains and railways were important milestones in European industrial revolution. Steam locomotives laid the foundation for the invention of trains, while the circulation of goods and free movement of people provided market demand for railways.

On September 27, AD 1825, the world's first public railway driven by steam locomotives was officially put into use. Its lines connected collieries near Shildon with Stockton-on-Tees and Darlington in Britain. Railways had many advantages over other forms of transport. They were fast, punctual, and not much affected by the weather, and most of all, they could carry a large quantity of goods. All these benefits prompted other Western countries to follow suit.

After the First Opium War, railway technology gradually became known to the Chinese. Western merchants also came to China, trying to promote railways to Chinese government officials. In AD 1864, British engineer Robert Stevenson was invited to China by Jardine Matheson Holdings Limited to research railway construction. Later, Stevenson proposed a blueprint. The idea was to build a railway network with Hankou at the center. Geographically speaking, Hankou was almost the midpoint of China. It could be connected to Shanghai in the east, Beijing in the north, Guangzhou in the south, and Myanmar and India in the west.

Another reason why Stevenson put Hankou as the center rather than Beijing was because Hankou was an economically advanced city. It could form an economic zone with other metropolitan cities such as Shanghai, Guangzhou, and Tianjin.[1] Stevenson also wanted to connect China via railway with India, a British colony at the time. If his plans had been implemented, the British could enter China proper easily without using the sea. Knowing Stevenson's intentions, Chinese government officials opposed his plans. However, most Chinese officials had never heard of railways. As a result, Stevenson's plans were tabled. Frankly speaking, though, his plans had some merits. For example, it might significantly improve local economies. Many years later, China did construct railways connecting Hankou and Guangzhou, as well as other transportation hubs.

As Stevenson's plans had failed, Western merchants thought about building a real railway to demonstrate its advantages to the Chinese. In August AD 1865, a British merchant called Durand built a 500-meter-long railway outside Xuanwumen in Beijing. The train, however, had to be pulled by man-power because it was not equipped with locomotives. The noise of the compartments moving on the rails shocked local audiences. Many people regarded the train as a monster. In the end, Beijing guards ordered the railway to be demolished.

Despite this unfortunate incident in Beijing, the first public railway in China was officially put into use in Shanghai shortly afterward. Shanghai was only a mid-sized city before AD 1840. Since the 1830s, the British had been looking for an ideal spot along China's coast in terms of politics, economy and military

---

1. Mi Rucheng, *Railways in Contemporary China*, vol. 1 (China Taipei: Wenhai Press, 1977), 5.

affairs. Shanghai was on their shortlist for this sought after location. After the Qing government lost the First Opium War, five cities were forced to open as ports to Western countries—Shanghai was one of them.

On 17 November AD 1843, Shanghai Port was officially opened. One disadvantage of the port was that ships were easily stranded in Huangpu River due to its thick, sandy residue. In the early days of the port, foreign ships were mainly sailing ships, with an average tonnage of 300 tons and a draft of 10 feet or less. Meanwhile, the sand residue in Shanghai became thicker and thicker. Foreign embassies and chambers of commerce had urged the local Qing government to clear the sand residue. The Qing government naively believed that the accumulation of silt could prevent foreign warships from entering the Huangpu River, thinking it was Heaven's way of protecting Shanghai. Additionally, the Qing didn't have enough money for the clearing; somewhat conveniently (for the Qing), the sand residue only affected bigger Western ships, not smaller ones. Therefore, government officials held an indifferent attitude toward the status quo.

Western merchants thought about a plan B. They wanted to build a railway from Shanghai to Wusong Port where the bigger ships disembarked. In this way, ships did not have to enter the Huangpu River. Instead, they could discharge

Locomotives used on the Songhu Railway

cargo in Wusong, transport the goods to Shanghai by railway, and then further into other areas along the Yangtze.

In March AD 1866, British diplomat Sir Rutherford Alcock (阿礼国) submitted a request to the Foreign Office of the Qing government, asking for permission to build a 30-*li* railway between Wusong Port and Shanghai funded by British investment. However, his request was turned down.

Shanghai also aroused interest in America. In AD 1872, with support from the American Ambassador and the State Department, Oliver Bradford, then-Vice-Consul-General of the American Consulate in Shanghai, established the so-called Wusong Company. However, due to financial difficulties, the company was later sold to Jardine Matheson Holdings Limited and was renamed Wusong Road Company.

Its board members knew that the Qing government would refuse to build a railway. Therefore, they lied to Qing government officials and said they were constructing a road only. The officials believed this and sold them the rights for road construction from Hongkou of Shanghai to Wusong Port. In March AD 1873, the company bought the land stretching from these two cities—at 14 meters in width and 14.9 kilometers in length. On January 20, AD 1876, tracks were laid on the rails. On June 30, the section of railway from Hongkou Tianfei Temple (located north of the current Henan Road Bridge) to Jiangwan Xu Family Garden was completed, with a total length of 5 kilometers.

Back then, trains were powered by coal or charcoal. The Chinese referred to them as "Fire Chariots." There were fences built along the railways, which were 4 *chi* (尺, one *chi* = 31.1 cm) in width. At first, every train had only 5 compartments. Later, it was extended to 8 or 9 compartments, each accommodating 30–40 people.

On June 30, AD 1876, the railway was first used publicly. All passengers were foreigners; it took them 17 minutes to reach Jiangwan from Shanghai. On July 1, all passengers were Chinese—having been invited by Wusong Road Company. The *Shun Pao* reporter's pen has a detailed report: "Shortly after one o'clock, I, along with Mr. Chu and Mr. Chen, went to Hongkou. At that time, there weren't many people around. We saw a total of five passenger vehicles … Among the attendees were women, children, and even courtesans from the brothels, their heads adorned with magnolia and gardenia flowers, emanating a pleasant fragrance … Suddenly, we heard the sound of a horn, and Westerners nearby

Scenic views in and around Shanghai

also blew whistles. The vehicle then started to move. Initially, it moved slowly but gradually picked up speed. All we could hear was the loud noise of wheels on tracks, and in a flash, it sped away like a lightning bolt. Both the passengers and onlookers were all smiles, expressing their amazement and considering this experience unparalleled. It took fifteen minutes to reach Jiangwan. By the time we arrived, there was already a large crowd ... In a short while, the five vehicles were filled to capacity, with some even standing in the aisle. Yet, more people kept coming, and the Westerners had to wave them away. As a result, many left disappointed. However, it further illustrated the public's immense fascination with novelty and innovation."[2] Farmers working in the cotton fields on both sides of the railroad suddenly saw a train full of six people passing by, stopped their work, and saluted in the direction of the railway. On December 1 of the same year, the entire line from Shanghai to Wusong was opened to traffic, with a total length of 14.5 kilometers. The first-class ticket cost 1 yuan, which could buy roughly 80 catties of rice at that time, which shows how expensive the ticket was, but it was still crowded with visitors.

Songhu Railway in the newspaper

---

2. *Shun Pao*, July 3, 1876, 2.

The railway began with a lie and was doomed to fail. During its construction, the company dug up many tombs to create space for the railway. This was extremely offensive to local Chinese, who held great respect for their ancestors and believed strongly in the importance of their resting place. They couldn't accept what the company had done: as an act of revenge, they vandalized facilities along the railway. After the completion of the Shanghai–Jiangwan section, the locomotive's chimney burst during a test run, killing and injuring some onlookers and causing a public mob. Later, the train killed a Chinese soldier who was walking along the tracks.[3] Fear started to spread among the Chinese and rumors abounded that the trains would hurt Shanghai's *feng shui* (Chinese geomancy). Chinese curiosity then turned to anger and finally they protested to local officials.

Most of the Qing government officials did not know what trains were. Even though some officials in Shanghai had actually seen the trains, they were ignorant and fearful of them—superstitious perhaps. They feared that the foreigners building roads and laying tracks would change the status quo. They were afraid of the roaring and shaking when the train started, believing these would disturb the spirits of the mountains and rivers. If these spirits were angered, droughts and floods would occur continuously, potentially leading to chaos throughout the land. One such official, called Feng Junguang, said he would rather lie on the rail track and be driven over by a train than let them continue to exist.

Foreigners in Shanghai found it hard to understand. Later, the two parties reached an agreement on the railway: it would be sold, including locomotives and compartments, to the Qing government for 285,000 *liang* of silver (两, one *liang* = 0.37 kilos). The Qing government had to complete the payment within one year. Before the fee was paid, the Wusong Road Company could continue its business.

On October 20, AD 1877, the Qing government finally cleared its payment. The Wusong Railway Company prepared a special car and invited Feng Junguang of Shanghai to inspect the whole line and carry out the handover procedures. This "not afraid of death" master resisted the temptation of the British and inspected the line in a palanquin carried by human beings, thinking that he had maintained the authority of a heavenly official. The right of way of the Wusong Railway was a correct and necessary action taken by the Qing government to protect the sovereignty of the country. However, in the fear of the Qing officials toward new

---

3. See Mi Rucheng, *Recent Chinese Railway History Materials*, vol. 1, 41.

things from abroad, in the blind and ignorant xenophobic action of some people, the Qing government was able to take the right way back. The Wusong Railway trains ran for the last time. Immediately afterward, the railway was dismantled and its parts were transported to Taiwan for preservation. The first railway in China, which had transported 160,000 passengers within one year, disappeared.

Map of Shanghai Special City zones[4]

2. Xiyuan Railway and Attitude Shifts toward Locomotion

Wusong Railway was gone. Yet the debate on trains did not cease among Qing government officials. The arguments mainly focused on whether or not China should build railways and what the pros and cons would be.

On December 3, AD 1880, then-Provincial Military Commander (later the first Governor of Taiwan), Liu Mingchuan appealed to the Emperor in favor of railway construction. "The benefits of the railroad, in transport, relief services, commerce, mining, determination of donations, and travel, cannot be described,

---

4. Collected from Bureau of Land in Shanghai, *Map of Shanghai Special Zones*, 1927.

and in the use of military especially cannot be slow. China is a vast country. The north stretches for thousands of miles, adjacent to the Russian border; the seaports of commerce, and with the common countries. Draw the border and guard; it is defensible, chasing the traffic, it is too long to reach. But once the railroad is opened, the east, west, north, and south breathe together, depending on the trend of the enemy, the camera response. Even if thousands of miles away, it can be reached in a few days; amongst millions of people, they can gather with a single call."[5] However, his opponents refuted that the Qing government didn't have the budget for railways. They also argued that railways would make people compete for luxury and fame.

In AD 1881, the first Chinese-built railway was completed. It connected Tangshan and Xugezhuang in Hubei, not far from Beijing. The purpose of this was to transport coal from the Kaiping Coal Mines in Tangshan to Xugezhuang, and then to Tanggu via canal. The coal was to support the Beiyang Fleet.

However, since Tangshan was close to royal family tombs, many people opposed the construction. Minister Li Hongzhang then put forward a compromise—to pull the trains using donkeys and horses. In this way, the noise would be kept to a minimum. Only on this condition did the Qing government agree. This was also dubbed the "Horse Railway."

In AD 1882, the Qing government finally resorted to steam locomotives. At the time, the Chinese had built their first light-weight steam locomotives by themselves, becoming the 56th country in the world to possess railways. After that, the focus of debate among Qing government officials shifted to where to build railways—in inland China, or on the borders. The Regent Empress Dowager Cixi kept silent and didn't express her opinion on the matter. Minister Li Hongzhang made every effort to convince Emperor Guangxu and Empress Dowager Cixi that trains were to their benefit.

In AD 1885, Emperor Guangxu and Empress Dowager Cixi were given a set of toy trains as a gift. Previously, the toys belonged to Li Hongzhang, who received them from an American merchant. Li then presented it to Yixuan, father of the Emperor. Yixuan was so fascinated by the gadget that he showed it to the Emperor and Empress.

---

5. "Book of Communications," vol. 1, in *History of Qing,* book 16 (Beijing: Zhonghua Book Company, 1976), 4427.

Chapter Eight

Portrait of Empress Dowager Cixi

In AD 1887, Yixuan, the Marine Minister, and Li Hongzhang took the opportunity to persuade Empress Dowager Cixi to build a railway in the royal garden of Xiyuan. The railway had a total length of 1,510 meters. In order to facilitate the daily passage of horses and cars, a "Huoan" railroad was designed. That is, the tracks were installed before the train passed, and the tracks were removed after the train passed. The railroad was called Xiyuan Railway and Ziguangge Railway. All the equipment of the whole line was imported from France, and there was one locomotive and six coaches, and the interior of the coaches was in two rows facing each other, with a capacity of 28 people, so it was a narrow-gauge train.[6] It was first estimated that the cost to build the railway would

---

6. See Yang Naiji, "The Small Railway by the Taiye Pond," *The Forbidden City*, no. 3 (1982).

reach 6,000 *liang* of silver using the budget from the Marine Ministry. However, the actual cost far exceeded the budget. The contractor, France Xinsheng, and the bank paid out about 40,000 *liang*, which is also a considerable amount of "advertising costs."

The locomotive with the dragon flag flying

In the winter of AD 1888, Xiyuan Railway was completed. Royal family members were invited to travel on the train and Empress Dowager Cixi was extremely pleased. At that time, Empress Dowager Cixi had declared her return to power and moved to Xiyuan, using the Qinzheng Palace as the place for political affairs and the Yiluan Palace as her sleeping palace. She used Jingqing Study in Beihai as her temporary residence. In the morning, the Empress Dowager Cixi went from the Yiluang Palace to the Qinzheng Palace to hold court, and after the court was adjourned, she and Emperor Guangxu, along with other royalty and nobles, took a train to Jingqing Study for lunch. The train was extremely luxurious, being exclusively for the imperial court. "Within the six carriages, there was one first-class carriage, two second-class carriages, all beautifully made with fine workmanship; two more second-class carriages, and one luggage carriage, all made of clean materials."[7] The windows of the carriages were covered with first-class silk curtains. The Empress Dowager Cixi and Emperor Guangxu were in the imperial yellow silk carriage, while other royalty and nobles used red and blue silk. The efforts of Li Hongzhang finally paid off. "But hoping to benefit the nation without harming the people, once a steadfast and unchangeable strategy is determined, it can be resolutely implemented without the need for lengthy deliberations and planning." On 5 May AD 1889, the Qing government announced that railways were important to China's development and construction was allowed.

Empress Dowager Cixi was a superstitious person. Before the construction of the Xiyuan railway, a geomancer was especially consulted to determine the lucky dates for starting work at various locations. Legend has it that she believed the vibration of steam engines was an ominous sound that would attract punishment from the gods and disrupt the vital energy of the imperial city. After the railway was opened, she ordered the engines to be thrown aside and ropes to be tied around the passenger cars to be pulled by eunuchs whenever trains ran. The conservative figure, Weng Tonghe, who was the teacher of Emperor Guangxu, wrote in his diary: "The steam engine races through Kun Lake, the rail tracks cross Xiyuan, the electric lights shine in the forbidden forest ... When I look at the situation, I feel worried. As a minister, can I avoid the shame and regret?" Compared to the Wusong railway, the Xiyuan railway had a relatively long life, operating for a total of 12 years. In AD 1900, the Eight-Nation Alliance invaded Beijing, and Empress Dowager Cixi and Emperor Guangxu fled west in a panic. With the owner gone, this royal railway lost its former glory and was left to be destroyed by foreign soldiers at will. It was not until three years after Cixi's death in AD 1908 that the railway was never restored. The intelligent but superstitious Cixi probably did not anticipate that three years after her death, the Qing Dynasty would be overthrown by the revolutionary party, and the spark was related to the railway—the robust railway protection movement that broke out in Sichuan and other places.

---

7. Yang Naiji, "Supplement to the Small Railway by the Taiye Pond," *The Forbidden City*, no. 2 (1983).

On May 9, AD 1911, the Qing administration stated that the railway was nationalized, and the policy of nationalization of the railway was implemented: "China has a vast territory and remote borders, stretching for tens of thousands of miles and requiring several months of travel. The court always thinks about border defense and is exhausted day and night. To control and regulate, the only solution is to build railways ... After careful planning, the country will surely have roads crossing the four borders, which is sufficient to support administration and control the central hub. Previously, the plans were not well-made, and there was no definite way, causing confusion and disorder in the road administration throughout the country, without branches and without measuring the strength of the people. A paper was submitted and approved for commercial operations ... All the trunk roads set up by private companies and stockholder companies in the provinces before the 3rd year of Xuantong should be taken back by the state and quickly built."[8] This policy, on the surface, seemed to speed up the pace of road construction in various places, but in reality, it contained the hidden goal of attacking and suppressing the rising Chinese capitalist class. At that time, the commercial railway companies in each province were the only private capitals that could compete with the national capital and foreign capital, and they were also the strongest civilian capitals.

On May 20, Minister Sheng Xuanhuai signed a loan agreement with banks from Britain, Germany, France, and America. The agreement literally gave the rights of railway construction to foreigners. When the news got around, the Railway Protection Movement broke out in China. It first started in Hunan, Hubei, Guangdong, and Sichuan, among which, Sichuan was the most active. Altogether, over 130 local governmental officials from the province joined in the movement.

The Qing government panicked and ordered Zhao Erfeng, then-Chief Commander of Sichuan, to crush the movement. While the Qing army focused on Sichuan, revolutionary organizations in Wuchang, Hubei, took advantage of the chaos and rebelled against the Qing government. This was known in history as the Xinhai Revolution. Mr. Sun Yat-sen, the first president and founding-father of the Republic of China, said the Wuchang Revolution would have been postponed for at least one year had there not been the Railway Protection Movement.

---

8. *Political Chronicles of Xuantong*, vol. 52, April 11 of Xuantong's third year; photocopy version of *The Qing Chronicles* by Zhonghua Book Company, book 60, 937.

3. The Beijing–Hankou Railway and Yuan Shikai Fished in Huan River

The Beijing–Hankou Railway was initially named Luhan Railway, meaning it connected the Lugou Bridge in Beijing to Tongji Gate in Hankou, Hubei. Later, the starting pointed was shifted to the Front Gate of Beijing and the destination to Yudai Gate in Hankou.

It was the first long distance railway to connect Beijing and central China, via three provinces—namely Zhili (Hebei), Henan, and Hubei. China Railway Company borrowed loans from the Belgian Government to build this. The construction began in April AD 1897, and was completed on April 1, AD 1906, lasting 9 years. Funding of the railway was composed of two parts: the Chinese regime invested 13 million silver and borrowed 4.5 million British pounds and 12.5 million francs in loans.

In the first year of the Xuantong era (AD 1909), outside the city of Zhengde on the Beijing–Hankou railway, lived a powerful figure who had fallen from grace. He was Yuan Shikai, the former Minister of War and head of the Ministry of Foreign Affairs of the Qing Dynasty. Yuan Shikai rose to prominence through his training in Tianjin, selling out the Guangxu Emperor, and suppressing the Boxer Movement. He had a successful official career and eventually became the Minister of War and head of the Ministry of Foreign Affairs of the Qing government. Most importantly, he controlled the most powerful army in the Qing Dynasty at that time, the Beiyang Army. The Beiyang Army consisted of six divisions, each with over 12,500 soldiers. Apart from the first division, which was led by a Manchu noble, the other five divisions were under Yuan Shikai's control. This formed a massive military and political group in the Beiyang region, centered around him, which posed a serious threat to the Manchu-led Qing ruling group. Some people predicted that Yuan Shikai would be the new Cao Cao at the end of the Han Dynasty or Liu Yu at the end of the Eastern Jin Dynasty.

Emperor Guangxu and Empress Dowager Cixi died in AD 1908. Before Cixi died, she ordered Puyi to assume the throne. In November of that year, Puyi was coronated at the age of three. He was the last Emperor of China, also known as Emperor Xuantong. Puyi's father, Zaifeng, acted as Regent. As soon as Zaifeng came to power, he wished to remove Yuan Shikai.

After deliberations, Zaifeng published an imperial edict at the end of AD 1908.

The edict read: "Grand Minister of State, Yuan Shikai, was unable to assume his responsibilities due to his foot disease, which made him unable to walk. Thanks to the kindness of his Highness, Yuan will be removed from his current position for rehabilitation."[9] In fact, Yuan's feet only suffered a minor disease resulting from cold weather. To say that Yuan was unable to walk was far-fetched. Obviously, Zaifeng was simply looking for an excuse to get rid of him.

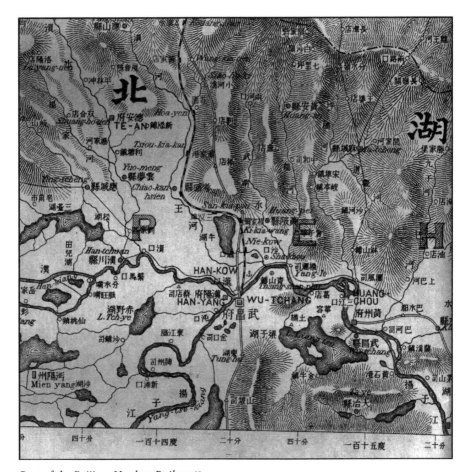

Part of the Beijing–Hankou Railway[10]

---

9. *Emperor Xuantong's Governance*, Dec. 1908; *Records of Qing Dynasty*, photocopy ed., book 60 (Beijing: Zhonghua Book Company), 74.
10. *Map of Beijing–Hankou Railway*, late Qing Dynasty and early Republic of China print ed.

When Yuan Shikai learned that he had been deprived of his job, he realized that it would be dangerous for him to stay in Beijing. So he moved to Zhangdefu (Henan), where the Beijing–Hankou Railway passed by. Yuan's hometown was in Xiangcheng County, in the east of Henan. The reason he didn't choose to go back to his hometown was because he bore a grudge with his brothers (and they with him).

When Yuan was still the Governor of Zhili Province (modern Hebei), he had already purchased a handsome collection of properties in the areas of Zhangdefu and Weihuifu. He had never explained to anyone why he wanted to buy houses there. However, one could find some clues from the map. The two places were on the borders of Henan and Zhili. Among all the locations in Henan, they were closest to the capital. What was more important, was that the Beijing–Hankou Railway had stops in both Zhangdefu and Weihuifu, making it very convenient for transportation.

Portrait of Yuan Shikai

Yuan Shikai's residence was located in Huanshang Village outside the northern gate of Zhangdefu. It had a beautiful view of the Taihang Mountains on its right and Huan River in the front. However, Yuan understood the dark sides of politics only too well: he wanted to fool his opponents by pretending that he was enjoying his retired life. He named his house "The Garden of Longevity" and was often seen fishing in his pond. To crown it all, he even hired a photographer to picture him relaxing and published it in Shanghai's *Oriental Magazine*—then the most influential magazine in China.

It gave people the impression that Yuan was no longer interested in politics, and that he had become a hermit. In reality, however, he had his old friend Yang Shixiang, then-Governor of Zhili Province, install a telegraph room in his house. Telegraph operators were hired to connect Yuan with his old friends and subordinates. Every day Yuan would spend around two hours working on the information he got through telegraphs and letters so that he could keep updated with the news and make orders.

Yuan's opportunity finally came. On October 10, AD 1911, revolution broke out in Wuchang. Soon, the Revolutionary Army conquered Wuchang's neighboring cities of Hanyang and Hankou. On October 12, the Qing Government appointed Yin Chang as Army Commander to fight back. General Feng Guozhang led the first legion of the Beiyang Army to counter the Revolutionary Army along the Beijing–Hankou Railway. The railway greatly helped the Beiyang Army in deployment.

As the war continued, a former subordinate of Yuan Shikai, General Feng, visited Yuan in Huanshang Village, while on his way to Wuchang. Yuan ordered Feng to contain his forces in Hubei and not to make any movement so that he could bargain with the Qing Government. Consequently, Regent Zaifeng had to give in to Yuan.

On October 27, AD 1911, Yuan Shikai was appointed Imperial Envoy, commanding the armies and navy in Hubei Province. On October 30, Yuan left his home in Zhangdefu and went to Hubei. On November 1, the Beiyang Army retrieved Hankou and on November 8, senior ministers voted Yuan Shikai the Prime Minister. Since Zaifeng was forced to retire, Yuan assumed total control of the Qing Government.

Later, the Beiyang Army retrieved Hanyang, forcing the Revolutionary Army to an armistice. Yuan successfully made Emperor Xuantong (Puyi) abdicate his throne on February 12, 1912, with threats from the Revolutionary Army at the gate. Backed by the Beiyang Army, Yuan later forced Mr. Sun Yat-sen to give up his title of Acting President of the Republic of China. He himself was then "elected" as the Acting President.

On June 6, 1916, Yuan Shikai died. He was very unpopular with the Chinese people. On June 28, his coffin was transported from Beijing to his home in Huanshang Village. The Beijing–Hankou Railway authorities prepared three trains for this event. One was for Yuan's coffin, modified from the hearse of Longyu, the Empress Consort of the Guangxu Emperor; the second was to transport bodyguards and Yuan's horses; and the third was for government officials and Yuan's former subordinates. On this day, the Beijing–Hankou Railway stopped its services for passengers.

4. Mr. Sun Yat-sen's Blueprint of China's Rail Networks

On February 13, 1912, Mr. Sun Yat-sen formally resigned as the Acting President of the Republic of China. Afterward, he devoted his time to building China's railway.

Sun Yat-sen carefully researched the railway systems. As early as AD 1894, Mr. Sun proposed his ideas to Li Hongzhang, then-Governor of Zhili. It was a utopian ideal. Mr. Sun dreamed of a country where "all people can demonstrate their talent, land resources can be fully explored, all material can be used according to their potential, and all goods are freely transported," and "The nations of the earth now regard railroads as their lifeblood."

He drafted the proposal to pool resources from businessmen to build a railway. He argued that many countries in the world had already put building railways at the top of their agenda. After the Republic of China was established, Mr. Sun believed that industry and business should be the main focus of new China. He argued: "If there were no railways, it would be difficult to transport goods. How could industries develop without transportation? Therefore, transportation is the basis for all industries. And building railways should be the top priority."

On June 25, 1912, Sun Yat-sen gave an interview to the *Minli* newspaper in Shanghai. He suggested, for the first time, a blueprint to build three major railway lines in China: the first line would start from the South China Sea, head through Guangdong, Guangxi, Guizhou, Yunnan, Sichuan, and Tibet and then end south of Tianshan Mountain; the second line would start from the Yangtze River, connecting Jiangsu, Anhui, Henan, Shaanxi, Gansu, Xinjiang, and Yili; the third line would start from Qinhuang Island, connecting Liaoning Peninsula, Mongolia, and Tannu Uriankhai.

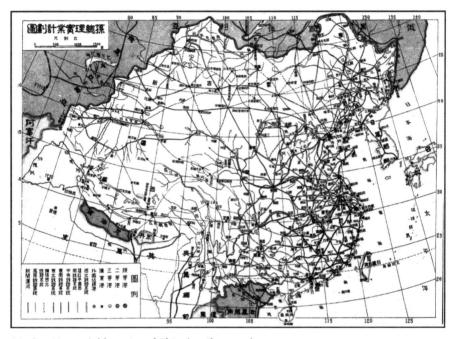

Mr. Sun Yat-sen's blueprint of China's rail networks[11]

After the interview, Mr. Sun was invited to Beijing by Yuan Shikai. The two met a total of 13 times, yet Mr. Sun did not see the true colors of Yuan. He reassured Yuan that he could count on his support in becoming the new president. He even promised Yuan that he would not enter politics for the next 10 years. Apart from all this, Mr. Sun also reported to Yuan many times on his plan to build railway networks in China, and he was also willing to "run the railroad by himself" and build 200,000 *li* of the railroad.

---

11. Collected from Hong Maoxi, ed., *The Latest Map of China* (Shanghai: Shanghai Oriental Yudi Press House, 1934).

Signed commission by Acting President Yuan Shikai

Starting from September 6, 1912, Yat-sen went to inspect the railway systems in North China. This included the Beijing–Zhangjiakou Railway built under the guidance of Zhan Tianyou; railways connecting Taiyuan, Shijiazhuang, Shanhaiguan, Tianjin, Jinan, and Qingdao as well as factories there. On September 9, Yuan Shikai named Sun as Head of the National Railway Bureau, in charge of establishing China Railway Company.

On October 3, Mr. Sun finished his inspection and returned to Shanghai. On November 14, China Railway Company was established in Shanghai. Mr. Sun telegraphed Yuan Shikai, the Congress, and provincial governors about the opening of China Railway Company.

The inspections in North China had enriched Sun's knowledge of railway construction immensely and his plans were better prepared. In the final days of the Qing Dynasty, debate still raged over whether or not railways should be built. Sun Yat-sen, however, believed that building railways was of life-and-death importance to China. He said, "A country must build its own railways in order to develop its economy." He used every opportunity to promote the importance and urgency of building railways to his countrymen. Mr. Sun said, "Industries would be in grave peril, if there were no railways in China. How could we restore our economy without railways? One can tell if a country is rich or poor judging by railway mileage. The distance of a city to a railway can determine its people's joy and pain."

Mr. Sun also compared railway mileage between China and America. This had already exceeded 230,000 miles in America in the 1910s—arguably the richest and most powerful country in the world by then. Even though China had vast territory, it was poor and weak without railways. In order to restore the national economy, Mr. Sun Yat-sen planned to build up to 100,000 miles of railroad in China in 10 years. According to his plan, this should consist of five major railway lines—Central, Southeast, Northeast, Northwest, and Plateau, to create a railway

Portrait of Song Jiaoren

transportation network that covers the entire country and is accessible from all directions.

However, Mr. Sun's plan was disrupted by gunshots in Shanghai's railway station. While Mr. Sun Yat-sen was promoting his idea to his countrymen, Mr. Song Jiaoren, another leader in the Kuomintang (KMT) Party, was trying to import Western political systems to curb the power of Acting President Yuan Shikai. In early 1913, the KMT won majority votes in both the House of Representatives and the Senate, counting over 390 votes.

On March 20, 1913, Mr. Song Jiaoren and other newly elected KMT party members planned to travel together by train from Shanghai to Beijing. At 10:45, Mr. Song, Mr. Liao Zhongkai, and Mr. Yu Youren left the congressmen lounge and were about to board the train.

Just as they were having their tickets checked, a gun shot was fired, followed by a second and third shot. Mr. Song stumbled and dropped onto the iron chair next to him. On March 22, Mr. Song died in Shanghai. Investigations showed the assassin was sent by Yuan Shikai. On July 12, Mr. Sun launched the second revolutionary war against Yuan Shikai. In the meantime, Yuan removed Mr. Sun's title as China Railway chief. China Railway Company, established by Mr. Sun Yat-Sen, came to an end, without building a single kilometer of railway track.

A BRIEF CHRONOLOGY OF CHINESE HISTORY

Xia Dynasty		2070–1600 BC
Shang Dynasty		1600–1046 BC
Zhou Dynasty	Western Zhou Dynasty	1046–771 BC
	Eastern Zhou Dynasty	770–256 BC
Qin Dynasty		221–207 BC
Han Dynasty	Western Han Dynasty	206 BC–AD 25
	Eastern Han Dynasty	AD 25–220
Three Kingdoms	Kingdom of Wei	AD 220–265
	Kingdom of Shu	AD 221–263
	Kingdom of Wu	AD 222–280
Jin Dynasty	Western Jin Dynasty	AD 265–317
	Eastern Jin Dynasty	AD 317–420

Southern and Northern Dynasties	Southern Dynasties	Song Dynasty	AD 420–479
		Qi Dynasty	AD 479–502
		Liang Dynasty	AD 502–557
		Chen Dynasty	AD 557–589
	Northern Dynasties	Northern Wei Dynasty	AD 386–534
		Eastern Wei Dynasty	AD 534–550
		Northern Qi Dynasty	AD 550–577
		Western Wei Dynasty	AD 535–556
		Northern Zhou Dynasty	AD 557–581
Sui Dynasty			AD 581–618
Tang Dynasty			AD 618–907
Five Dynasties		Later Liang Dynasty	AD 907–923
		Later Tang Dynasty	AD 923–936
		Later Jin Dynasty	AD 936–947
		Later Han Dynasty	AD 947–950
		Later Zhou Dynasty	AD 951–960
Song Dynasty		Northern Song Dynasty	AD 960–1127
		Southern Song Dynasty	AD 1127–1279
Liao Dynasty			AD 907–1125
Jin Dynasty			AD 1115–1234
Yuan Dynasty			AD 1206–1368
Ming Dynasty			AD 1368–1644
Qing Dynasty			AD 1616–1912
Republic of China			1912–1949
People's Republic of China			Founded on October 1, 1949

INDEX

A
Ai Ruose, 172–73
Aksu River, 84
Aleni, Giulio (Ai Rulüe), 156, 169, 170, 176
Altay Prefecture, 15
Amami Ōshima, 88
Amu Darya River, 43, 63
Anhui Province, 7, 9, 21, 29, 32, 50, 92, 93, 97, 123, 133, 203, 209
Anotatta Lake, 62, 63
Antiochia, 45, 46, 47
Anxi (now Iran), 44, 45, 46, 70, 71, 83
Anyang, 18, 82, 134
Atlantic Ocean, 167, 169

B
Balkash Lake, 44, 45
Ban Chao, 45, 47
barbarians, 38, 44, 53, 65, 76, 78, 87, 101, 131, 150, 165, 183
Ba-Shu (present-day Sichuan), 25, 36, 37, 38, 39, 49
Beijing, xv, 21, 33, 66, 67, 70, 71, 99, 115, 118, 121, 122, 125, 127, 128, 132, 133, 134, 136, 141, 142, 155, 156, 163, 164, 169, 172, 173, 174, 177, 178, 179, 186, 193, 196, 198–204, 206
Beijing–Hangzhou Grand Canal, 121, 122
Beijing–Hankou Railway, 198–202
Beiyang Army, 198, 201, 202
Binghai Route, 28, 51
Bi Seas, 11
Bohai Sea, 4, 8, 10, 29, 50
Book of Documents, 2, 10
Book of Han, 21, 42
Bo Route, 37
Buddhism, xvi, 55, 56, 57, 59, 61–65, 82, 85, 86, 89, 90, 96, 97

C
Canghai County, 50, 51
cannon(s), 153, 156–65, 182, 183, 185
 light-weight cannon, 164
 red-clad cannons, 162, 164, 165
Cao Pi (Emperor of Wei), 55
Cape Hope, 172–73
carriages, xiii, xvi, 18, 19, 26, 27, 31, 39, 132, 145, 175, 195, 196
Catholicism, 153, 156
Central Asia, 13, 14, 43, 46, 62, 63, 114

Central China, xv, xvi
Central Plains, 52, 62, 87, 100, 101, 110, 113, 126, 146
Central Secretariat, 116, 120, 125
Chang'an, xiv, 41, 43, 44, 45, 47, 57, 60, 67, 69, 70, 77, 81, 82, 83, 86, 89, 95, 96
Chengdu, 71, 140, 141
China Railway Company, 198, 204, 206
Chinese ancestors, xiii, 1, 2
Chinese civilization, 10, 11, 13, 165
Chinese classics, 155, 165
Chinese scholars, 156, 165, 166
Christianity, 153–56, 170, 171, 174
Church of Flora, 154
"Commandery-County" system, 25, 31
Complete Map of the World, 166–67
Confucianism, 138, 156
Confucius, 1, 2, 22, 23, 31, 140, 156, 170, 171, 172, 174
Congling Mountains, 43, 84, 85
cultural exchange, 1, 24, 25, 55, 65, 76, 165, 167

D

Daming Temple, 89, 91, 93
Danyang Post Station, 117
Daqin (Rome), 45, 46, 54, 62, 75
Daxia, 20, 32, 44, 62
Dayuan (Fergana, Uzbekistan), 43, 44
Dayuezhi (present-day north Afghanistan), 43–45
Dayu Mountain, 76, 94
Dengzhou, 70, 71, 96, 97, 101, 102, 113, 162
Dingjun Mountain, 140
Dongting Lake, 33, 119
driveways, 28, 29, 30, 31, 67

E

East China Sea, 9, 10, 51, 62, 63, 143
Eastern Jin Dynasty, 60, 198
Eight Banners, 165
Emperor Gaozu of the Han Dynasty, 40, 43
Emperor Guangxu, 193, 195, 196, 198
Emperor Huizong of the Song Dynasty, 102, 107, 112

Emperor Wu of the Han Dynasty, 36, 37, 39, 43, 44, 47, 48, 50, 51, 52
Emperor Xuan of the Han Dynasty, 45
Emperor Yang of the Sui Dynasty, 65–67, 86
Empress Dowager Cixi, 193–96, 198
Ennin (Japanese monk), 95–97
ethnic minorities, xv, 6, 36, 38, 47, 128, 147
Europe, 13, 72, 153, 156, 166, 167, 169, 170, 171, 173, 174, 176, 177, 179

F

Fan Shouyi, 172–76
Faxian, 55, 56, 57, 59, 60, 61, 72, 86
First Opium War, 185–87
Five Dynasties and Ten Kingdoms, xiv, 110
Folangji, 157, 159–62
Four Remotes, 1, 12
Fuchō, 89, 91, 92
Fujian Province, 49, 80, 143

G

Ganges River, 59, 61, 63
Gansu Province, x, 7, 26, 71
Gan Ying, 43, 45, 46, 47
Gaochang (Turpan, Xinjiang), 70, 83, 84
General Wang Ben of Qin, 26
General Weiqing, 44
Genghis Khan, xv, 112–15
Goryeo, 71, 96, 97, 99–103, 105–12
Grand Canal, xiv, 65, 66, 67, 99, 121
Greater Nine Provinces, 8, 10, 11
Great Wall, 28, 133, 167
Guangdong Province, 49, 52, 72, 94, 130, 140, 144, 145, 153, 157–59, 166, 172, 173, 197, 203
Guangxi Province, xv, 34, 49, 94, 128, 130, 139, 140, 141, 142, 148, 149, 203
Guangzhou, 50, 52, 54, 60, 70–73, 75–81, 94, 151, 154, 173, 186
Guangzhou Port, 54, 71, 72, 76, 77
Guanzhong area, 25, 27, 28, 143
Guilin Prefecture, 149
Guizhou Province, xv, 39, 94, 128, 134, 143, 144, 145, 147, 148, 149, 151, 203

Guo Shoujing, 122

H
Hainan Island, 75, 93, 94
Haiyang River, 34–35
Han Dynasty, 29, 30, 35, 36, 37, 38, 40, 42, 44–52, 55, 62, 64, 65, 72, 166, 180, 198
    Eastern Han Dynasty, xiv, 21, 25, 40, 42, 45, 50, 51, 54, 55, 64, 72
    Western Han Dynasty, 15, 29, 38, 40, 44, 49, 55
Hangu Pass, 19, 31, 33
Hangzhou, xv, 28, 67, 77, 92, 99, 104, 120, 121, 122, 137, 142, 145, 146, 183
Hankou, 186, 198–202
Han Pass, 27
Han people, 44–46
Han River, 7, 20, 119, 140
Hebei Province, 4, 8, 39
Heilongjiang Province, 71
Henan Province, xi, 7, 8, 82, 118, 119, 121, 134, 142
Hengpu Pass, 76
He Ru (Inspector of Dongguan), 158–59
Hetao District, 43–44
Hexi area, 44
Hexi Corridor, 13, 44
Himalayas, 61, 63
Huai River, 6, 7, 9, 66, 67, 77, 121, 122
Huangpu River, 187
Huang Taiji, 162
Huan River, 198, 201
Hubei Province, 9, 201
Huitong Station, 126–28
Hunan Province, 9

I
Ibn Khurdadhbih, 72
Ili, 44, 177, 180
Ili River Basin, 177
India, xvi, 44, 53, 55, 57, 59, 61, 62, 63, 71, 72, 74, 75, 82, 83, 85, 86, 186
Indian Ocean, 56, 75, 169, 172

Indian Peninsula, 75
Indonesia, 172
Inner Mongolia, xv, 33, 43, 67, 178
Iraq, 45, 46, 74, 75, 78
Irtysh River, 177–78
Islam, 65, 72, 80

J
Japan, xiv, 4, 12, 13, 86–95, 97, 104, 108, 128, 155
Java, 53, 54, 73, 75, 128
Jiangnan Economic Zone, 67
Jiangsu Province, 6, 21, 32
Jiangxi Province, 9, 70, 118, 146
Jianye (present-day Nanjing), 54, 56
Jianzhen, 86, 88–95
Jiayu Pass, 177
Jibei Commandery (present-day Tai'an, Shandong), 31
Jingtu Temple, 82
Jinsha River, 149–50
Ji River, 4, 8
Johann Adam Schall von Bell, 162
Journals of Xu Xiake, 142, 148, 150
Jungar, 177

K
Kagarin, 182–83
Kaiyuan Temple, 91
Kangju (Kazakhstan), 43–45
Kang Senghui, 56
Kangxi Emperor, 153, 163–65, 171–74, 177, 179, 182
Kao Gong Ji (Records of Examination of Craftsman), 15, 16, 18, 19
Kazakhstan, 43, 177
Khitan, 100, 101, 110
Khokhan-Bulak (Jimusaer, Xinjiang), 83
Khotan, 44, 61, 63
Kingdom of Duyuan (modern day Java), 53
Kingdom of Huangzhi (southeast India), 53
Kingdom of Yichengbu (Sri Lanka), 53
King Hui of Qin, 26

King Mu of Zhou, 1, 12–14, 40
Kong Yingda, 12, 29
Korea, 51, 87, 101, 104, 106, 108, 110, 112, 128, 169
Korean Peninsula, 4, 50, 71, 87, 88, 101, 108, 121
Kuaiji Commandery, 33
Kublai Khan, 119
Kumalik River, 84
Kumārajīva, 56
Kunlun Mountain, 20, 62, 64
Kunlun people, 78, 79
Kunming Lake, 47, 48
Kunyu Tushuo (*Universal Encyclopedia with Illustrations*), 169
Kuomintang (KMT), 206
Kyushu, 87, 88

L
Lake Baikal, 178, 180
Langya Terrace, 32
Later Jin, 161–62
Liang Qichao, 151
Liaodong Commandery, 50
Liaodong Peninsula, 4, 28, 51
Liao Dynasty, 100, 101, 102, 112
Liaoning Peninsula, 203
Liaoxi Commandery, 50
Li Chengxun (Minister of Military Affairs), 160
Li Daoyuan, 64
Li Hongzhang, 193, 194, 196, 202
Li Linzong, 89, 91
Limadou, 155, 156, 166–70, 172. *See also* Ricci, Matteo
Li Mian, 77
Lingguan Route, 25, 36, 37, 38
Lingnan area, 25, 26, 32, 34, 36, 47, 52, 69, 72, 76, 77, 79, 80, 91, 94
Lingqu Canal, xiv, 34, 35
Liu Bang, 36, 40, 42
Liuzhou Prefecture, 149
Li Zhizao, 156, 166

Loess Plateau, 10
Luo River, 4, 6, 7, 66, 70
Luoyang, xiv, 21, 23, 31, 42, 56, 66, 67, 69, 70, 77, 82, 89, 96, 121
Lu Yundi, 100, 102, 106, 107, 112

M
Macao, 153, 154, 155, 161, 172
Malacca Straits, 75
Map of Mountains and Seas, 166–67
Maritime Trade Superintendency, 79
Mekong River Estuary, 75
Mencius, 23, 155
Meng Kangxiang, 64
Meng Tian, 28, 34, 43
merchant ship, 53, 60, 106
Mezzabarba, Carlo Ambrogio, 173
Mid Nine Provinces, 11
Ming Dynasty, xvi, 116, 125, 128, 132, 134, 138, 139, 142, 145, 153, 157, 161, 166, 170, 176
Mingzhou (Ningbo in Zhejiang), 88, 91, 92, 99, 100, 102, 107
Ministry of Foreign Affairs, 198
Ministry of Military Affairs, 126
Min River, 143, 149, 150
missionaries, 153, 156, 165, 170–73, 176
mosques, 81
Mount Hua, 4
Mount Tai, 4, 9, 32, 50, 147

N
Nalanda Monastery, 85, 86
Nan Huairen, 163, 164, 169, 170
Nanjing, xi, xv, 54, 56, 60, 94, 123, 125, 129, 131, 132, 136, 142, 155, 159, 172
Nanyue, 36, 37, 54
National Railway Bureau, 204
Needham, Joseph, 151
Nestorianism (Jingjiao in Chinese), 153
Nine Provinces, 1–4, 8–12, 32
　Jingzhou, 7, 8, 9, 70, 71, 82
　Jizhou, 4, 5, 8, 10, 94, 120, 122
　Liangzhou, 7–10, 71, 83

Qingzhou, 4, 8, 9, 10, 96
Xuzhou, 6, 8, 9, 10, 32, 60, 118, 120, 131, 143, 145, 150
Yangzhou, xi, 7–10, 33, 60, 70, 71, 80, 88, 89, 91–94, 96, 119, 123, 131
Yanzhou, 4, 8, 9, 101, 146
Yongzhou, 7, 8, 10
Yuzhou, 7–9
Ningbo, 88, 91, 92, 99, 100, 102, 109, 146
Northeast Asia, xiv
Northern Song Dynasty, xi, 67, 100, 101, 102, 110, 112
Northern Wei Dynasty, 64
North–South Grand Canal, 121–22
Nurhaci, 161

O
Osaka Bay, 87

P
Pacific Ocean, 169
Pamir Plateau, 13, 62
Panyu (present-day Guangzhou), 34, 36, 49, 50, 52, 71, 72
Pearl River, 25, 75
Pei Shiqing, 87
Pengcheng County, 32
Penglai Mountain, 104
Persia, 13, 75, 78
Persian Gulf, 45, 46, 74, 75
Pope Clement XI, 171
Popo Mituoluo, 83
Portugal, 172, 173, 174, 175
Portuguese, 153, 155–61, 175
Portuguese ship, 158
post offices, 39, 41, 42, 185
post stations, 39, 67, 77, 97, 99, 116, 117, 118, 119, 120, 126, 127, 128, 129, 130, 133, 134, 136, 141
Poyang Lake, 77, 141
Prefect Wang Pan, 154, 155
pre-Qin period, 8, 180
Provana, Antonio Francesco Giuseppe, 172
Puyi (Emperor Xuantong of Qing), 198, 201

Q
Qiantang River, 67, 77
Qilian Mountains, 13
Qin Dynasty, 26, 28, 30, 32, 33, 40, 42, 52, 57, 60, 76
Qing Dynasty, xv, 4, 134, 171, 177, 180, 183, 185, 196, 198, 204
Qing government, 163, 172, 177, 180, 183, 187, 188, 191–93, 196–98
Qinghai Province, 62
Qin Mountains, 9, 26
Qin Shi Huang, xiv, 25, 27, 29, 31–34, 43, 50
Qiu Chuji, 112–15
Qiuci, 43, 45, 61
Qizhou Ocean, 75
Quanzhou, 80, 120
Qunshan Island, 105, 110
Quwen Tai (King of Gaochang), 83, 84

R
Record of Buddhistic Kingdoms, A, 60, 61, 64
Record of Foreign Lands, 156, 169, 176, 179–83
Records of the Grand Historian, xiv, 13, 14, 21, 31, 42, 52
Republic of China, 197, 202
Revolutionary Army, 201–2
Ricci, Matteo, 153–55
Roman Colosseum, 176
Rome, 45, 167, 169, 173, 174, 175
Rōshu, 89, 91, 92
royal patrols, 31
royal road, 29–31
Ruggieri, Michele, 154, 155
Russia, 71, 177–82

S
Sanchuan Commandery (present-day Luoyang), 31
Sanskrit, 59, 61, 85, 181
Shaanxi Province, 7, 8, 9, 21, 26, 30, 33, 43, 97, 117, 118, 126, 127, 130, 134, 140, 160, 172, 203
Shandong Peninsula, 9, 51, 101, 124
Shandong Province, 4, 6, 8, 60, 70, 120, 122

Shang Dynasty, xiii
Shanghai, 9, 124, 135, 186–92, 201, 202, 204, 206
Shanxi Province, 8, 57, 70
Shendu (now India), 44
Shiniu Road, 26
Sichuan Province, 27, 117
Siku Quanshu, 119, 121, 123, 151
Silk Road, xiv, xvi, 28, 45, 46, 53, 54, 55, 71
Silk Road on the Sea, 53–54
Sima Guang, 47
Sima Qian, 11, 28, 31
Sima Xiangru, 37
Sima Yan, 55
Sishui Prefecture (Xuzhou, Jiangsu Province), 32
Situo River, 63, 64
Song Dynasty, xi, 79, 80, 81, 99, 100, 102, 103, 106, 108, 110, 112, 118, 143–45
    Northern Song Dynasty, xi, 67, 100, 101, 102, 110, 112
    Southern Song Dynasty, xi, 113, 122, 145
Song Jiaoren, 205, 206
South China, xiv, 49, 51, 52, 62, 63, 66, 73, 125, 143, 163, 182, 202
Southeast Asia, xiv, 52, 53, 72, 75, 169
Southern and Northern Dynasties, xiv, 55, 56, 65, 72
Southwest "Yi" Routes, 36, 38, 39
Spring and Autumn Period, x, 15, 19, 22, 27, 32, 47, 62
Sri Lanka, 53, 59, 60, 74, 75
State of Qi, 15, 21, 23
State of Qin, 10, 21, 24, 26, 27, 42
Stevenson, Robert, 186
Sui Dynasty, 65, 66, 67, 78, 82, 86, 87, 121
Sumatra, 54, 60, 73, 74, 75, 128
Sun Quan, 50, 51, 54, 72
Sun Yat-sen, 197, 202–6
Su Wu, 180
Suzhou, 21, 33, 50, 66, 123, 126, 127, 131, 135, 137, 172
Syria, 45, 46

T
Taihang Mountains, 8, 201
Taihang Route, 67
Taihu Lake, 142
Takeshima, 87, 105, 109, 110
Tang Dynasty, xi, 35, 42, 62, 63, 65, 67, 69, 74–79, 86, 88, 91, 92, 95, 96, 97, 100, 101, 110, 143, 144, 153
Tang Meng, 36–38
Tangshan, 193
Tarim Basin, 43–45
Tarim River, 43
Thoroughfares of the Universe, 130–31
Three Kingdoms Period, 42, 51, 52, 54, 55, 72
Tianshan Mountains, xi, 14, 44, 83, 84, 114, 177, 180, 203
Tianshan North Road, 14
Tianzhu, 57, 59, 61, 62, 74
Tibet, 13, 71, 100, 128, 203
Tonghui River, 122
Tongji Canal, 66
Torghut, 177–80
tower ship, 47, 48, 50
transportation networks, xiv, xv, 1, 4, 99, 118, 119, 132, 206
transportation systems, xiv, 1, 27, 185
transportation tools, 2, 3, 19, 137
Travels of Marco Polo, The, 97
Tsushima Island, 87, 88
Tulichen, 177, 179–82

V
Verbiest, Ferdinand, 163. *See also* Nan Huairen
Vietnam, 13, 49, 52, 73, 75, 95, 128
volcanic hot springs, 150
Volga River, 177–80

W
Wang Shixing, 133, 139, 140, 141, 142, 145, 146
Warring States Period, xvi, 2, 13, 15, 16, 19, 21, 26, 32, 39, 40
water transportation, 2, 35, 48, 99, 117, 121

waterways, xv, 1, 7, 8, 25, 36, 37, 49, 51, 99, 119, 122, 134, 135, 149, 176
Wei River, 7, 31, 84, 121
West Asia, 46, 72
western expedition, 12, 13, 15, 112
Western Protectorate-General, 45
Western Regions, xiv, xvi, 11, 13, 14, 15, 43–47, 56, 57, 63, 64, 71, 83, 97
Western Regions in the Tang Dynasty, The, 97
Western Xia, xiv, 100, 113
Western Zhou Dynasty, xiv, 15, 39
West Mongolia, 177
Wuchang Revolution, 197
Wuchi Road, 36
Wusong Port, 187, 188
Wusong Railway, 191, 192
Wusun, 44, 45

X
Xia Dynasty, 2, 16
Xiang–Gui Corridor, 34
Xiang River, 34, 35
Xianyang, xiv, 21, 25, 27–34
Xiaomei Pass, 77
Xinhai Revolution, 197
Xinjiang, xi, xv, 13, 15, 43, 45, 57, 63, 70, 83, 84, 86, 114, 115, 177, 203
Xiongnu, 26, 28, 36, 38, 43, 44, 45
Xixia clan, 14
Xiyuan Railway, 192, 194, 195
Xuanzang, 82–86
Xu Fu, 12, 32
Xu Guangqi, 155, 156, 161, 162
Xu Xiake, 139, 140, 141, 142, 147–51

Y
Yalu River, 121, 143
Yangtze River, xi, 7, 9, 25, 27, 28, 50, 51, 66, 67, 92, 93, 94, 104, 118, 123, 143, 145, 149, 167, 203

Yelang, 25, 36, 37, 38, 49
Yelang Route, 36–38
Yellow River, xi, 4, 6, 7, 8, 9, 13, 14, 15, 25, 26, 33, 55, 62, 63, 64, 66, 67, 69, 104, 105, 118, 121, 136, 143, 147, 167
Yellow Sea route, 86
Yinjiang Estuary, 99
Yki Island, 88
Yongji Canal, 66
Yongle Encyclopedia, 117, 120
Yongzheng Emperor, 173
Yuan Chonghuan, 161
Yuan Dynasty, xv, 99, 116–22, 126, 153, 180
Yuanmingyuan, 176, 183
Yuan Shikai, 198–204, 206
Yu Gong, 1, 2, 3, 4, 8–11, 143, 149
Yunnan, xv, 38, 39, 47, 71, 117, 128, 130, 134, 139, 140, 142–51, 203
Yuquan Mountain, 164
Yu the Great, 2, 3, 33
Yuyao County, 2

Z
Zangke River, 36, 49
Zhang Qian, 43, 44, 63, 166
Zhang River, 33
Zhang Yi, 24, 26
Zhan Tianyou, xv, 204
Zhaobao Mountain, 99, 100, 104
Zhao Rushi, 108
Zhao Tuo, 36, 52
Zheng He, xv, 166
Zhenjiang, 67, 121, 131
Zhili Province, 132, 147, 198, 200, 201, 202
Zhi Route, 28
Zhu Di (Emperor Yongle of Ming), 125, 132
Zhu Yuanzhang, 125, 126, 129, 130
Ziyan Island, 106
Zou Yan, 10–12

ABOUT THE CHIEF EDITOR

GE JIANXIONG, PhD, born in 1945, is a professor at the Center for Historical Geographical Studies of Fudan University in Shanghai, China. He is also a doctoral supervisor and Director of Fudan University Library. His research focuses on historical geography, population history, migration history, and cultural history.

Selected publications of Professor Ge include:

- *History of the Population in China*, editor-in-chief and author of Vol. I
- *History of Migrations in China*, editor-in-chief and author of Vol. I & II
- *History of the Development of Population in China*
- *A Perspective of Chinese History: Unification and Separation*
- *A Short History of Cartography in Ancient China*
- *The Changes of Boundaries and Administrative Divisions in China*
- *The Natural Environment for Human Being in the Future*
- *Biography of Tan Qixiang*, Vol. I & II

ABOUT THE AUTHOR

Fu Linxiang, PhD, was born in 1961 and is a professor at the Center for Historical Geographical Studies of Fudan University in Shanghai, China. Fu specializes in historical geography and the ancient history of Shanghai.

He is the first author of *History of China's Administrative Divisions (Vol: Qing Dynasty & Republic of China)* and the chief editor of *Encyclopaedia of China (Vol: Transportation-Postal System)*. His other selected publications include *Historical Atlas of Shanghai* (Deputy Editor), *New Perspectives on Evolutions of Wusong River,* and *The Partition of Jiangnan, Huguang, and Shaanxi Provinces and the Change of the Provincial System at the Beginning of the Qing Dynasty.*